Inventions of a Present

Also by the Author

The Poetics of Social Forms

I.   *Categories of the Narrative-Historical (forthcoming)*
II.   *Allegory and Ideology*
III.   *The Antinomies of Realism*
IV.   *A Singular Modernity / The Modernist Papers*
V.   *Postmodernism, or, the Cultural Logic of Late Capitalism*
VI.   *Archaeologies of the Future*

Studies

Sartre: The Origins of a Style
Fables of Aggression: Wyndham Lewis, the Modernist as Fascist
Late Marxism: Adorno, Or, The Persistence of the Dialectic
Brecht and Method
The Hegel Variations: On the Phenomenology of the Spirit
Representing Capital: *A Reading of Volume One*
Chandler: The Detections of Totality
The Benjamin Files

Theory

Marxism and Form: Twentieth-Century Dialectical Theories of Literature
*The Prison-House of Language: A Critical Account of Structuralism and
    Russian Formalism*
The Political Unconscious: Narrative as a Socially Symbolic Act
Valences of the Dialectic
An American Utopia: Dual Power and the Universal Army

Film

Signatures of the Visible
The Geopolitical Aesthetic: Cinema and Space in the World System

Essays

The Ideologies of Theory
The Seeds of Time
The Cultural Turn: Selected Writings on the Postmodern, 1983–1998
The Ancients and the Postmoderns: On the Historicity of Forms

Seminars

The Years of Theory (forthcoming)
Mimesis, Expression, Construction (forthcoming)

Inventions of a Present

The Novel in Its Crisis of Globalization

Fredric Jameson

VERSO

London • New York

First published by Verso 2024
© Fredric Jameson 2024

The author and publisher would like to express their gratitude to the publications in which the original versions of these essays appeared. Details of prior publication are given at the foot of each chapter title page.

1 3 5 7 9 10 8 6 4 2

Verso
UK: 6 Meard Street, London W1F 0EG
US: 388 Atlantic Avenue, Brooklyn, NY 11217
versobooks.com

Verso is the imprint of New Left Books

ISBN-13: 978-1-80429-240-2
ISBN-13: 978-1-80429-242-6 (US EBK)
ISBN-13: 978-1-80429-241-9 (UK EBK)

British Library Cataloguing in Publication Data
A catalogue record for this book is available from the British Library

Library of Congress Cataloging-in-Publication Data

Names: Jameson, Fredric, author.
Title: Inventions of a present : the novel in its crisis of globalization / Fredric Jameson.
Description: First edition hardback. | London ; New York : Verso Books, 2024. | Includes bibliographical references and index.
Identifiers: LCCN 2023049626 (print) | LCCN 2023049627 (ebook) | ISBN 9781804292402 (hardback) | ISBN 9781804292426 (ebk)
Subjects: LCSH: Fiction—History and criticism—Theory, etc. | LCGFT: Essays.
Classification: LCC PN3331 .J35 2024 (print) | LCC PN3331 (ebook) | DDC 808.3—dc23/eng/20240109
LC record available at https://lccn.loc.gov/2023049626
LC ebook record available at https://lccn.loc.gov/2023049627

Typeset in Minion Pro by Hewer Text UK Ltd, Edinburgh
Printed and bound by CPI Group (UK) Ltd, Croydon CR0 4YY

Il n'est pas de Présent, non—un présent n'existe pas . . . Faute que se déclare la Foule, faute—de tout. Mal informé celui qui se crierait son propre contemporain.

Mallarmé

Contents

Introduction

The scholar longs for a tiger's leap into the past; the book reviewer for flashes of the present. The novel, meanwhile, is time's relief map, its furrows and spurs marking the intrusion of history into individual lives or else its tell-tale silences. All novels are thus historical; but the viability of the full-blown nineteenth-century or "realist" novel rested on protagonicity, that is, the capacity of its central character to suffer history's lightning strikes and to survive in some memorable form, which might well simply be death (or its American equivalent, failure). Such chronicles were required to run the tripartite Faulknerian gauntlet of Experience, Observation, Imagination, the strongest passing triumphantly through all three.

Meanwhile, as the social raw material of these novels stabilized, the impression gradually emerged that the novel was, in fact, a genre or fixed form just like those that had preceded it (and whose breakdown, according to Lukács, accounted for its coming into being in the first place). Was then the continent of nineteenth-century "realist" fiction some uninterrupted temporal landmass one could cross by way of a continuous history? What is certain is that, in the twentieth century, this hypothetical mainland began to break up into any number of verifiable archipelagos and free-standing islands. We go on using the generic term, but each truly original or ambitious novel seeks formal judgment in its own right, even when it claims nineteenth-century readability.

A now conventional division between modernism and realism then begins to give way to some new arrangement where the mass culture—the airport and drugstore categories which replaced the older genres—begins to flourish in opposition to the formerly modernist "classics" of college humanities courses, while, under the force field of globalization, a newer novelistic production begins to sort itself out into categories of national origin, confronting us with Chilean novels and Bangladeshi ones, African novels and European (both Eastern and Western) products, the mass of these assimilated to the Greenwich Mean Time of a hegemonic English language whose American market is the ultimate target.

In the essays that follow, I have not planned a proper *tour du monde* of this new world literature. After a brief settling of accounts with the situation in which it leaves a presumably hegemonic American variety, I have scarcely even touched on the even more hegemonic Central and Eastern Europe. But I do feel satisfied with an attention to Eastern Europe running backwards to the past of World War II; as well as works which register the deeper histories of violence in Japan and Colombia.

Meanwhile, in yet another grouping, the question of the future makes its Utopian or dystopian appearance, throwing up some unusual national pairings, in which, for example, the classical pessimism of a Danish metaphysics is juxtaposed with life in the Norwegian supermarkets, and this whole itinerary is concluded spectacularly with the Messianic Jewish heresies of eighteenth-century Poland.

Is this not to say that, in opposition to the private lives of currently fashionable autofiction, these are historical novels which, in one way or another, foreground a public dimension of life which has become problematic? This is, at least, something a little more historically distinctive than the older conventional opposition between the individual and society—the latter here having become more massive and frozen than Gibson's cyberspace and more global as well, while the individual, if not already at grips with the notorious "death of the subject," is at least in the throes of those more recent clichés called reification and fragmentation.

Perhaps the secret is this: what is new and distinctive about the novel today, what is historically unique about the emergent situation of the works discussed here, is that they try to write the collective or at least register the crisis of the individual attempting to do so. Not even the nation-state functions any longer to frame our innumerable destinies, although it is still there to mark its failure to do so: still national-historical in their singularities, other forms of collectivity, residual or emergent, offer to heal a breach its subjects may not have been aware of until registered in the works examined here. On the other hand, to read these records and these symptoms with any accuracy demands a kind of formalism, provided it is a social or better still a materialist formalism capable of detecting the profound historicality of which these works are an archeological transcription.

"There is no present," cried Mallarmé, "no—a present does not exist . . . absent the voice of the Multitude, absent—everything. Poorly advised, those who would declare themselves their own contemporaries." In these novels we can begin to hear, however faintly, the voices of contemporaries.

These essays on the novel were mostly written for *New Left Review* and the *London Review of Books*. I have assembled them together at the suggestion of Perry Anderson, with whom I share the formative impact of Sartrean existentialism and a passion for the historical novel and its problems. It is therefore a great pleasure to dedicate the results to him, in comradeship and admiration.

1

Allegories of the Hunter

Vulgar Marxism has left its scars, particularly on what American intellectuals feel a Marxist interpretation of literary works sets out to do. Marxist criticism is supposed to be "reductionistic," and to see the work of art as a mere function or reflex of the socio-economic context. It is rumored to search for the "social equivalent" of art (e.g., Was Jack London a working-class or a petty bourgeois writer? Are Faulkner's characters really peasants?). Finally, its aesthetic judgments are suspected to be little more than old-fashioned ethical ones disguised as political assessments: thus, to say that a work is progressive or reactionary would mean little more than to give the code word for moral commendation or castigation.

From the historical point of view, we might observe that many of the stereotypical features of the older Soviet criticism derive from Belinsky rather than from Marx, and similarly, a good deal of the positivistic clumsiness of the older American Marxist criticism can really be traced back to Parrington rather than to the Marxist tradition. Still, let us try to deal with these objections on their own merits.

They seem to me to reflect two kinds of fears: 1) that a Marxist criticism is bound to substitute social and economic considerations for a genuine formal analysis of the text; that it wishes, in other words, to replace discussion about literature with discussion of what T. S. Eliot

"The Great American Hunter, or, Ideological Content in the Novel," *College English* 34(2), November 1972.

used to call "some other thing"; and 2) that a Marxist point of view is, in the long run, anti-aesthetic and anti-cultural and will have the effect of making us stop reading a lot of writers and works we now admire, on the grounds they are politically suspect (and it is certain that, since so much of modern American culture is politically suspect, such an eventuality would not leave us with very much to read).

As for the first of these two objections, it can readily be agreed that a Marxist criticism which does not have anything to say about class conflict or about the nature of capitalism is not likely to end up having much that is Marxist about it. But such considerations do not always take the form you might expect. Certainly, when we are dealing with works of the past, we are obliged, by the very nature of the object itself, to restore its historical context, for it is the context of the past which is, by definition, no longer there: and such a restoration is bound to involve the transmission of a certain amount of nonliterary social and economic data. But, when we are dealing with contemporary works, with the literature of our own country and our own time, this is no longer the case. The context of these works is simply the American scene itself, which we share with them. And, insofar as that scene is torn by class conflict and class hatred and distorted and dehumanized by the most extreme structures of post-industrial capitalism, we are ourselves permanently preoccupied with these matters whether we know it or not: they stand as the permanent situation within whose framework we make all our decisions, they contaminate our every thought in the form of ideological introjection, and our very passions and fantasies are fed by them in deep subterranean ways of which we are not often conscious. But, if this is so, then to speak truly about a work of contemporary literature is already to be talking about all these things, whether we like it or not; and real literary analysis cannot be separated from a critique of the cultural situation to which the literary work stands as a complicated and vital response.

To put it this way is, in other words, to raise the question of ideology, and of the relationship between ideology—conscious or unconscious, the reader's or the writer's—and the literary work itself. This is, in effect, to turn to the second of our objections, and to ask ourselves what the attitude of a Marxist critic ought to be towards works which are clearly non-Marxist and even unprogressive. For surely the bulk of our literature can be considered as no more than liberal in its conceptual content, when not downright conservative—which is to say, in both these cases, profoundly middle class in its ideological focus. Is it not the task of the

Marxist critic to denounce such ideological content wherever they find it, and does this not commit them to a resolutely negative and destructive attitude towards our contemporary literature as a whole?

Such is the problem suggested by a reading of two recent works in a very old American genre, the wilderness novel, or the tale of the great American hunter. The first of the books I have in mind is James Dickey's bestseller, *Deliverance*, which tells the story of four town dwellers on a boating expedition through a wild area about to be submerged. The protagonists, however, suffer less from hostile nature than they do at the hands of human beings, if one may thus term men who are released by the very wilderness setting from the constraint of human law and the norms of human society, and whom the author evidently intends to represent that fundamental, bestial cruelty at the very heart of human nature ascribed by the maxim *homo homini lupus*. The heroes' eventual triumph over their pursuers, their laborious return to civilization, thus amount to a victory over Nature in general, so that the novel is by way of being an initiation ritual or *rite de passage*, if one can so characterize something that happens to middle-aged men. So, from the very outset, in its choice of subject matter, this book reflects a fashionable right-wing preoccupation, popularized by such writers as Robert Ardrey: that of the necessity of violence, both on the individual and the social level. For, if violence is a necessary component of existence, or so the argument runs, if it is indeed the very heart of life itself, then modern civilization has robbed us of the supreme experience we can have as men. In this the primitive world was wiser, for the institutionalized rituals it prescribed for adolescents taught the ultimate lesson of bodily pain and fear. These rituals had much to do with the stability of the village structure, from which our modern restlessness for some indeterminable, yet absolute Experience—for some a Romantic, for others a typically American, phenomenon—was thereby effectively exorcized. The advantage of an adventure story like Dickey's lies in the way it permits the exercise of a kind of ideological double standard: on the individual level, it allows you vicariously to experience and to satisfy this "ineradicable" instinct for violence, which is then the object of your critique on a social and political level, where it causes you to posit the need for Leviathan, or the authoritarian state, to hold the disorder and the anarchy of individual violence and of human nature in general in check. So, the strategy of the adventure tale allows you to reconcile the apparently contradictory demands of your own individual license and your authoritarian political leanings simultaneously through the same series of events.

At any rate, Dickey's characters are out to prove themselves: "they tell me," says one of them, "that this is the kind of thing that gets hold of middle-class householders once in a while." So Dickey's wilderness expedition would seem to emerge from some more basic dissatisfaction with the structure of middle-class life (the dullness of routine, the renunciations of family living, the nagging frustrations of work and of the reality principle), if not, indeed, from some "insufficiency principle at the very heart of life itself" (Georges Bataille, quoted in epigraph to *Deliverance*). In actual practice, however, you never do prove yourself in general, you always try to prove *something* to yourself in particular; and one cannot long for Experience without locating it symbolically within some individual experience of a concrete and determinate kind, which is to say that what looked metaphysical at the outset is nonetheless, in the long run, obliged to realize itself in a social world through actions and choices invested with social and historical values. So, when we observe Lewis, the ringleader of the expedition, it is not so much his *ennui* as his sheer technical and instrumental capability that strikes us:

> Lewis was the only man I knew who could do with his life exactly what he wanted to . . . He was one of the best tournament archers in the state and, even at the age of thirty-eight or -nine, one of the strongest men I had ever shaken hands with. He lifted weights and shot arrows every day in a special kind of alternating rhythm and as a result was so steady that he could easily hold a sixty-pound bow at full draw for twenty seconds.

Such an account makes it clearer than in most sports stories (e.g., the mystiques of Hemingway and Faulkner) that the sport is not only a symbolic realization of some deeper project (as in the killing of animals), but also a preparation for something, a way of training the body and the self for some impending, if often imaginary, ordeal.

So, we are only mildly surprised when we find out what it was for which Lewis was preparing himself; and the prudent reservation of Dickey and of his narrator is just a precautionary measure:

> "I just believe," Lewis said, "that the whole thing is going to be reduced to the human body, once and for all . . . I think the machines are going

to fail, the political systems are going to fail, and a few men are going to take to the hills and start over." What kind of fantasy led to this? I asked myself. Did he have long dreams of atomic holocaust in which he had to raise himself and his family out of the debris of less strong folk and head toward the same blue hills we were approaching?

But this is Dickey's form of irony, his way of having his cake and eating it too: those of us who don't swallow Lewis's motivation can identify with the narrator and with his bemused reaction. A process of *displacement* is involved, in the Freudian sense of the word: the rational surface of the mind accepts the objection, while the unconscious remains symbolically and unconsciously committed to Lewis's enterprise.

Surely, however, the technological fear cannot be a primary one. I have always felt that the terror of atomic destruction, which is, no doubt, for some an existential reality, only masked some deeper social and political apprehension. And as for the fear of technological breakdown, reflecting as it does the computerization of modern industry, the decentralized systematization of monopoly capitalism, the net drawing tight, sweeping everything into an irrevocably total organization, here surely, it is the very *existence* of the great computerized industries which is the nightmare, and not the, in any case, distant and improbable prospect of their collapse.

The same ambivalence marks the presence of the ecological theme in a work like this. For the expedition was organized in the knowledge that this partially unexplored wilderness area would soon be flooded in order to make an artificial lake. In this perspective, we rejoin that old theme of the imminent destruction of the wilderness which Cooper sounded in the earliest volume of the Leatherstocking series, and which has, in our own time, received its strongest mythical expression in Faulkner's *Go Down Moses*. Yet the tragic spirit of such a theme is no guarantee of its intellectual adequacy: for the sense of tragedy springs from the feeling of the inevitability of the destruction of nature, and it is as consistent with Cooper's belief in the desirability of progress and the unavoidable necessity for civilization to displace the lower barbarous or savage forms of life, as it is with a Romantic hatred for civilization and the city in general. The first of these positions, indeed, can be squared with a systematic apologia for the worst business practices, the worst excesses of the acquisitive instinct, while the second is able to repudiate socialism itself in the name of a revolt against regimentation and a refusal of industrial organization and planning. Both "tragic" view-points thus remain imprisoned in the ideological myth which opposes Nature to Civilization, so that whichever alternative is chosen, it perpetuates the feeling that there is some radical incompatibility between individual life and the social order.

At this point, no doubt, it will be observed that Dickey's novel is in reality a *myth*, and that a myth-critical analysis of the book can quite adequately account for the disparity we have been feeling between Lewis's conscious motivation and the deeper logic of the wilderness journey. And, no doubt, it would not be altogether wrong to see the latter as a journey into the unconscious itself, back to primal origins: a descent into the underworld, from which, after a battle with ogres or giants, limping painfully, one man lost and two others disabled, the heroes are at length able to make their way back up into the light of day, bearing with them a story which can never be told. In the process, the most essential function of myth has been fulfilled: the creation of the Hero—not the Hercules of the outset, the henceforth crippled Lewis, who is, as it were, a mere traveling companion and elder Mentor—but, rather, the narrator himself, on whom the entire responsibility of the return journey falls, and who may thus be seen as a representative of some newer generation of more human and less legendary heroes.

Yet we must observe, in this context, that the characters—and, with them, the writer and the reader—never do make it all the way back to the earth's navel, to the place of primal origins: we have to do here, in short, with a myth incompletely realized, with a kind of imaginative short-circuit, in which, for whatever reason, the deeper logic or intent of the mythic wish-fulfillment finds itself abruptly blocked by the intrusion of alien realities or impulses.

On one level, of course, such imaginative incapacitation is part of Dickey's sociological raw material, and it is hardly astonishing that his characters—these slick and typical professional men of the post-industrial world, men sophisticated enough to choose the good life of small business and a relatively rural environment, and to make the money they need at the same time that they appreciate folk music and camping—are constitutionally unable to shed their America for something radically different. In this sense, the cheapness of Dickey's style, the meretriciousness of his imagination, only faithfully reflect the shallowness of his characters as of contemporary American life in general. Such is indeed the burden of his own prize poem, "The Firebombing,"

where the World War II saturation bombing of Japan serves as the archetype for the pathological indifference, the numbed gum-chewing
ataraxia, of such American push-button war making, for which only
middle-class suburbia is real:

> It is that I can imagine
> At the threshold nothing
> With its ears crackling off
> Like powdery leaves,
> Nothing with children of ashes, nothing not
> Amiable, gentle, well-meaning,
> A little nervous for no
> Reason a little worried a little too loud
> Or too easygoing nothing I haven't lived with
> For twenty years, still nothing not as American as I am, and proud of it.

Only Dickey's poem is *about* this phenomenon, it takes the lack of imagination as its object; whereas *Deliverance* presupposes precisely the exercise of that projective imagination, of that vision of where and what you
are not, of which "The Firebombing" sung the absence. So, from beyond
the irrevocable boundary line of monopoly capitalism, a post-industrial
America—as sealed and disinfected as an astronaut's capsule, brainwashed, as Norman Mailer will put it, "until it smelled like deodor-
ant"—gazes with fatal incomprehension at other cultures and, indeed, at
its own past as well.

Something of this inability to cope with difference is vividly conveyed to
us by the climax of Dickey's story, where the heroes confront their human
enemies; and, no doubt, to have your heroes rather than your heroines
raped is a new twist posited as much on the conditioning and the shock
potential of your audience as on any genuine deeper content or logic.

Still, when we look more closely at these new arrivals, something in
their mode of narrative presentation catches our eye, something like a
nagging distortion of perspective, an odd discrepancy in the form, some
stylistic incongruity that alerts us to the presence of some deeper structural imbalance. The new characters suggest a combination of hillbilly
inbreeding and degeneracy on the one hand and the most proverbial
barnyard perversion on the other. Nor are we the only ones to receive
these stereotyped impressions: "'Escaped convicts' flashed up in my
mind on one side," the narrator tells us, "'Bootleggers' on the other." To

see these figures juxtaposed beside the novel's heroes, those standard-ized plastic men of our own business society, is to have a curious feeling of aesthetic anachronism, of the mixture of historical styles: it is as though Dickey's subconscious had been rummaging inside the wrong box of costumes, had grasped the wrong set of characterological conven-tions by mistake; and it is an eerie experience, in among the brand new equipment, the bow-and-arrow set from Neiman Marcus, the electric guitars, and the suburban houses financed on the most modern credit plans, to come across these ghosts from an older past, from the Dust Bowl and Tobacco Road, faces that stare at us out of the old Evans and Agee album, that listened to Roosevelt over the old radio speakers and rode the Model-T Ford and voted for Huey Long.

Now, perhaps, we are in a better position to understand what kind of a confrontation it was for which Dickey's heroes had prepared them-selves: it was the Thirties they went forth to meet—in some obscure way they journeyed into the wilderness to settle their accounts with the great radical tradition of the American past. Not technological breakdown, not some nagging sense of the unfulfillment of middle-class life, not atomic holocaust, not the heroic attempt to overcome nature or to find the very outer limits of the self, no, the new heroes whose legend *Deliverance* passes down to us are the frightened men of the modern American suburb, men for whom Nature is a kind of unconscious syno-nym of underdevelopment, and whose systematic and self-punishing gymnastics are, like the classic Western theories of counter-insurgency warfare, a way of beating the enemy at his own game.

The hillbilly figures are, of course, a disguise and a displacement: for if the 1930s still call to mind that older indigenous heritage of American resistance and insubordination from Roger Williams to Eugene V. Debs, the threat to the middle-class way of life today has taken another form: that of the peoples of the Third World, of the Blacks, of the intransigent and disaffected young. For a political fantasy, however, which does not wish to know its own name, these images of the Thirties provide an eminently suitable manifest content behind which the deeper logic of the story can be concealed. For the Thirties are dead, both figuratively and literally, and the triumph of the heroes over their class enemies can thus be draped in the mantle of historical necessity, the fantasy seeming to be confirmed by the very outcome of history itself. Even the political coloration of these substitute figures is useful camouflage, for, since the beginning of the civil rights movement, the redneck as a political symbol has changed his meaning, and tends rather to set in motion associations of knownothingism and reaction than of the agrarian populism of an older era: thus there is nothing in Dickey's symbolism itself which risks giving the game away and warning that you have passed beyond the bounds of a respectable and conventional political liberalism.

That the encounter should be couched in terms of violence and perversion is scarcely surprising, for the propertied classes have always understood the revolutionary process as a lawless outbreak of mob violence, wanton looting, vendettas motivated by ignorance, senseless hatred and *ressentiment*, terms which are here translated into degeneracy and general disrespect for life. As for the rape itself, however, some of Jean-Paul Sartre's analyses in *Saint Genet* suggest that, as an event, its choice is not quite so gratuitous as we might at first have thought: for, in Sartrean terms, rape, in which the body is treated like an object and exposed defenseless to its enemies, is essentially a process of being *seen*. Being looked at is a rape, being raped is being looked at: such an interpretation suggests the deeper social import of that horrified powerless indignation of Dickey's heroes, who are thus seen as though for the first time by a hostile class which rises up against them as an equal, able to think its own thoughts about you and to see you for what you are with an inexorable severity that puts your own good conscience and your own comfortable images of yourself forever in question.

James Dickey's novel is thus a fantasy about class struggle in which the middle-class American property owner wins through to a happy ending and is able, by reconquering his self-respect, to think of himself as bathing in the legendary glow of a moderate heroism. But Dickey's artistic fault was not in expressing such content. For surely such fantasies are among the most inescapable facts about contemporary American daily life. And the therapeutic function of literature lies in its value as a "talking cure," as a way of bringing such buried fantasies to expression in the broad daylight of social consciousness, rather than wishing or arguing them away in some facile optimistic manner. Dickey's book is thus repellent for some reason other than that of its content as such, and I am defending something a little more complicated than the proposition that bad politics makes bad literature. What is the matter with Dickey's treatment of these social terrors is that he is himself possessed by them; he is as unaware, as profoundly unconscious, of their shaping presence as are his readers. His story is thus not an instrument of ideological demystification, but rather an outright political and social wish-fulfillment and as such it reinforces the very tendencies which it is the function of genuine art to expose.

When we turn from *Deliverance* to a book which seems to share many of the same conscious or unconscious preoccupations, namely Norman Mailer's *Why Are We in Vietnam?*, we may well have the feeling that its attitudes and values are if anything more objectionable than those implied, rather than overtly expressed, in the Dickey novel. I'm not referring, by this, to the Free Speech Movement quality of the narrator's language, which may momentarily prevent us from noticing the perfectly chaste character of the novel's plot, in which a teenager becomes disillusioned with his Texas corporation executive father during an expensive hunting trip in northern Alaska. The disparity between the language and the events ought therefore to be enough to make us realize that sex here always stands for something else: for power relationships, for imposing your own ego; and it is the vital locus of the things that can happen to your ego when you lose, so that in this world egodamage is translated into sexual malfunction.

But this Reichean component of Mailer's vision (which might well, as in Reich himself, be genuinely revolutionary) is harnessed to a value of a far more doubtful character—namely that strident cult of *machismo*, of maleness and courage, which Mailer inherited from Hemingway, not without giving it a few twists of his own. In its origins, machismo is the sexual and familial ideology or value-system of the Mediterranean world, from Greece and the Arab countries to Sicily and Spain and beyond them to Latin America: socially, it is at one with patriarchal authoritarianism and with the segregation and subordination of women. Like all such psychological ideologies—like Puritanism, for instance, which it resembles in its potential for psychic damage if in little else—machismo takes its toll of oppressor as well as oppressed and imprisons men in their superiority just as surely as it maintains women in their inferiority. In Reichean terms machismo is a "character structure," that is, a kind of internalized psychic compulsion system which serves as the vehicle for the enforcement of social authority within the individual; and surely one of the most fundamental aims of any genuinely revolutionary movement should be to eliminate the vestiges of such ossified inner structures, which play something of the same role in our own profoundly subjectivized world as did religious remnants in the time of Marx.

Yet Hemingway's machismo cult is scarcely the expression of some deeply rooted cultural and social institution of this kind, but rather simply a personal myth; it does not, in other words, reflect anything fundamental about the American family structure but only something fundamental about Hemingway himself and his psychology, and to put it this way is to begin to wonder just exactly what social function this ostentatious myth of virility might play in the lives of intellectuals like Hemingway and Mailer. The American intellectual, indeed, suffers under a double burden of social guilt: first, in that as a bourgeois and as an American, he finds himself deeply and inextricably implicated in the values of the acquisitive and counterrevolutionary society, values which he cannot but abhor on a purely intellectual level; and then, inasmuch as he is an intellectual, he finds himself rejected and spewed forth by the very business society which is his milieu and his public and the predestined arena of his life's work. Hence the strategy of machismo: he pitches his appeal to be received back as an equal into the collectivity on the more fundamental physical basis of sex itself. For being a male is something he shares with the businessmen (and with the workers); sex (and its accompanying symbolic expressions in the realm of personal courage, sports, hunting, warfare, and the like) is the one subject with which he can talk to them without a feeling of his own difference and his own exclusion. It thus becomes the privileged place of his self-dramatization and of his attempt—through the fantasy-work of his own creation—to overcome the tensions of his unhappy consciousness and to be reunited with the social order itself.

That something like this is true for Dickey's work as well—allowing for the greater class informality among white men in the states of the Old South—seems clear enough; only it is cruder and more instinctive, and a kind of indifferent representation of violence of all kinds seems in that context to be enough to show that you can take it. It is quite different from the thematic articulation which Mailer brings to the various ways you can go about achieving manhood. In *Deliverance*, as we have shown, a generalized sense of proving yourself, a quest without an object on the conscious level, was united with a very precise unconscious class antagonism, and with the unconscious setting of a goal which amounted to nothing less than the destruction of the class enemy. In *Why Are We in Vietnam?*, on the other hand, the object of the quest is given at the outset: the grizzly bear, fiercest animal known to man, "coming at them from thirty yards away with the roar of nothing D.J. ever heard, like a foghorn fire siren about to burst, cause some congested hell in a whirlwind has come thundering with rocks down a hill out of its foghorn throat . . . wall of fur coming fast as a locomotive barreling on that trail." And because, in this work, the precise object is given, its characters and Mailer himself are far more lucid about the deeper purpose of the expedition, which is nothing more nor less than, as in the fairy tale, to *learn fear*, to find out what the worst fear that you can experience is and how you will stand up to it, to measure yourself against the most frightening experience man can know.

This is the level on which the struggle between the son and the father takes place: for as far as D.J. is concerned, the hunt for the grizzly bear gives the father one last chance to cleanse himself of all the other-direction and ego-involvement and all the gray facelessness of corporation life. For D.J., as for Mailer himself, fear is thus the privileged moment in which the psyche can purify itself of its accumulated poisons. But Rusty fails the test when he destroys the dying bear, so that his own fundamental corruption is identified with senseless violence (and thus ultimately with the violence of the Vietnamese war).

So it is already apparent that Mailer's treatment of violence has an explicit ethical and political dimension which was almost wholly lacking in *Deliverance*; but to leave it at this would be to give a rather Faulknerian and elegiac picture of Mailer's novel because we have not yet touched on D.J. himself or on the "positive" and systematic side of Mailer's vision, most notoriously embodied in that strange private religion of Manichaean struggle and obsession with smell, with decay and breath and rot, which has so singularly transformed Mailer's work since "The White Negro."

It is a religion which has its medical as well as its metaphysical dimension, and, for Mailer, every instinct which remains unrealized turns back upon the organism and sours it, triggering that most emblematic of all American diseases, cancer:

> who knows? this may indeed be the day when the first of the exploited cells takes that independent and mysterious flip from one life into another—from the social, purposive, impoverished, and unspeakably depressing daily life of an obedient cell, to the other life, wild-life, the life of the weed or the hired gun, rebel cell growing by its own laws, highwaymen upon the senses, in siege to the organs, rife with orgiastic speed, the call of the beat drumming its appeal to the millions of cells, for if other-life is short, it is wild as well, and without work.

The body with its decay is thus a visible sign or manifestation of the way
we live, so that Mailer's religion, like other versions of the occult, turns
out, in reality, to be a way of fleeing the absurdity and contingency of life
itself. To claim that we have the diseases we deserve is, at one stroke, to
abolish our anxiety before the unjustifiability of accident and disease
and to make of all life a secretly meaningful process, transparent to initi-
ates. If his ethic remains aggressive and anti-middleclass, confronting us
inexorably with the amount of death inherent in the way we live, Mailer's
metaphysic, on the contrary, holds out the false comfort of all
mystifications.

Does Mailer actually believe his own system? Probably not in the way
in which Zola "believed" his analogous notions of bodily heredity and
determinism: not scientifically or positivistically, but perhaps aesthetically. For the novelist, indeed, these occult paraphernalia amount to a
kind of *stylistic superstition*: they permit the writing of vivid sentences
and constitute a new kind of characterological shorthand. Thus the
evocation of Rusty's breath in the following passage allows Mailer to
dispense with a good deal of what in some older naturalistic tradition
would have been dramatization and background material, scene,
dialogue, and events designed to illustrate character:

> It got a hint of middle-aged fatigue of twenty years of doing all the
> little things body did not want to do, that flat sour of the slightly used
> up, and there's a hint of garlic or onion, and tobacco, and twenty years
> of booze gives a little permanent rot to the odor coming off the lining
> of the stomach, and there's even a speck of caries, one bit of dental rot
> almost on the agreeable side (for face it, fellow Americans, there are
> secret freaked-out grope types who dig dental rot if its subtle kind of
> high clean funky smell, how often, after all, does a nose get near a
> living nerve?) but with all this detraction, fatigue, booze, Nick the
> Teen, garlic and cavity, it's still a good breath, it got muscle and a big
> happy man with that clean odorless white American flesh . . .

In such a perception, a whole life and a whole lifestyle are thus condensed,
but at the same time, as D.J.'s parenthetical interjection shows us, it is not
merely a question of some useful and appropriate symbolism, but, rather,
a way of working in up close to the American reader, body against body,
naming with relish precisely those things which have been repressed by
the deodorized culture, using a revulsion as much social as personal to

revive the reader's numbed perception of the state of the organism among the computers. So, what looked like private obsession and arbitrary sensory symbolism turns out to be an implied political commentary on the American way of life itself, as well as a new and more direct and exasperating way of relating to readers formed in that way of life.

This physiological symbolism is, at length, capped by a theology and an ultimate vision of the nature of life and the universe itself. Increasingly, for Mailer, the very heart of Nature is madness, rage and unutterable hatred, a violence and a longing for revenge lashed and exacerbated by our own essential powerlessness: such is the message emitted, characteristically, by the breath of the dead wolf:

> just dead air from the dead interior, but raucous breath, all the fatigue of the wolf running broken ass to the woods and the life running the other way from him, a crazy breath, wild ass odor, something rotten from the bottom of the barrel like the stink of that which is unloved, whelp shit smell, wild as wild garlic, bad, but going all the way right back into the guts of things, you could smell the anger in that wolf's heart (fucked again! I'll kill them!) burnt electric wire kind of anger like he'd lived to rip one piece of flesh from another piece, and was going to miss it now, going to miss going deep into that feeling of *release* when the flesh pulls loose from the flesh . . .

So it is that at the climax of the novel, when the two teenagers hike up into the Arctic Circle, we come upon one of the most sensational visions of the Absolute in American literature since the closing page of *The Narrative of Arthur Gordon Pym of Nantucket*, a delirious hallucination in which the entire Arctic Circle is revealed as the "MagneticElectro fief of the dream," as one immense psychic crystal, receiving into itself and storing up and retransmitting all the vibrations and lusts and instincts, all the noxious energies generated out of the daily routine and frustrations of the inhabitants of the North American continent and then flushed back to them in the form of unclean dreams and unconscious impulses. It is, in short, for the body of the globe itself, something comparable to Mailer's vision of the psychic economy of the individual body. At length, when this malign atmosphere begins to tell on the travelers and to make its power felt through the generation of homosexual fantasies in them (and, for Mailer, homosexuality as a direct struggle for virility between men themselves is always a murderous symbol, a sign of impending Evil), there is vouchsafed a glimpse of the nature of the deity itself, God as Satan, as the Prince of this World, whose instinctual command is a kind of never-ending murmur pulsing throughout creation itself, the ultimate mesmerizing admonition, "Go out and kill—fulfill my will, go and kill."

With such a vision, we are evidently at the very heart of Mailer's explanation "why we are in Vietnam," with all its fundamental ambiguity. No doubt, insofar as Mailer's God is nourished by all the rot and poison of American life, his religious vision also amounts to a social commentary and offers a striking figure for the violence which, as has so often been observed, lies concealed and sleeping within the most placid externalizations of American life. In this sense, it holds open the possibility that such violence would not necessarily be secreted by other social forms which offered some fuller mode of instinctual satisfaction and of personal realization in general.

And, no doubt, as in Poe, the vision is a way of ending a book otherwise somehow structurally unresolvable: what cannot be articulated in further action, in the concrete working out of the plot itself, is here projected as static and almost visual decoration, a resolution through image in default of event. But this already has something symptomatic to tell us about how much of American reality we can express through literature, which is to say, through an unmediated vision, and confirms our fear that it is only too difficult to convey the historic socio-economic causes of American violence through the medium of a narrative about individuals and individual experience. The recourse to myth or symbol thus stands as an admission that the artist has not been able to do his job, has been ultimately thwarted by the recalcitrance of his raw material.

Still, it will be observed that the book includes social and political comment of a far more explicit type than we have so far suggested: this is the point of the whole Texas background, and obviously enough, just as the earlier *Presidential Papers* and *An American Dream* amounted to an imaginary dialogue with Kennedy, so *Why Are We in Vietnam?* turns around the writer's ambivalent and fantasy-charged relationship to Lyndon B. Johnson, of whom, in the memorable public address described at the beginning of *The Armies of the Night*, Mailer declared himself "the dwarf alter ego." Such ambivalence characterizes Mailer's relationship to his Texas material in general, with which he identifies as profoundly as it revolts him: hence the ambiguity of his hero, for D.J. is, at one and the same time, quintessentially Texan and explicitly at odds with the values embodied in his father's way of life.

Of course, to use Texans as symbols of Americans, and to blame the Vietnamese war on the corporations and the big oilmen, on Dallas and Lyndon B. Johnson's lust for power, is to have recourse to stereotypes at least as hackneyed as those we have already found to be at work in *Deliverance*. Once again, however, the self-consciousness of the process results in a qualitative difference, and, for Mailer, such stereotypes are the very signs of an intimate knowledge of American life itself; they show whether you know the score and how American society really functions. In this sense, the writing of the novel is the very first arena in which you prove your manhood, in which you show whether you are really capable of appropriating the social totality itself, in the way a businessman appropriates it when, by making his million, he shows that he knows the facts of life of that otherwise "untotalizable totality" which is America today. Conversely, failing the test is being taken in by all the myths and ads, all the sugarcoating and the politicians' explanations, which are prepared for the dutiful consumption of a brainwashed public: hence Mailer's instinctive anti-idealism, hence the reflex of cynicism automatically triggered by any kind of socialistic or ameliorative perspective, which he instinctively assimilates to the naive credulity of liberalism itself. The use of social stereotypes in Mailer thus corresponds not to the truth-requirements of some naturalistic aesthetic of representation or mimesis, but, rather, to this new and as yet imperfectly characterized process in which the making of the book itself dramatizes the novelist's fundamental subject anew, symbolically on the level of the relationship between writer and reader.

There remains, however, the question of the ultimate adequacy of Mailer's explanation, even on a sociological level. There can be no doubt but that his novel generates a picture of the power elite sharp enough to stimulate all the elements of a healthy class antagonism, isolating and identifying the corporation men who represent America and for whom violence comes as a release from frustration and sexual impotence (see the long list of Rusty's political beliefs in Intro Beep 7). Still, it remains a psychological explanation and one is tempted to wonder whether these business types are worth hating in their own right, whether they have not, in their turn, been programmed by their own system. The notion of the "organization man" is, in other words, a kind of displacement of the older Marxian socio-economic description. By giving you psychology rather than economic functionalism, the description of a stratum rather than a class, Vance Packard rather than C. Wright Mills or Malcolm X, it risks deflecting your attention from the political to the merely folkloristic.

Indeed the very force of Mailer's novelistic evocation of such characters is inextricably linked with the structural defects of his account of the war and of American violence in general: in order to dramatize such violence, in order to re-create from within characters who may in one way or another be identified with it, Mailer finds himself committed to an imaginative sympathy with violence which forbids him any kind of historical or dialectical perspective on it. Hence the central ethical paradox of *Why Are We in Vietnam?*: D.J. is disgusted with the corrupt business world of his father, but what he chooses to put in its place, what he appeals to for purification and renewal from that corruption and that competition, is merely an intensification of the latter itself. Struggle, fear, aggression: these are *already* the laws of Rusty's world, and to move from Dallas to the Brooks Range, to exchange the anxieties of the corporation for the terrors of the hunt itself, is not to shed one set of values for a different one, but only to revive and restore the basic values of the competitive society itself, grown fat and stale and too comfortable in the atmosphere of the new post-industrial affluence. So, it would be a mistake to think that D.J. rejects the value system of his father's existence (but it is a mistake of which D.J. himself is probably just as guilty as some of his readers): on the contrary, his cult of fear and of courage is a way of being *more* faithful to those values than Rusty himself.

A comparison with Faulkner's *The Bear* makes the difference very clear: in Faulkner, Uncle Ike renounces violence itself when he renounces hunting, just as he renounces the whole economic system based on violence and his own inheritance along with it. One can therefore speak here of a genuine conversion to a different system of values, even though Uncle Ike's gesture is, no doubt, a sentimental and elegiac one, a purely individual renunciation devoid of social significance inasmuch as it can scarcely be thought to reflect the goals and aspirations of a class or determinate group. But Faulkner is well aware of this: hence the dreary isolation of the old man's life, his childlessness, his survival as a kind of lonely anachronism, all of which underscore his value as a static symbol or moral image rather than as a sign of some genuine possibility of action. Still, insofar as he represents the imaginative attempt to conceive of some concrete alternative to the world of the hunt, such a character is inconceivable in Mailer's novelistic universe, where, as we have shown above, those who withdraw (e.g., idealists, liberals, radicals, and the like) convey gutlessness, cowardice, the great refusal, rather than some concrete existential option in their own right.

I suppose that, in one sense, this simply means that Mailer's world is more advanced and more irrevocably developed than Faulkner's; his is a world in which there are very few vacant lots left and very few empty places where a man like Uncle Ike can still pursue a marginal existence. But, in another sense, this increasing social claustrophobia is peculiarly Mailer's own and brings us face to face with what is surely the originality of his work as a whole. And not only of his work: of his lifestyle as well, as it has been carefully reported and dramatized for us, not least of all by Mailer himself. The combativeness, the studied caprice and unpredictability, that peculiar egomania which distinguishes itself radically from the self-satisfied mannerisms of ordinary vanity in that it aims at exposing the ego anew, at reopening all the wounds and daring you to make a fresh assault upon it—all of these characteristics are inflamed at the prospect of indifference in the interlocuter; they aim at getting under your skin in the most fundamental way, probing for your weak points, exasperating you into some new and direct form of contact; they foresee a crumbling of our characterological defenses, a kind of pained and astonished lashing back which in Mailer's scheme of things amounts to the most genuine and immediate form of interpersonal recognition; and we have already had occasion to see how such a relationship, under the guise of whatever sporting metaphor you will, obtains in the uneasy distance between Mailer the writer and his readers as well. This wary boxer's stance, these eyes on the alert for the most fundamental signs of life in those approaching, the impatience with which the comfortable security of social institutions and interpersonal conventions are short-circuited on behalf of some more primary form of the *agon* or ontological combat—surely all of these psychological and behavioral preparations point not so much to unresolved aggressive impulses or to the random violence of repression but rather to some hypostasis of *competition* itself as a social and historical mode of being. It is as though within the competitive society Mailer had chosen not to repudiate the dominant value but, rather, to adopt it with the fanatical exaggeration of the newly converted, to live it to its ultimate existential limits, to extremes of intensity no ordinary businessman has ever known, giving his own personality over to a kind of symbolic possession by what would otherwise look like an alien force, transforming his life and work into a sacred reenactment of what cannot apparently be exorcized any other way. And, indeed, I believe that, for modern psychology, such a total alienation of the self to threatening forces, such a total identification with what otherwise menaces consciousness from within or without, is one of the classic ways by which the psyche seeks to maintain its precarious stability.

By which I do not so much mean that Mailer is sick as that the society itself, in all the ways we know only too well, is sick itself and manifests this sickness through him: Mailer's is merely the immemorial gesture of the artist who takes this sickness upon himself symbolically and tells us about ourselves through the medium of the "egotistical sublime" of that symbolic identification. His social and historical value for us, and his greatness and integrity as an artist, can thus be measured by the degree to which he has actualized everything which in and around us is only potential, to which he has lived out and articulated for us the very essence of that competitive "instinct" which is the very low-grade element of our public and private lives and for that very reason often imperceptible to us.

Yet such symbolic identification is not a game, nor is it achieved without paying a price, both psychological and artistic; and something of that price emerges vividly from that odor-laden perceptual universe of which we have already spoken and which here indeed finds its secret and most fundamental justification. For, to be sure, our bodies themselves are sick and poisoned with all the industrial waste of the market civilization, which we relive in the taste in our mouths and the smell of our sick perspiration, in muscle fatigue and the ripe middle-aged decay of the sense organs; and of all this Mailer is the poet, the individual and biological drama of the aging of an individual for the first time meeting that historic and specifically capitalist phenomenon which is the devastation of nature and the systematic adulteration of the human environment. Yet all this is but an external figure for the intoxication and contamination of the very spirit, and I put it this way in order to emphasize the increasing dependency of the mind on its own disease: the point is that as an artist, Mailer cannot afford to be cleansed of his poisons. His sickness is his raw material: so his eventual cure, the prospect of some definitive and permanent disintoxication, runs the risk of putting an end to his productivity as a writer. Nor does this amount to a revival of the old Romantic notion of the relationship between genius and sickness (e.g., in a Thomas Mann): for it is, in reality, a dilemma peculiarly characteristic of the artist under capitalism, one exacerbated by the increasingly total and dehumanized organization of post-industrial society, in which the writer finds himself increasingly compromised by the materials with which he is called upon to deal.

Nor is it the artist's dilemma alone, but, rather, that of cultural revolution in general, and we are all, in some sense, infected by the very poisons for which we seek a cure. In his phenomenology of the stages of spiritual and historical development, Hegel described the transitions between one moment or form and another as a kind of *death*, in the sense in which the religions speak of conversion as a kind of dying to the self; and from within the commodity reification of American society—a reification so thoroughgoing that we have even forgotten what the older human world felt like—we may well look forward with a kind of terror to the society of the future as to a kind of loss of self, in which all of the intoxications to which we are the most feverishly attached are taken from us.

Thus, the novelist has a kind of vested interest in his raw material, and this is why Mailer clings with incorrigible tenacity to everything he denounces. So, Kate Millett has observed that "he seems to cherish even the notion of guilt in men, a generalized guilt associated with sexual activity itself, giving it the piquancy relished best by a puritan sensibility." And we have already seen how he instinctively protects his vision on a political level: he refuses the terms of that radical and Marxist critique which, in offering some ultimate intellectually coherent and satisfying account of that preoccupation with competition and violence which makes up his novelistic vision, risks dissolving it as a vision altogether.

So, with the case of Mailer, at length we glimpse the elements of a solution to the problem raised at the beginning of the present essay: that of the place of ideology in the novel, and the relationship between the character of that ideology and the artistic value and force of the work itself. We may now perhaps understand a little more concretely what Lucien Goldmann meant when he insisted that the greatest works are not those which are most unique, but rather those in some profound sense most *representative* of their age:

> The writer of genius seems to us to be the one who realizes a synthesis, whose work is *at one and the same time* the most immediate and the most philosophically lucid, for *his sensibility coincides with the ensemble of the historical process and the evolution of history*; the one who, in

order to speak about his own most concrete and immediate problems, implicitly raises the most general problems of his age and of his culture, and for whom, inversely, all the *essential problems* of his time are not mere intellectualizations or convictions but realities manifesting themselves in living and immediate fashion in his feelings and his intuitions.

And, indeed, we have tried to show above how much of the force of Mailer's work springs from this coincidence in it of the personal obsession and the historical contradiction, from the way in which he has been able to experience an objective historical institution (the competitive nature of life under capitalism) as a subjective, psychological, indeed often purely stylistic phenomenon, thus evolving a literary construct which is both socio-historical and psychological at once, or better still, which transcends the limits of the purely sociological document on the one hand and the psychological case history on the other.

Still, the problem remains of the nature of Mailer's ideology, and it will be said, particularly inasmuch as we have shown its affinity with many of the values in *Deliverance*, that our analyses here have ended up proving the opposite of what we initially intended, and may be ultimately reduced not to some qualitative difference between two ideologies but rather to the simple difference in talent between two writers themselves. All of which, it will be said, only goes to show that whereas a mediocre writer is bound to produce a mediocre novel, a writer of talent like Mailer can transform the same objectionable materials and ideas into a work of art of great quality. And, if this is the case, then, of course, artistic quality is ideologically neutral and may be wholly and completely separated from the political convictions and attitudes of the author himself.

But I think we have been able to see a little more than this, for the essential difference between Dickey's social attitudes and those of Mailer turned out to be that the first were unconscious and inarticulate, informing the work after the fashion of blind and deeply held prejudices; whereas the ideology of Mailer proved to be a supremely self-conscious construction, constantly dramatized and reexamined by the author himself. Is it, then, enough for a writer to systematize his attitudes and to transform his implicit feelings into some coherent and personalized worldview?

The writer's worldview or system of ideas—Lawrence's as well as Thomas Mann's, that of Malraux just as much as that of Proust—is evidently an intellectual object of a type very different from the various abstract systems of the philosophers; and to say this is perhaps to raise the additional problem of the differentiation of literature from the various abstract disciplines—philosophy or psychology or sociology—which aim at replacing concrete experience or historical data with some abstract model. Literature, on the contrary, offers an immediate vision of the coherence and significance of the concrete, one unmediated by abstractions, in which meaning becomes visible within the things themselves, and is articulated, rather than illustrated, by the organization of the narrative. On the other hand, it is clear that a Marxist criticism must go much further than the conventional literary investigations into the themes and world of a given author, in that it insists on understanding those themes not as mere formalism or aesthetic play, not even as the symptoms of deeper psychological conflicts, but rather as the expression of some genuinely concrete social and historical experience. Thus, once again, for Marxism, the investigation into the world or worldview of a given author slowly seems to veer about into that problem of the author's ideology with which we began.

Some remarks of Louis Althusser suggest a way of resolving these problems: "Art," he tells us,

> makes *visible* and makes available in the mode of *seeing, perceiving* and *feeling* (which is not that of abstract *knowing*) that *ideology* itself from which [the work of art] springs, in which it bathes, from which it detaches itself as a work and to which it makes *allusion* . . . Balzac and Solzhenitsyn furnish a "point of view" on the ideology to which their works continually allude and which sustains them, a point of view which presupposes a certain *remove*, the *establishment of a certain inner distance* with respect to that very ideology from which their novels emerge. They thus, and as it were *from within* and through a kind of *inner distance*, cause us to "perceive" (but not to know abstractly) the very ideology to which they remain prisoner.

So, the great writer always tends to *thematize* their ideological raw material, not because they aspire to the condition of philosophy or of abstract knowledge and formulations, but, rather, because this is the privileged way in which such ideological material can be lifted to consciousness and made available to us as an object in its own right. Art thus allows us to walk all around these otherwise latent and implicit unconscious attitudes which govern our actions; to see them isolated as in a laboratory experiment for the first time, spread out and drying in the light of day where we are free to evaluate them consciously. This explains why the writer's personal attitude towards that ideological material is not so important, why it does not ultimately matter whether Balzac was a reactionary, or whether Mailer is a sexist, a dupe of the myths of American business, and so forth. For his essential task as a writer, faced with such ideological values both within and without himself, is, through his own prereflexive lucidity about himself and through the articulations of his fantasy life and the evocative ingenuity of his language, to bring such materials to artistic thematization and thus to make them an object of aesthetic consciousness. After that has been accomplished, his own distance from the ideological object in question is no more privileged than ours, with which we are free to replace it.

This is not to say that, under certain conditions, a writer cannot achieve a genuinely political perspective on his raw materials. Such a genuinely militant literature—one which did not scorn the tasks of agitation and propaganda in their most incandescent revolutionary sense—would be to the literature here under consideration as a kind of metaliterature: one which reunited the two types of consciousness which here fall asunder, rejoining the hitherto separated realms of literature and criticism, of private experience and public commitment, of the expression of ideology and the evaluation of the ideology thus expressed. Such a political literature—henceforth providing its own explicit theoretical commentary on its own themes—would not necessarily make criticism superfluous but would absorb the latter's political content, the latter's techniques of ideological analysis, back into itself. More is involved here than the mere assimilation of overtly political materials into the artistic medium: Mailer's own journalism does that already, and does it with gusto. Rather, a genuine political literature would aim at the politization of everything hitherto considered to be nonpolitical, of private life and psychology, perception and the emotions; it would imply an expansion of form and a refinement of the artistic fluoroscope such that the political character of the most remote and specialized areas of experience stands revealed to the naked eye. Works like those of Brecht, or, more recently, of Godard, yield a glimpse of what such a fully political and fully conscious literature might be.

Until it exists, the Marxist critic and teacher, who is always, of necessity, a Marxist student as well, faces the task of dealing with a prepolitical literature in political terms, of raising to consciousness that political and ideological infrastructure of literary works which is so often unconscious as far as the writer is concerned, and imperceptible to the reader trained in the traditions of idealistic thinking. I hope to have shown that such analysis does not involve the imposition of extraneous themes and concerns but, rather, provides a more thoroughgoing exploration of the deep structures of works than the current formalist criticism is willing to undertake. Is it necessary to ridicule the idea that it is because the critic is a Marxist that he or she practices a Marxist interpretation of literature rather than some other kind? Not we, but reality itself is Marxist in its structure; and the Marxist is not a member of some peculiar sect, with its own determinate beliefs and terminology, but rather one who tries as best they can to approximate that reality and to come to active terms with it, in literature as elsewhere. Faithfulness to the text is an excellent slogan, but one which commits us, even more than we may be aware, to an enterprise which cannot stop short of history itself.

2
Limits of the Gringo Novel

"But thou wouldst not think how ill all's here about my heart; but it is no matter."

Hamlet

I want to start with a proposition, namely, that the culture of late capitalism is not merely an empirically impoverished one, but one doomed structurally and tendentially to enfeeblement, whence its desperate need to revitalize itself with transfusions of the foreign and the exotic, the Other (this is then the "exogamy" of my title). It is a proposition I would actually be willing to argue in relation to all three current centers of late capitalism, not merely the North American superstate but also Japan and post-1992 Europe. The paradox is, of course, that very few societies have been quite so saturated with culture (in another sense) as this one, in which the effacement of the boundaries between culture and the noncultural (or superstructure and base, if you prefer) and the penetration of culture into the most remote crannies of social and individual life are well-known phenomena that have motivated the invention of new sociological conceptions, such as those of image society, media society, the society of the spectacle, and so forth. The cultural sterility I have in mind, however, in no way excludes the existence, in all three

"Americans Abroad: Exogamy and Letters in Late Capitalism," in *Critical Theory, Cultural Politics, and Latin American Narrative*, ed. Steven M. Bell, Albert H. LeMay, and Leonard Or (Notre Dame: University of Notre Dame Press, 1993).

superpowers but particularly in Europe and Japan, of spaces of extraordinary elegance at their upper reaches while the lower ones are suffused with commercial narratives and entertainment forms of all kinds. But the vital source of language production is in them sapped, as we shall see later; their older indigenous philosophical traditions have been colonized by Anglo-American analytic philosophy to the point where very little of the critical or the transcendent remains, and the content of their finest literary production can be shown, on closer inspection, to be borrowed from what reality persists outside their own immediate national and linguistic borders.

It is just such a closer inspection I propose to make here, of one of the most remarkable novels of the decade that has just ended, Robert Stone's *A Flag for Sunrise* (1981). I am going to take this book as the exemplar for a genre I want to define as the "gringo novel," which is to say, the novel written by gringos about Latin Americans, in this case an imaginary country in Central America. I shall also have to keep reminding us that this book (and some others I will mention) are not mediocre products of the North American imagination but, rather, are very good writing indeed, and better than most fiction produced here: for that is the strong form of my argument, that at its very best and most intense the literature of late capitalism needs to borrow from its Others.

Otherwise, the literary production of the superstate would seem essentially to boil down to two basic categories, leaving aside that whole area of cultural production which is so-called paraliterature or the subgenres (such as detective stories, science fiction, Harlequin romances, and the like), and leaving aside also the literatures written for the new publics of the so-called new social movements or microgroups (such as gay literature or feminist literature or ethnic literature or neo-ethnic literature). Thus, the mainstream of white American cultural production would seem to nourish two distinct areas and to articulate two distinct types of raw material, which can also be characterized in generic terms as the soaps, on the one hand, and regionalism, on the other. The soaps, a category that today encompasses most North American bestsellers and most "serious" North American filmmaking, offer narratives organized around a fundamental category of North American life, called, in media language, the "relationship." It would be wrong to think that this term designates private life alone, or the subjective or existential: rather, as a result of the effacement of the distinction between private and public, business realities and the public realm of the profession and of success are also now included within the objectified and depersonalized category of the "relationship," reified not least because it thus bears a peculiarly abstract name. The aesthetic point one wants to make here is that such commodified and pseudopsychological categories have so deeply entered the very substance of North American life that it is impossible to use the "relationship" as literary raw material without at the same time admitting the objectified trash of this language and its "concepts": we thus here witness the terminal stage of a process that began with Flaubert and his clichés and commonplaces, and it is a stage that no longer admits of internal innovation let alone of change— since the commodification and packaging of subjective goods have too great a functional stake in such pseudopsychological categories for fresh subjective experience to emerge, on the one hand, while, on the other, the commercial colonization of the North American psyche is too far advanced to permit any ironic distance or satiric perspective, save perhaps the Utopian wish to imagine a world utterly denuded of "relationships" in the first place.

As for regionalism, it was, with the Faulknerian narrative apparatus, one of the last great North American literary technologies to have been successfully exported all over the world, and this second area of North American literary production essentially consisted in the invention of a vertical regionalism that included history and the experience and memory of historical catastrophe within its local surveyor's map. It would not be fair to point out the obvious, that in a situation in which nature and the land have been abolished, these things can scarcely be revived in the imaginary as a form of national salvation or cultural therapy: after all, regionalism in its present form came into being precisely because of the postmodern abolition of nature and as a response to it. Indeed, if Faulkner is in any way the patron saint of the new regional literature, then, imperialism or not, we have to add that his new forms are our great gift to the rest of the world, and, in particular, to the Third World, whose extraordinary cultural production from García Márquez to the Chinese is inconceivable without Faulkner's invention of a vertical regionalism that includes history and the experience of historical catastrophe within its small local confines. But a regionalism after Faulkner not merely takes place in a South or a West that has superhighways and shopping malls just like everywhere else; it also governs regions from which obscure and ancient historical catastrophes have faded away, at least from the memory of white people. But the question of what a regionalism can possibly be worth that has no history left can also be reframed sociologically, and in a stronger way than in the opposition between country and city. For one would think that authentic and vibrant regionalism depends for its condition of possibility on the existence of a peasantry, something Faulkner had but which agribusiness has replaced by migrant workers (a substitution which at once raises the very constructional problem we will be confronting in the present study, that of the transcription of foreign speakers). So, regionalism does not offer an authentic alternative to the inauthentic commodification of the soaps but, rather, confronts us in turn with its own internal contradictions.

A gringo novel like Stone's will now, outside the territorial limits of these two vast North American generic entities, combine their mutual specialties in ways that modify both. The novel will go on dealing with "relationships," and very peculiar and historicized period relationships at that, '60s relationships, as distanced as specimens from the pathology lab, but will do so against the backdrop of regions that do not belong to us spiritually and culturally and thus are registered as exotic. But this is no longer tropical literature: Stone no longer has anything in common with *Under the Volcano* or with Graham Greene, let alone with *The Plumed Serpent*; meanwhile, the replacement of Mexico by Central America is more than a mere change of scene, it is also a fundamental shift in time, as we shall see in a moment.

But it is also worth mentioning a few other possible generic categories for this unclassifiable book: the spy novel, for example, which is, in my view, an essentially theological genre that turns on the cosmic confrontation between Good and Evil in the universe, or the political novel itself—most problematical of all genres—which ought a priori never to be possible, so that when it rarely and miraculously comes into being it is its unexpected existence that needs to be explained and not, as with the other genres, its absence and its lack.

Meanwhile, even though the historical novel has become problematical in a different way—insofar as everything is history but yet the present is more historical than the past (and the future perhaps even more historical than the present)—it would be paradoxical but appropriate to advance the suggestion that *A Flag for Sunrise* is not only one of the rare great political novels of the period but is also one of the rare historical novels, even though situated in the present of its own writing. But this is so, for a reason that will situate it sharply in historical time and that will mark it fundamentally: it is a paradox one can only express by saying that, despite but also on account of and through its Central American setting, this is a novel about Vietnam, a novel marked in all conceivable ways and scarred beyond any healing by the climactic encounter of the superstate with its Other. It is not only the fact that most of the characters of *A Flag for Sunrise* have lived through the Vietnam War itself; it is also the ominous and bewildering fact that Central America really is Vietnam, is still Vietnam; and not the least unnerving moments of this book are the ones when, like drugs repeating on you, unexpectedly and without warning everything turns back into Southeast Asia:

> As they passed the palace gatehouse the smells, the sight of the sentry box in its well of light under the jacaranda, the brown sawed-off soldiers in MP's helmets brought Holliwell such a Vietnam flash that he was certain they must all be feeling it together [i.e., the other post-Vietnam Americans in the car with him]. It awakened in him so potent a mixture of nostalgia and dread that in spite of the morning booze-up which was still fouling his blood, he began to feel like a drink.[1]

Here's the story: a small mission on the Atlantic coast of the Central American dictatorship called Tecan houses the remains of an order, an old alcoholic priest and a young middle-western nun who are scheduled for repatriation back to the United States. But the government and its North American masters have the feeling that these religious (Catholic missionaries being, as one of the characters puts it, nothing but "a pack of reds" [FS 188]) are somehow involved in local politics, that is, have connections with internal subversive groups. So, the protagonist is set in motion, an alcoholic anthropologist and former "expert" in Vietnam, who, invited to give a scholarly lecture in the neighboring "democracy" of Compostela, is encouraged in a variety of ways to take the opportunity to visit Tecan as well and provide some more reliable eyewitness evidence about the mission's activities. Meanwhile, in the subplot, a young speed freak who has deserted from the Coast Guard gets himself involved in an arms-smuggling venture that will also end up on the

---

1   Robert Stone, *A Flag for Sunrise* (New York: Knopf, 1981), p. 163. All further references to this work will be given within the body of the essay and the work designated as FS.

eastern coast of Tecan, near the mission, in the middle of the predictable revolutionary explosion. He escapes along with the anthropologist Holliwell, and not the least tactful and aesthetically expert feature of the novel is the utter ignorance in which it leaves us about the fate of the revolution itself (all we find out is that the president has fled to Miami, something which could obviously have any number of different sequels). The young nun, however, is tortured to death, and Father Egan presides over the return to peace and quiet in the jungle in a state of irreversible alcoholic decomposition.

The novel's great formal triumph is that, unlike Stone's earlier *Dog Soldiers*, it does not reduce in the mind or the memory to a set of strings of individual destinies or plot-lines: out of the two or three that can be coldly and analytically enumerated in hindsight, the impression of a far greater multiplicity is disengaged, and this seems to me to be so for two fundamental reasons. The first is that these individual characters are themselves at distance from their own destinies, which therefore break down into a series of ungeneralizable experiences; while the second has to do with something like the doom of the historical process itself, transindividual if not collective, which rises above its individual participants or victims and grips them together in a cluster in its mighty convulsion.

What is it now that North Americans are able to experience in this setting that they cannot find back home, in their own language? Violence, for one thing, of course: which is to say violence unmotivated by crime as such, or the familiar categories of criminal motivation. None of these characters, however technically illegal, is a criminal in the tradition of North American television police procedurals. But even the great Sartrean theme of sadism and torture—impressively revived in this novel—becomes reduced to clinical and juridical banality when reimagined within the continental US. Our own cultural representations are thus forms that domesticate the scandal of violence and reduce it to the known quantities of already catalogued and named categories. The law-and-order shows in the US service the cause of order in two different ways and on two different levels: they frighten the public and enlist its support for increasing funding and repressive legislation; but, in some deeper well-nigh metaphysical way, they reassure the public that the bewildering forms of violence with which it is sometimes confronted, or imagines itself to be confronted, are already under the control, as Foucault might put it, of the knowledge system itself, which has drawn up exhaustive tables of the acts in question and can explain them all to your satisfaction. The very act of *naming* a form of violence, as Stuart Hall and his colleagues have so dramatically shown for the category of "mugging" when it is deliberately imported from the United States into Britain,[2] is an act of social control and remastery, and the naming substitutes an ideological idea of the thing for the thing itself.

It is that name and ideological idea which Stone's non-American restaging seeks to strip away, albeit at some cost, since one never manages to get outside of ideology in any absolute or ultimate sense. The price here, as I will try to show later, is the lurid reawakening of the old category of Otherness, along with the inevitable slippage from politics into ethics. Yet this is done, in some sense, in the name of politics itself: for the other great experience—linked, to be sure, to violence—that is unavailable within the North American borders is the experience of classical revolutionary politics: this also has become an exotic, imported, when not to say tropical, product, that we have to get from abroad. We are told that nowadays (in late capitalism) the category of revolution or of total social transformation by way of the political level is irrelevant and philosophically incoherent, a view that sometimes strikes one as parochial First World wishful thinking. As a form, however, Stone's novel itself must stand or fall with the validity of this category (however the practical chances of revolution are in it assessed). If revolution is henceforth meaningless in the postmodern sense, therefore, Stone's novel is as extinct as the dinosaur or as dead and mummified as the voluminous dissident and Gulag literature of the Eastern European countries, which must now also be consigned to the ashcan of History.

But we may begin this inquiry on a more formal level, which has to do with style and perception, landscape and the body. Clearly, when one raises the question of style today, one activates the problematic of postmodernism, for which a personal or individual style of the older modernist type is no longer possible. Stone's novels are, of course, representational or realistic in the classic North American (if not bestseller) sense, a sense from which the most obvious earmarks of modernist experimentation, but also of postmodern textuality, have been repressed or effaced. Stylistically, however, the book is peculiarly thinned out, as

2   Stuart Hall, Chas Critcher, Tony Jefferson, John Clarke, and Brian Roberts, *Policing the Crisis: Mugging, the State, and Law and Order* (New York: Holmes and Meier, 1978).

though deliberately detoxified of the rich cholesterol of description and physical sensation; nor is this the ostentatious Hemingway-style silence and stoicism of omissions and renunciations: rather, it is something like a convalescent sensorium, about which then the other most important thing to say is the apparently contradictory, but obviously dialectically constitutive, appearance within this perceptual impoverishment of the "sublime" itself, rare enough at any moment of aesthetic history and here reinvented in the diving sequence, as we shall see in a moment.

What accounts for this peculiar combination of moments of great perceptual intensity and an otherwise seemingly constant indifference to the physical facts of life, to descriptions of the physical appearance of the characters for example? We find, at least, an emblematic key in Stone's next novel, the disappointing *Fields of Light*, about Hollywood and alcoholism, disappointing not least because, preceded by *Dog Soldiers*, with its motif of drugs and smuggling, the weight of the evidence thereby threatens to infect *A Flag for Sunrise* in its turn, rewriting it back into a drama of controlled substances, where the omnipresence of uppers and downers, rum, booze, dope, among all the main characters, now seem on the point of turning the political content of the novel into a mere excuse and pretext to deal with the now obsessive-seeming motif of addiction.

Yet it is important not to let this novel turn into yet another stereotypical rehearsal of the perils of the tropics for Northerners, yet another archetypal print-out of the well-known alcoholic disintegration of imperial bureaucrats in the heat of the Southern tier. As I have said, *A Flag for Sunrise* has, in fact, very little in common with Graham Greene or *Under the Volcano*. What saves *A Flag for Sunrise* (perhaps uniquely in Stone's work) from the specialized category of the novel of addiction is, in fact, the completion of what I began to say about Vietnam a moment ago: there comes a point in reading this book, indeed, when you realize that Vietnam is itself here an addiction, and perhaps the most powerful one of all—that searing experience of the outer limit which, no matter how horrible, empties the lesser experiences of peacetime of their savor and thus persists in the mind as an absent, obsessive fixed point. Once you realize that, however, all the other more local physical addictions in the book suddenly themselves become political, allegories of Vietnam, rather than the other way around.

And this can also account for the stylistic peculiarities just mentioned, which we can now see as incorporating the irritability of the ex-addict,

the withdrawal and privation of a disconnected sensorium. For that irritability and discomfort is itself the condition of possibility for the occasional electrifying stream of sensations, in a situation in which perception itself is little more than an exasperation of the sensory stimuli to
which the external world condemns us in our vulnerable and hypersen-
sitive, fragile condition. And that also accounts for the human relations
here, and the dialogues in which people work up very close to each
other, so close you can feel each remark inside the other's system. It
probably has something to do with the relatively muted emphasis on
description and the physical: very little of the heavy insistence on
appearance and the body that most modern literature has found its
satisfaction in; the rare sex scene is exceedingly disembodied, as is the
climactic moment of torture (although you certainly do not remember
it that way afterwards). But to this idiosyncratic synthesis of susceptibil-
ity and anesthesia we also owe the great sensory breakthroughs, the
momentary lifting of all of this, a suspension of all this, a suspension of
irritability, and, in particular, the wondrous descent into the deep-sea,
one of the great bravura pieces of modern contemporary writing and a
new kind of opening onto the ontology of earthly space, such as we have
not known since Lawrence: "It had been years since he had taken so
much pleasure in the living world," the novel comments tersely, within a
world full of excitements and intensity but virtually without pleasure.

But the diving sequence, in which alone the splendor of the created
universe is retained, beneath a surface above which an atmosphere
much more horrible than pollution reigns, is also the path towards some
deeper, ultimate truth in this universe. That is a truth, not of the skin
and of sensory perception, but, rather, of deep feeling tone and of something no longer even related to emotions in the older sense, and for
which Heidegger's notion of *Stimmung* is now too weak; it is the ultimate bad trip or fear itself, "the Fear," as Burroughs's characters call it
("I've got the Fear!"), something very different from the energizing anxiety of the old existential period. Here it is, as without any physical
embodiment (we never see the shark, or even learn whether there is
one) it begins to resonate throughout this exotic tropical beauty:

> He was at a hundred and ten and his pressure gauge, which had
> pointed twenty-five hundred p.s.i. at the jump-off, now read slightly
> under eight hundred. It was all right, he thought, the tank had no
> reserve and no J value; he would have enough to climb back as the

pressure evened out. At a hundred and twenty, his exhilaration was still with him and he was unable to suppress the impulse to turn a somersault. He was at the borders of narcosis. It was time to start up.

As soon as he began to climb, he saw shimmers of reflected light flashing below his feet. In a moment, the flashes were everywhere—above and below. Blue glitters, lightning quick. The bodies of fish in flight. He began pumping a bit, climbing faster, but by the book, not outstripping his own bubble trail.

Some fifty feet away, he caught clear sight of a school of bonito racing toward the shallows over the reef. Wherever he looked, he saw what appeared to be a shower of blue-gray arrows. And then it was as if the ocean itself had begun to tremble. The angels and wrasse, the parrots and tangs which had been passing lazily around him suddenly hung in place, without forward motion, quivering like mobile sculpture. Turning full circle, he saw the same shudder pass over all the living things around him—a terror had struck the sea, an invisible shadow, a silence within a silence. On the edge of vision, he saw a school of redfish whirl left, then right, sound, then reverse, a red and white catherine wheel against the deep blue. It was a sight as mesmerizing as the wheeling of starlings over a spring pasture. Around him the fish held their places, fluttering, coiled for flight.

Then Holliwell thought: It's out there. Fear overcame him; a chemical taste, a cold stone on the heart. (FS 226–7)

The condition of possibility of this splendor, but also its inner hollowness—which one might, in a postmodern age, designate as the scriptibility of the media image or the filmic travelogue—shows what a displacement of region can afford in the gringo novel; the displacement of relationship is much more complicated, because it involves the mimesis, not merely of an image, but, above all, of a language, and of the language of the Other at that. This is indeed the deeper topic of my present remarks, and one of the fundamental problems posed by a world system to other national literatures, namely, whether it is possible to transcribe the substance of one national life, with its specific language, into the language of another one. Can the novel be subtitled? Such is the dilemma in which cultural envy and translation meet, only to face the problem of pidgin as a stylistic dilemma; nor is this a problem of transcribing the English spoken by foreigners, something born mimics can always bring off, but, rather, that more critical one of inventing an

English for what people say in their own language—something that would seem to present an absolute barrier and to stand as the fundamental experience of otherness itself. This moment is also the crucial place of the literary flaw, the point at which the stress on form itself becomes virtually unbearable, thereby releasing the symptom and the clue for any thoroughgoing form-historical analysis.

As for language, I would like to pose the principle that, in late capitalism at least, its life is always the surest space or place of contradiction. Living language—if I may revive so quaint an expression—cannot be programmed or technologically organized and produced. The penetration of late capitalism into the hitherto uncommodified area of language can be observed in the elaborate computer technologies of language and composition teaching, whose necessary failure designates the seam between the commodified and the uncommodified more surely than the media of yesteryear and that now-familiar and even old-fashioned commercialization of the aesthetic (or reification of fantasy). The businessmen's complaints—that help to know how to write a letter is no longer available—are socially and historically a little more significant than mere organizational variants on the shortage-of-domestic-labor crisis: like the concept of "mugging" and with equally racist overtones, these complaints unerringly pinpoint the place at which machines cannot replace living labor in the production process, the place, I am tempted to say, where the labor theory of value is still alive and minimally capable of undermining the post-industrial hypothesis about the primacy of knowledge over production. We need to be very careful about reviving the old language-as-production theoreticism of the '60s; careful also about awakening more spiritualistic doctrines of human creativity.

My hope is that both these misunderstandings can be contained as well as possible by a rigorous historicizing of the present in which what is here affirmed about language is understood to be applicable only to this system, which we call late capitalism, and even, if you like, only to this moment of that system. The thesis would therefore need to take a form like this, and to suggest that, in a world of universal commodification and standardization such as our own, while stored human labor of unimaginably stacked varieties remains the basis of social appearance, human labor as such, labor nakedly visible to the living eyeball, can only be glimpsed in a few unique and privileged places, one of which is the production of real sentences. I put it that way to remind us that a great many unreal or false, imitation, sentences are also produced all around us, and that it is often a desperate matter, of more than tact and delicacy, to tell the difference any longer; maybe we should also add the qualifier that real sentences have a very short lifespan when exposed to the outer atmosphere and are at once subject to cooptation and reification.

In Stone's novel, the moment of truth comes when he finds himself obliged to portray the Central American revolutionaries themselves, for whom no English equivalent can be found. For the comprador bourgeoisie, complicitous with the English-speaking power structure, are easier to do and more class-homogeneous, even though some nimble footwork is still required. We are never shown any of the ruling elites of Tecan, for example, only the sadistic Lieutenant Campos, about whose "evil" some ultimate questions must then be asked. But we are shown a sample of the neighboring bourgeoisie, in the nonrevolutionary client state of Compostela: Stone brings it off by a tactical displacement of a classic, indeed well-nigh archetypal, fashion—instead of showing us people, he shows us intellectuals. And indeed, it must be asked and wondered now whether the fact that one of Stone's two or three major protagonists and point-of-view figures is an intellectual and a professor may be thought to be a structural weakness or flaw, in a global situation in which all kinds of technicians and experts now have university connections (a situation sometimes, I believe, called "post-industrial society"): Holliwell was, in any case, himself just such an expert technician in Vietnam. So perhaps we are not yet in David Lodge after all, but in more suitable proximity to the war novel (even though the latter's protagonist tends to be that ambiguous kind of intellectual called a journalist, rather than an academic).

But the urgency of this question is not only determined by the anti-intellectualism of a business society as well as by the transformation of that society into a technocracy in which the new functional space of the university is both an ivory tower from which reality and experience (sometimes also figured as manhood and virility) are absent, and a place from which manipulative guilt and criminal complicity emanate: those new features are present, but it is easy to see how they also add up to a very old stereotype of the intellectual as well (who doesn't know real life but kills people anyway). I suspect that in the novel it is always the functional or structural distance of intellectuals from the constitutive social classes that is at stake and that renders precarious the use of an intellectual as a representational camera eye, no matter how keen his or her perceptions. So much stands or falls with the question of whether Holliwell is just a professor or is, in fact, a characteristically maimed product and veteran of Vietnam.

At any rate, the scene in which he makes contact (dead drunk) with the Compostelan bourgeoisie taps deep unconscious fantasies at the same time that it enables an expected and untimely kinship with Melville to find expression. Holliwell's drunken lecture, in which he explains the meaning of the United States, is a pendant to Father Egan's equally drunken sermon, in the jungle, among the Mayan stelae, in which he tells assorted lounging hippies about the meaning of the universe: the great interpolated text— the inserted pamphlet from another world of discourse—was not Melville's invention (in *Pierre*), even though through it formally designated a profoundly modern impatience with the indirection of traditional narrative meanings and ripped his book apart in a way only healed by its ultimate replay in *The Magic Mountain*, where Mynheer Peeperkorn's prolix disclosure of the meaning of life is drowned out by a waterfall. On the other hand, at least in Holliwell's case, the lecture situation, vulnerable, unprepared, to a hostile public, is, as so often in Hitchcock films, the narrative equivalent of any number of archetypal nightmares of exposure and extreme social danger. The abortive lecture is thus also the antechamber to what I can no longer, owing to media debasement, call paranoia, but which is better characterized as sheer physical fear.

Here is now, in any case, Holliwell's lecture, which reveals the "secret culture" of the US to an elite right-wing public in Compostela:

"Let me tell you now some of the things we believed: We believed we knew more about great unpeopled spaces than any other European nation. We considered spaces unoccupied by us as unpeopled. At the same time, we believed we knew more about guilt. We believed that no one wished and willed as hard as we, and that no one was so able to make wishes true. We believed we were more. More was our secret watchword."

"Now out of all this, in spite of it, because of it, we developed Uncle Sam, the celebrated chiseling factor. And Uncle Sam developed the first leisured, literate masses—to the horror of all civilized men. All civilized men—fascists and leftist intellectuals alike—recoiled and still recoil at Uncle Sam's bizarre creation, working masses with the money and the time to command the resources of their culture, who would not be instructed and who had no idea of their place. Because

Uncle Sam thought of nothing but the almighty dollar he then created the machine-made popular culture to pander to them. To reinforce, if you like, their base instincts. He didn't think it was his job to improve them and neither did they. This debasement of polite society is what we are now selling you."

Again Holliwell paused. Voices were being raised but he was not being shouted down. He could make himself heard.

"I have the honor to bring you hope, ladies and gentlemen and esteemed colleagues. Here I speak particularly to the enemies of my country and their representatives present tonight. Underneath it all, our secret culture, the non-exportable one, is dying. It's going sour and we're going to die of it. We'll die of it quietly around our own hearths while our children laugh at us. So, no more Mickey Mouse, *amigos*. The world is free for Latinate ideologies and German ismusisms . . . temples of reason, the Dialectic, you name it." (FS 109–10)

This reproduces the now-familiar left diagnosis of imperialism in terms of consumerism, although the "lecture" certainly strikes out in a number of directions and seeks to satirize a certain left as well as a certain right (in any number of countries). I shall return to the ideological content of this view of the world system later on.

For the moment, what interests us is how it negotiates the representation of the Latin American Other, for it is within the lecture situation that the collaborators are able to emerge, from spiteful academics all the way to a very interesting woman minister of culture, all speaking English to Holliwell in order to humiliate him and, in general, allowing the class resentment of a pro-American bourgeoisie to be, if not overdetermined, then at least redoubled and overlaid, by the more familiar gesturality of intellectual mediocrity associated with academic politics. Meanwhile, in Tecan, the only putative Hispanic or indigenous counterrevolutionary is a Cuban, whose psychology and ideological character structure is by now, since the Bay of Pigs and beyond (to 1898 itself), familiar to us and, as a former colony, virtually a part of North American culture. (It would, however, be useful here to have a characterological equivalent for Bakhtin's conception of the chronotope, as an equivalent of some similar structural unity of ideology, historical experience, and character type in the actantial realm.) Thus, we must return to the left as virtually the only space in this novel in which a genuine approach to absolute otherness can and must be executed.

Stone's ideological position on the Christian left gives his still ambiguous answer a certain representational coherence, and he does all this
better than any other living writer I can think of, without, nonetheless,
giving full satisfaction. The relationship between the various political
figures is nicely salted or spiced by tacit personal appreciations: one is a
dandy and a turncoat, another a cleric, another an Indio small businessman and activist, the new leader an art historian and painter trained at
UCLA, and the returning leader of the older generation a man formed
by the Spanish Civil War ("now we'll be off to Spain," thinks the younger
leader sarcastically; "always Spain. Why not Algeria? Why not Angola,
Vietnam, China?"). This silent subconversation of characterological
tropisms is not altogether a concession to the aesthetics of the bourgeois
novel and its commitment to individual character and personality as
some ultimate intelligible unit of social life: for one thing we are shown
how these distinctive individual personalities have all been forged in
class situations and bear—or are even constituted by—scars of history
that are not mere colorful accidents. This impression of narrative skill is
then strengthened by the remarkable portraits of the "other side," of the
American advisors, the mercenaries, the State Department and CIA
people, as well as their local or indigenous collaborators: all of this is
immeasurably superior to the demonology of Stone's previous novel
(*Dog Soldiers*). The ideology of counter-revolution is persuasively
analyzed, as we shall see in a moment, not least because it corresponds
to a state in which the agents of that ideology are themselves conscious
and self-conscious of it and ready and willing to express it themselves:
nor is that any mere personal accident either (as was the case, for
instance, with the Kurtz of *Apocalypse Now*, or the other maniacal
figures as which alone the American "liberal imagination" has hitherto
been able to represent the darker forces of domination within US society). Stone is indeed very clear that the new foreign policy lucidity that
gives his political figures their authenticity is itself profoundly historical
and the result of a very special moment in American history, namely, the
defeat in Vietnam (in this sense, also and again, *A Flag for Sunrise* is in
the deepest sense a Vietnam novel).

And this is why it is sad and embarrassing, but not unexpected, to
report that the revolutionary scene, with its pidgin Spanish, climaxes
with an all-too-familiar megalomaniac paroxysm on the part of the
younger revolutionary leader, in which "power" is again affirmed as the
ultimate drive in political praxis. Shades of Orwell, or of my favorite

political villain, the evil genius of *Barbarella*, who murmurs, as at the
end he disappears into the magma, "Earth, you have lost your last great
dictator!" That the great dictator novel is a specific Latin-American
genre with its laws, constraints, and internal traditions, does not entitle
other national writers to go and do the same. Is anything more tiresome
today—in full postmodernism and organizational standardization, after
the well-known death of the subject (which seems to have different
consequences than either the equally wellknown death of God or the
newly famous or infamous end of history)—than this demonology of
power-lust, as though power were any more stimulating for today's
jaded postmodern subjects?

If language now marks the limits of political representation and
understanding in *A Flag for Sunrise*, we need to turn to the other formal
limits of this book, about which I have not yet said that, besides being a
great political novel, it also has some claims to being a great religious
novel, in ways I now want to explore. It may or may not come as a
surprise, then, that the fundamental worldview of *A Flag for Sunrise* is
what used to be called nihilism, but for which I now think we ought to
find a better term. To be perfectly candid about it, and if we really want
to be serious about ourselves, I think we have to admit that white
America is characterized by two basic features: we are hypocritical as a
people; and we are shallow (in the Russian sense of *nykulturny*, uncul-
tured). This is an old tradition with us that probably goes back before
capitalism proper to Weber's "Protestant ethos." But it means that only
one form of collective authenticity remains open to us, and that is cynicism, which constitutes at one and the same time the repudiation of our
hypocrisy about ourselves and our motives, and the acknowledgment of
what a world looks like that is reduced to only those things and forces
that North Americans can perceive and understand. Under these
circumstances, cynicism is not some mere posture or momentary attitude: to become fulfilled, cynicism has to take on, as it does in this book,
the proportions of an extraordinary gleaming nonhuman thing of
tremendous purity and otherworldliness—a cynicism so absolute that it
rejoins nihilism in the aesthetic museum of fundamental metaphysical
worldviews.

Stone's achievement of this metaphysical resonance is, however, not
unique in our recent period: it is indeed in one way or another shared by
the other novels that would make up a little corpus of significant gringo
novels, among them Joan Didion's *The Book of Common Prayer* (1977)

and *Democracy* (1984), as well as a remarkable novel by Robert Roper that was published last year and has not yet received the kind of attention it deserves, entitled *Mexico Days*. In all these novels, the precondition for the achievement of an absolute and metaphysical cynicism is, of course, the Vietnam War. Their spiritual task, as it were, is the transcription of such a worldview, its notation and endowment with form; but the forms involved inflect the historical explanation of their subject matter in varying (and ideologically distinct) directions. Two (*The Book of Common Prayer* and *Mexico Days*) attribute the emergence of absolute cynicism to the sixties as a unique internal or domestic North American condition in which youth and politics and, to a secondary extent, drugs are involved; the other two (*Democracy* and *A Flag for Sunrise*) more appropriately attribute it to the Vietnam War itself. There is a way in which Stone's preceding novel *Dog Soldiers* combines both explanations, but their value and consequences are in fact quite different and should be separated.

For the explanation by way of the sixties ends up attributing everything to the New Left, to political troublemakers who are, in effect, liberal bleeding hearts or worse. The narrator's sister, in *Mexico Days*, is mixed up with a group called No Pasarán, whose policy is to liberate all black prisoners from American prisons; her brother is a dope dealer—it is important to understand how these two destinies or choices are identified and seen as being somehow equivalent. The originality of *Mexico Days* is to expand the time frame in which this diagnosis is effectuated and to blame both vices on the father, a wealthy mafia lawyer, whose allegorical significance thus now draws in the thirties and the forties and gives this work a kinship with Doctorow's wonderful *Billy Bathgate*. The relationship to Mexico here thus spans two historical periods, as it were from Dolores del Rio to the DEA, and has the merit of including the Mexican political sixties along with the North American one, in the form of the massacre of Tlatelolco. In this one, then, our Other changes along with us and becomes, in some sense, our equal, even though the obligatory gringo scene of the "horror" of Mexican prisons is retained. In *The Book of Common Prayer*, a somewhat different Other is at stake, the now more familiar Central American Other, with its political terror and its death squads; indeed, the heroine ends her life in a round-up in one of those archetypal sports stadiums turned into a concentration camp. But the signifying equation here is again with the North American political sixties, in the person of the absent daughter, who is a kind of fictionalization of Patty Hearst. Here, too, then, whatever the other messages, something is being said about the infantile leftism of the North American sixties, and it is being said by way of a representation of a different, foreign, Latin American society in which evidently politics still exists or really exists.

In Stone, these judgments are much harsher, and it is important to be clear about the essential and constitutive relationship between his "cynicism" (in our broader sense) and his repudiation of the left—in *Dog Soldiers*, both lefts, new and old, since hilarious portraits of old thirties' veterans are interlarded in the implacable indictment of the drug-smuggling journalist-protagonist, whose left-liberal lies about the one positive figure in this book (a dead soldier who seems to offer the glimpse of an "attitude in which people acted on coherent ethical apprehensions that seemed real to them")[3] finally come to seem the sin for which his troubles in this book are the atonement, even though he himself escapes safe and sound, leaving the Nietzschean Vietnam-veteran "hero" dead behind him in a kind of martial apotheosis. Ethics rather than politics: that is essentially the perspective against which *A Flag for Sunrise* will attempt to confront politics itself.

What this will mean is, essentially, that sainthood is possible, whereas socialism is not. "Do you really think the other guys are going to *resolve* social contradictions and make everything O.K.?" the CIA man asks the protagonist. "Worker in the morning, hunter in the afternoon, scholar in the evening—do you really believe that's on, Frank?" "No," Holliwell replies (FS 24–5). And, later on, in his infamous lecture on North America's manifest destiny, Holliwell tells us: "I regard Marxism as analogous to a cargo cult" (he's an anthropologist, remember), "it's a naive invocation of a verbal machine" (FS 110). On the other hand, the revolutionaries exist; and, in the peculiar double standard of all these novels, what is inauthentic at home takes on a very different resonance abroad, whether it is ultimately possible or not.

Sister Justin will now be in some sense the link between these two opposite mirror-images of sixties' politics: ethical at home and political abroad (rather than the other way 'round). "In her eyes, the hunger for absolutes. A woman incapable of compromise who had taken on compromise like a hair shirt and never forgiven herself or anyone else, and then rebelled. She could, he thought, have no idea what that look

---

3   Robert Stone, *Dog Soldiers* (Boston: Houghton Mifflin, 1973), p. 261.

would evoke in the hearts of smaller weaker people, clinging to places of power. She was Enemy, Nemesis, Cassandra. She was in real trouble" (FS 343). But this, which motivates her final martyrdom in a nonpolitical way—the torturer, classically Sartrean, seeks to destroy this image and this look—is in Stone imaginable only in terms of sainthood, even though it might well apply to any number of the other doomed heroines in these books, from the Marin of *A Book of Common Prayer* to the Marta of *Mexico Days*.

As for Sister Justin's own political commitment—the quality of it, and its potential ambiguity as well, whether it can equally well be read as something ethical that takes the place of politics—besides her ill-considered involvement with the guerrillas (she supplies them with medicines), we have only a few remarks, like this one: " 'Am I ego-tripping?' Justin asked. 'Isn't it supposed to bother me that people starve so America can have Playboy Clubs and bottomless dancing?' " (FS 35).

This is, at least, interestingly ambiguous, in how it faintly raises the question of puritanism or prudery behind the political passion (either in the character or in Stone himself). But it is more important to underscore the consonance of the remark with Stone's general analysis of imperialism in this novel, which is politically intelligent and economically and socially up to date. Indeed, the flaw in many otherwise admirable political novels or films can often be located in the nonchalance and irresponsibility with which the stage is set, the pretext for the narrative is disclosed in passing, and the preconditions for political unrest are dispatched, as though, in the outside world, revolutionary ferment were a constant possibility that did not need precise materialist analysis. Stone is very lucid about the inadequacy of simply endowing an imaginary Central American country with a revolutionary movement a priori and without further justification. Its condition of possibility here is explained by the pressures on the Atapa Indian population in the interior, whose farmlands are being destroyed by new government mining operations on the one hand (the main chance of a poor supplier of valuable raw materials in the new world system) and the expansion of multinational tourist industries and installations on the other: base and superstructure—the combination of a sixties' economic explanation of neo-imperialism with an eighties' and nineties' cultural and media expansion version of that explanation.

As for Sister Justin, I am not qualified to make any sensitive or reliable theological judgment on the quality of this sainthood, reached at the other end of torture and physical agony. Certainly, its theological framework depends very much on that conquest and appropriation of, commitment to, construction of, conviction of, the cynicism already evoked. Father Egan's sermon at the stelae is a vision of cosmic horror; human, social, and historical cynicism now projected through the cosmos; and absorbing elements of cultural and religious otherness such as the cult of human sacrifice in the pre-Columbian era, a howling bloodlust literally embodied in the homicidal maniac Weitling: "'Oooh, he is terrible,' Weitling sang . . . 'He is more terrible than you can know. His face is like Indian corn, of colors. Then sometimes invisible, the worst. The hair of him is blue. He is electricity. Arms and legs are made of worms. The power. And it is like space beneath you, you are falling. I fall, I, poor myself, I fall. He crushes me'" (FS 365).

But as a cosmic principle human sacrifice turns out to be funnier and more banal than that, not quite as American as apple pie, but fully as mindless as the supermarket and the shopping mall:

> A man came here once from the national museum. They took rubbings of those stones and they picked up everything that could be moved. They said it was for the museum's collection, but of course it was for the President's family to sell. They picked up bone carvings and shards with graffiti on them. The man said he thought the graffiti might tell him something about everyday life here long ago, about how people went about life. But it turned out that he was wrong, it turned out that every single stroke represented human sacrifice—even the graffiti. It was as though there was no everyday life. Only sacrifice. (FS 368–9)

This is, then, alone the condition, I may even say the experimental condition, the laboratory precautions and arrangements, under which Father Egan can posit the existence, under the tons of garbage and dead meat, of a barely perceptible form of life: "a glimmer? . . . who knows down in that mess? But maybe there is something. A little shard of light" (FS 318). The two things go together: the "living" can only be grasped "among the dead" (FS 319); sainthood can only become momentarily imaginable under the most extreme and inhuman, abominable suffering. It is, as I've said, a plausible worldview, in a situation in which not many traditional ones are plausible any more.

But I want to make the other point, in our context, that the achievement of this particular worldview, its representability, the possibility of grasping it and entertaining it even momentarily, is altogether dependent on and inconceivable without a fundamental preliminary condition of possibility, which is the cultural iconography of the Aztec or pre-Columbian other—in short, a set of images and representations that does not belong to us gringos and that is henceforth illegal to export. I do not particularly care what Mexican artists and writers have excessively done with these materials, which are their own business (although Diego's great jaguar-clad resistance fighters haunt the mind as they desperately grapple with the conquistadors). My point is rather that, restricted to purely North American materials, this vision could not be represented and would shrivel to the banal proportions of this or that serial murder (which is what the Weitling figure in reality amounts to); the great metaphysical *frisson*, the "scream of blood running through the cosmos" (as the Norwegian painter Edvard Munch once called it), would thereby be utterly missed. Manson offers a thrill certainly but is much too American to afford you any satisfactory picture of absolute Evil, any more than—for our writers and novelists—the North American political hippies and students of the 1960s seemed able to afford any satisfactory image of true politics and political praxis as such. But this can surely not only be the result of a collective national inferiority feeling in the superstate and its citizens and artists.

This does not prove that Stone is a bad artist; on the contrary, it is because he is a very great artist indeed that we can get a glimpse of these representational limits. Meanwhile, I think we have to be clear about the reason why this representation of Evil fails—it fails because all such representations fail, since, in that sense, Evil does not exist, it is a figment of the specifically ethical worldview and thus an optical illusion. What is more relevant for our present purposes is the nature of that illusion, which is fundamentally based on the category of absolute otherness. Evil is otherness, and only the Other is absolutely evil: that is the ultimate reason why we have to ransack exotic storerooms and foreign cultures for its representation, under conditions of increasing social standardization (I hesitate to call it democratization except in the very sociological sense of plebeianization, the universalization of wage labor), from which otherness has increasingly been excluded. (Don't get me wrong about this: Chacmool and the Hispanics are by no means the only source of "evil" in this novel: indeed, the North American CIA figures in A Flag for Sunrise are a good deal less scary than the Englishman who works for them; and I have already said that the North American villains in *Dog Soldiers* do not make my flesh creep at all. Maybe we really are innocents abroad after all, as Henry James and so many others have thought! Only what we do abroad is rarely innocent.)

But evil brings us back to the matter of formal and narrative contradiction with which I began, and with which I conclude here. Briefly resumed, the point I have been trying to make is this: the imperial power cannot represent itself to itself, cannot come to any authentic form of representational self-knowledge, unless it is able to include within that representation the represented realities of its own colonies. This is something we have long since understood in individual terms, in terms of an individualizing psychology: if you are a jailer, for example, your truth cannot adequately be represented without your prisoners; if a tyrant, without your subjects; if a torturer, without your victims. It cannot be any different when we come to collectivities; and this is something we have gradually come to understand for the past, for the older or classical system of imperialism—whose central power was Great Britain— namely, that something peculiar happens structurally and formally to a literature that is forced by the nature of things to exclude those Others that, in many respects, constitutively define it.[4] The new world system is structurally very different from the old system of rival imperial powers; but the proposition that something similar holds culturally for it seems to me to be the formal lesson of the gringo novel as well.

---

4   See, for further reflections on this, my "Modernism and Imperialism," in Terry Eagleton et al., eds., *Nationalism, Colonialism, and Literature* (Minneapolis: University of Minnesota Press, 1990), pp. 43–66.

3

Form-Problems in Henry James

I expected these fine and stimulating essays to be criticisms of my scanty and sometimes unfair treatment of Henry James, an approach I would certainly welcome. Many of them, however, have taken the (very flattering) line of comparing my work with that of James in one way or another, and that is an approach I am not qualified to pass judgment on, however interesting or outlandish I may find the results.

I am also reluctant, but more willing, to add a somewhat more autobiographical note and to confess that James was one of the only three American writers who meant something to me in my intellectual formation (otherwise mostly foreign and principally French). The others were Pound and Faulkner, and I suppose it is worth noting that two of those three were exiles, while the third was well out of the American mainstream, being, as it were, the citizen of a conquered foreign country under American occupation, much as an East German might feel in the triumphantly recentralized "west" Germany of today. But Faulkner never wrote about that occupation or those occupiers, which is why, for me, despite the far more aestheticized vocations of my other two influences, his work still strikes me as the one that most fully embodies the aesthete's ideal of the autonomy of art, owing to the self-contained existence of Yoknapatawpha County.

"Remarks on Henry James," *Henry James Review* 36(3), Fall 2015. This essay was originally written as an afterword to symposium in *Henry James Review* 36(3), Fall 2015.

He, too, then, like the others represented a kind of anti-Americanism, and, more than ever, I feel that "provincializing America" ought to remain our central cultural task at a time when American hegemony seems about as permanent as that of ancient Rome in its heyday. That is, in fact, always how I understood Pound: if you're going to rule the world, he seemed to be telling us, then at least do it right and inherit world culture, indeed construct a world culture in which your best moments (Jefferson!) take their place modestly enough alongside China, Greece, the Renaissance, and modern revolution (although I would have preferred the place of honor for Lenin rather than for Mussolini, who did, after all, begin his career as a socialist). The epic as a poem that includes history, indeed, that includes economics: there was Pound's lesson, and, in an age of world literature and world political upheaval and transition, it still seems to me to have its uses.

You can still read his tribute to James in Canto VII. May I confess that James's Anglophilia bothers me more than Pound's fascism (my feeling being, to paraphrase Horkheimer, that you can't seriously talk about fascism unless you are willing to talk about conservatism in general, of which it is a subset). That James's one great political gesture should be his adoption of British citizenship during World War I seems to me a little less glorious than Proust's youthful circulation of pro-Dreyfus petitions.

It is said, by the way, that James wrote Proust a letter of appreciation after the publication of *Swann's Way*. I have never seen it, nor do I know whether the story is apocryphal, but it makes a useful lead-in to a topic that does interest me, namely James's fluency in French. France was, for him, I take it, the homeland of literature as such (as it was for so many of us until a few years ago): the country of professional writers such as Flaubert and Zola (may I add Turgenev?), with whom he had personal and professional relations. England had plenty of socializing and social relations, social raw material (plus the common language), but neither James nor Pound was able to feel that London was a real intellectual capital. Like Conrad and unlike Beckett, however, James was unwilling to adopt French as a professional language, nor does he ever seem to have contemplated doing so.

I now want to introduce a notion of Bakhtin's that has always fascinated me, namely that of "alien speech." He meant by that the way in which religions tend to enhance their authority by couching their rituals in an alien language—Roman Catholicism in Latin, the Assyrian rituals in Sumerian, etc. This has, I believe, a more subtle and interesting equivalent in literature and literary language and text, namely, the infiltration of the national language by the syntax of another, foreign and indeed alien one. Milton is the obvious example, but I would also point to triplication in Flaubert and some absent pull of Anglicism in Mallarmé's strange French (something less surprising insofar as he was an English teacher in the first place).

But then there is the secret presence of French within James's peculiar style, or at least his late style, of which Seymour Chatman has given us a useful grammar.[1] In all these instances, the secret foreign language at the heart of the colloquial one rescues the latter from mere orality and ephemerality; it lends it a density (as cornstarch does to sauce); it endows it with matter and assists it in its approach to aesthetic reification (for Adorno the most effective defense against an increasingly omnipresent system of commodity reification). Mahler, who composed his narratives with the massed sonorities of the different instruments as (sometimes antagonistic) characters, invented a type of moment that may convey this effect more dramatically, a moment in which two distinct instruments—an oboe, say, and a flute—project a single note in unison in such a way that their sounds cannot be distinguished but nonetheless produce an unclassifiable and dense tone. Such is the mystery of the unison of the two different languages, the inner foreign one and the public or demotic words, when they combine, taking on a unique autonomy and objecthood of their own. Oddly enough, all of this vanishes away the moment you read the sentences aloud and follow their meandering turns effortlessly in the medium of orality.

I think that, for Melville, it was Shakespeare who functioned as that inner "alien speech" and lifted American to the status of a "culture language" (as the Germans might put it). The hexameter did something similar for Whitman, and, in both cases, the need would seem to have arisen from uncertainty as to what "the American language" was or whether it really existed in the first place. But we would be wrong to think that James simply decided to become an Englishman and adopt the English language of England, as T. S. Eliot so successfully was able to do (unless—doing the police, as he did, in different voices—the whole thing was pastiche rather than interiorization). I think that British

---

1   Seymour Chatman, *The Later Style of Henry James* (New York: Barnes and Noble, 1972).

English simply compounded the uncertainty and the dilemma and demanded the line of flight of a more personal, although not yet modernist, solution.

Still, this is only part of the picture: we need to come back to the question of modernism and its relationship to language. To be sure, James's most peculiar sentences are not to be found in his own prose but in the dialogue inserted into it. Thus, an essentially spoken if idiosyncratic style—it is well known that, stylistically, his late period begins with the typewriter and his adoption of dictation—a style that can be corrected by replacing it in the medium of its original oral delivery, becomes incorrigibly mannered and Mallarméan when that oral production attempts to imitate orality.

Yet this is not, I think, a matter of style and of orality and writing alone. The modernists (of all kinds) began to emerge when the institutions that guaranteed their social status (and their income) fell prey to market forces and excluded any number of ambitious and productive talents from relatively secure social positions. At this point, the practice of a métier is gradually replaced by the fantasy image of the *poète maudit* and the solitary "artist." I repeat this oversimplified narrative in order to insist that James was still on the other side of this historical divide. Just as, later on, Walter Benjamin will assure one of his Weimar correspondents that he wanted to become "the greatest literary critic in Germany,"[2] so in this earlier period James's ambitions ran less to some fantasy image of art than to that of the still extant "man of letters" (*sic*). His voluminous book reviews, often of the most mediocre commercial productions, abundantly demonstrate this (as do Benjamin's).

But, from our current vantage point in this symposium, it is the Gloriani cycle that gives the clue. Its "retour des personnages" suddenly reveals James's deepest literary affinities and his fundamental ambitions. They certainly do not lie with Flaubert's painstaking and artisanal labor over the individual sentence—one need only read James's savage review of *L'Education sentimentale* to be convinced of that.[3] Nor, for all his elaborate politeness, do they lie with his English-language contemporaries, whose mediocrity must have given him satisfaction and spurred

---

2   Walter Benjamin, *The Correspondence of Walter Benjamin, 1910–1940*, ed. Gershom Scholem and Theodor W. Adorno, trans. Manfred R. Jacobson and Evelyn M. Jacobson (Chicago: University of Chicago Press, 1994), p. 359.

3   Henry James, "The Minor French Novelists," *Galaxy* 21 (February 1876): 219–33.

his own efforts. No, they stand with the immense figure of Balzac, always the legendary Master hidden away behind all these literary daydreams. One finds him again in Faulkner, who must have pored over the multi-volume "complete works" owned by so many American households and placed side by side with those of Sir Walter Scott. It is an interesting juxtaposition, not only because Scott was also Balzac's master but, above all, because it foregrounds an initial and fundamental opposition between realism and romance, or rather their initial identity in the romance of realism and the realism of romance.

Understanding James, then, first and foremost demands a sense of the presence of Balzac in his work and of Balzac's own (fantasy) ambition of becoming the complete man of letters, the Walter Scott of his generation and nation. This is why, if the question is not already simple-minded, James could not write in French: the place was already taken. Nor was an American Balzac conceivable, for the reasons ruminated on in James's Hawthorne book.[4] And, as a colonial, he could scarcely identify with the history of his adopted place of work and residence. James was thereby thrown back on the raw material of high society individual gossip and the fate of the innocent abroad.

There is more: I claim that, for economic (and publishing) reasons as well as on account of his conception of the métier, James was essentially a writer of short stories. The novellas and the novels themselves are flukes: happy accidents in which, without warning, the "subject" of a short story suddenly expands beyond conventional "treatment," takes on a life of its own, sets its own goals and laws, and grows accordingly. To be sure, the complete man of letters needs to be a novelist as well, and books like *The Portrait of a Lady* and *The Bostonians* are, for all their greatness, still relatively conventional novels. It is in the late novels and the novellas that James "happily" (as he might put it himself) loses control and does something inimitable. But the life of letters, the literary life, remains essentially a matter of book reviews and short stories, in as many venues as possible (along with the networks of an active social life).

I need hardly add that it is in the theory, in the prefaces, that James suddenly becomes modern. This kind of reflexivity (unmatched even in Flaubert's letters) is the new hallmark and springs from the crisis of form itself and from a consciousness of form as a reality in its own right,

---

4   Henry James, Hawthorne (London: MacMillian and Co, 1879).

with its own history and destiny, its own dilemmas, a consciousness that will henceforth become indispensable in theory and practice alike.

But all this remains anecdotal unless we make a stab at the heart of the matter and venture into speculation as to what drives the content of this production, what constitutes its deeper "moment of truth." I want to dispel the notion—but it is probably no longer very current anyway—that the biographical, and along with it the psychoanalytic, remains an "extrinsic factor" in the work of art. This is, to quote myself somewhere, an age of great biography, and, as befits biographical work in the age of surveillance, of a particularly nosy and scandal-mongering kind of biography at that, with details of every public lunch the subject ever ate as well as all the private and intimately personal encounters that can be unearthed (for James, not many). The word has fallen into disuse, perhaps fortunately, but it is often as not of psychobiography we are speaking. My argument has always been that such biographies make up the life of yet another text, which can be added in alongside the official and published ones, and that therefore to draw on this or that suggestive gesture revealed in the biographical text is sometimes to identify a thematic *gestus* that, showing up in a variety of key points in a narrative, sheds new light or is somehow "suggestive."

All this to preface my claim that the deeper drive in James, which illuminates almost everything, is that of voyeurism, something rather different from the identification so many novelists bring to their characters and that also, in its inherent shamefulness, necessarily demands precautions both stylistic and narrative. I range suspicion under this, and am, therefore, certainly not at odds with my fellow critics here.

One does recall the great Faulknerian dictum and wonder where James is to be positioned with respect to it. Novel-writing, says Faulkner, requires three distinct faculties: Observation, Experience and Imagination; in a pinch any two, but the greatest novelists require the simultaneous exercise of all three. Of experience, the Jamesians seem agreed, James had very little; of imagination in its most novelistic sense, which is to say, sheer invention, not much. But observation absolutely, very much like that naturalist novelist in Proust, who, asked what he is up to sitting in the corner of the salon all by himself, candidly replies, "J'observe." Now, normally, the almost exclusive exercise of this particular faculty would result in a "textual production" familiar and at once easily identifiable, namely gossip. (We will return to gossip in a moment.) However, it is as though James was aware, in advance, of the Faulknerian requirements and of his own deficiencies with respect to them and as an answer, with prodigious energy, expanded observation as such to fill both their empty places. So it is that observation became his experience, and not only his but that of his characters as well (we will speak of the "subconversation" in a moment). And, as for imagination, well, what is voyeurism but precisely that, the traces of the observable converted into the most lurid imaginary suppositions possible? Which I would not identify with the sexual exactly, but rather maintain the reverse: they become what we call sexuality in this period. The "stain" indeed! They are the child's curiosity about the primal scene, and James knew it only too well. If we have to talk about homosexuality, then only because it compounds the risk and makes the curiosity even more unavowable, demanding subterfuge and indirection, strategies of evasion and disguise.

Hence the late style, which, in search of "le mot juste," turns out to avoid it. Mallarmé, whose problems were, to be sure, of another order, once memorably detained a would-be interviewer in mock horror with this *cri de coeur*: "*Attendez, par pudeur, que j'y verse, au moins, un peu d'obscurité!*" The hesitations and elaborate over-qualifications, the inter-jections and parenthetical clauses are not rhetorical (in either the tradi-tional or the Burkean sense); they do not aim to shape the sentence but to slow it down and render it provisional. They do not aim for a unique style, as the modernists would, even though they are certainly unique, and there ends up being such a thing as a Jamesian style or late style. Rather, they aim to undermine the sentence and to implicate the reader in that process: if they are mimetic of anything, then precisely of the voyeurism and the suspicion, the hermeneutic ferreting out, the curios-ity of a self-doubting speculation that must both keep itself alive by remaining in the dark, by preserving the secret of the primal scene, at the same time that it enlists our own commitment to the urgency of the search. This kind of sentence resists the parsing method of Stanley Fish's notation of the multiple possibilities a sentence opens up, even as it shuts them down in the next moment and with the decision for the next word. Instead, in a sense, the Jamesian sentence tries to do all this simul-taneously, incorporating its own contradictory possibilities by way of its own peculiar temporalities.

This "late style" is Adornian only insofar as the novel itself incorpo-rates that rift between subjectivity and objectivity by way of the form's constitutive gap between style and narrative, *syuzhet* and *fabula*.

Adorno's emphasis on old age, or at least the old age of a productive, perhaps even over-productive career, in which Beethoven exhausted the forms he practiced (and even initially invented), that emphasis is only interesting when the old age is that of the form rather than of the practitioner. It becomes even more interesting when the form reflects the old age of the social formation itself. In the case of James, there would seem to be room for doubt as to that second experience of lateness. He was not, I think, particularly perceptive (à la Proust, for example) of the fragile destiny of the limited society he moved in, nor as intensely aware as the Edwardians of the effects of the imperial vocation on England itself, let alone as apprehensive as his brother of the toxicity of a nascent American imperialism. Perhaps it is true that these novels of marriage still, despite all the adulteries and on the far side of Jane Austen's nuptials, worry the question of living happily ever after as a dog worries a bone. Meanwhile, a bachelor is poorly placed to observe the mutation of the family into the dynasty in this period and its historical experience of entropy as a fundamental ideologeme.

So, however intimately it has become associated with "point of view," irony is not in James particularly historical or political in its effects. I do appreciate the efforts of the participants in this symposium to avoid the term, but I suspect that various strong analyses of the inner multiplicity of the practice of point of view—all those windows looking down at you from the house of fiction—are so many attempts to revive the function of irony without its now dated overtones, tainted as it was by Cold War liberalism.

This is perhaps the moment in which another autobiographical digression is unavoidable. Several participants here refer to my alleged dispute with Wayne Booth (as well as that, equally alleged, with Kenneth Burke), and I'm happy to have the chance to clarify these exchanges. Wayne Booth was my freshman English teacher and the best teacher I ever had. We had frequent, often heated discussions about Aristotle, Marx, criticism and theory, Henry James, modernism, pedagogy, and writing, discussions that were indispensable for me and formative, even when (especially when) we disagreed. The offending public critique of Booth quoted here was at fault in an ambiguous use of the word "conservative." I largely endorsed his own negative view of the doctrine of "point of view" (which I've repeated many times) and also of the notion of irony, with this difference: that Wayne felt able to distinguish stable ironies (good) from the unstable ones of a Flaubert or a Céline, which he felt to be immoral or amoral, and certainly rhetorically ambiguous and, in that sense, ineffective. What I singled out was the literary conservatism of a return to the stable ironies you find in Fielding, for example, or that some people here have located in *The Wings of the Dove*. But I never thought he was politically conservative in the slightest (except to the degree that a good liberal is not really as progressive as he or she may think), and I also never saw the counterattack on me in the second edition of the *Rhetoric of Fiction*.[5] He meanwhile never saw my dedication to him of *A Singular Modernity*, since Verso printed it on the "verso" of their title page and thereby rendered it invisible to most readers. We met again much later on in our lives, but this particular misunderstanding never came up.

As for Kenneth Burke, a different kind of misunderstanding was involved. I felt that his use of the term and concept of ideology (whose copious use in his own work he was able to document in great detail) was still the rather limited one of a 1930s left, which I proposed to replace with something far more broad and all-encompassing. He rightly sensed, then, that I was relegating him to the past, something people don't much like you to do. But the matter had little bearing on his major achievement, the dramatistic system, which I still admire and occasionally draw on.

Returning now to the Jamesian sentence, I would argue that its fundamental historical achievement, by whatever happy accident to which you may wish to attribute it, was the discovery of what Nathalie Sarraute will later on call the subconversation, the unspoken tropisms (again Nathalie Sarraute!) of our sensing of the positions of the other, our subtle readjustments and silent renegotiations of our own quasi-physical stances and *gestus*, the kind of strange circling with friendly or hostile others that more visibly characterizes animals' behavior with their own and other species, rather than what can be seen from the outside in the exchanges of human speakers.

However much the subconversation—that imperceptible, hidden, far more intimate, engagement of two characters with each other in the Jamesian *agon*—however much this contact may do double duty as the primal scene the voyeur reconstructs between his characters, it is also an index of the more general repudiation of reification in the modernist

---

5   Wayne C. Booth, *Rhetoric of Fiction*, 2nd edition (Chicago: University of Chicago Press, 1983).

period. For it wishes to elude the naming of un-nameable things, to shun the verbal stereotypes at the same time that it stakes out the space for unique interpersonal feelings that have no name in the first place—a space of apposition and anaphora, the enigmatic references to an "it" the writer has not identified but which we are supposed to recognize and to remember. At any rate, it is this virtual discovery and revelation of a whole layer of human relations that are not unconscious but which the literary apparatus had hitherto been too primitive to register, that is, to my mind, James's most enduring claim to greatness, and not the doctrine of point of view, which should surely be credited to Percy Lubbock's formalization and propagandizing rather than to the Master himself.[6]

Such is then the world of James's sentences, a surface world that must nonetheless be explored by this or that depth hermeneutic. As for *fabula*, and the narrative organization we have so far evoked only at a distance, maybe the following will be sufficient.

I have characterized Henry James as a short-story writer, a practice almost absolutely dependent on that discovery of the proper "subject" of which his journals provide an abundant record. Here we find what André Jolles would have called the "simple form" of the anecdote and the social reality of gossip.[7] I have elsewhere celebrated gossip for its Utopian dimension: the proper activity of a human world from which nature and economic contradiction have been eliminated, so that our fundamental preoccupation can become that which concerns our own species and its peculiarities (and I have even quoted Adorno to the effect that, in Utopia, individuality will be itself little more than just such assemblages of the weirdest personal peculiarities). So far so good. But, in a sexually obsessed society and for those afflicted with voyeurism as a life-passion, gossip can, no doubt, be a toxic habit, like food cravings or erotic obsessions. The most revealing stories, like "In the Cage" or a (suppressed) novel like *The Sacred Fount*, testify to James's own consciousness of this temptation and to the willpower with which he is able to draw it back within the formal elaboration itself, as he so triumphantly does in *The Ambassadors* but with the odd result of an unwitting confession: for Strether's great outburst—"to live!"—is so clearly the voyeuristic moment of truth as to disfigure the novel itself with its

6   Percy Lubbock, *The Craft of Fiction* (London: Jonathan Cape, 1921).

7   André Jolles, *Einfache formen* (Darmstadt: Wissenschaftliche Buchgesellschaft, 1958).

vacuity, its utter lack of content. Any determinate passion would have been preferable, but here, fatally, the empty signifier, to which James could not, by virtue of his own unique life and work, give meaning in any way, is bound to be colonized by a not exactly unspoken sexuality and the disgrace of the "stain." He catches himself and, in the obverse of this tale, in that incomparable masterpiece that is "The Beast in the Jungle," recaptures the right way to do it.

As for the moments of unexpected expansion, they can be explained by the way in which a simpler narrative scheme—a "libidinal apparatus," as Jean-François Lyotard would have called it—suddenly provides the occasion for the absorption of a content hitherto alien to it. So it is that an "interesting subject"—for example, the peculiar triangular situation of *The Wings of the Dove*, both a national and a libidinal allegory, and rather Hegelian in its insistence on the mediation as such—is then suddenly infected with the virus of a dynamic foreign body—money!—which propels it far beyond its natural limits into complexities and developments, episodes and profundities, a differentiation of back-ground and minor characters to which it could not have initially laid claim. We may not wish to endow this novel with all the usual political and social connotations of the word "realism," but, surely, this diagnosis of the viral dynamic of money and its toxicity yields an x-ray of nine-teenth-century social reality whose shadows even betoken social class itself.

As for plot and the novel, I think it is more productive to substitute another mode for that of "romance" in our thinking of "realism" (in any case, to me a not very rewarding topic to raise on the occasion of Henry James), and that is melodrama as such. We need to interrogate the place of melodrama in the novels in order to evaluate them in that history of the nineteenth-century novel whose most pressing dilemma is the persistence of melodrama and what to do about it: eliminate it, as George Eliot so triumphantly does, or transfigure it, revel in it as though in some new and more obscene formal orgy, or diagnose it medically and politically. In James, I think one can observe the visible persistence of the two historically determinate forms melodrama takes in this period.

First of all, there is the *ancien régime*: this is the Satanic or Byronic villain, from Lovelace to Dracula, the quintessential domineering husband, as in Eliot's Grandcourt, whose role is in James so memorably taken by Osmond of *The Portrait of a Lady*. I believe that our fascination with *The Wings of the Dove*—and our obsessive return to the problem of "irony" it imposes—can be explained by the subtlety with which James negotiates the dilemma of villainy here, distracting us by projecting it onto minor characters (and may I salute the Greimassian square of those secondary characters Alexander Woloch has so usefully theorized for us[8]), and using point of view to blind us to the tawdriness of the plot, however well-intentioned.

Meanwhile, the hedonistic peace of *The Golden Bowl* draws its serenity from the disappearance of the problem and, if I may put it that way, the *Aufhebung* of adultery itself: this should be the moment of achievement of a properly Jamesian sublime. That it is not may be the most opportune place in which to grasp the limits of our writer, as considerable as he may be.

But we must not neglect the allegorical levels in all this: the Gothic and *ancien régime* villain is obviously the survival of the oldest American political ideology, the hatred of old Europe and its hierarchies and aristocracy (despite decisive French help!), while the Americans are still the innocents abroad, potentially at the mercy of these would-be sharks, the "suckers," the country boy in the hands of city slickers, etc. Just as clearly, of course, the Americans already have the money, so twentieth-century developments are proleptically registered.

At this point, something new enters the picture: it is the dead girl, the dead cousin, encrypted à la Abraham and Torok, at the very heart of things, the unassuageable melancholy that seeps through all the superficial, social relations, and those of villainy and vice as well. It is of this impossible work of mourning that James's great victims—the Milly Theale of *The Wings of the Dove*, the Isabel Archer of *The Portrait of a Lady*—are the objects. And, surely, their creation is what will cut through the voyeurism at the crucial moments of this oeuvre and will guarantee a passion, but also a potential sentimentalism, whose absence would have otherwise condemned this work to journeyman status.

Yet I must not omit to disagree about the "free choice" that converts Isabel Archer's exploitation into a kind of happy ending. On the contrary, I believe that this ending represents James's participation in one of the great ideologemes of the nineteenth-century bourgeoisie, that of *Entsagung* or renunciation. If a choice, then a forced choice if you prefer,

---

8 Alex Woloch, *The One vs. the Many: Minor Characters and the Space of the Protagonist in the Novel* (Princeton: Princeton University Press, 2003).

the consent to choose failure: it is there already in Goethe and persists at least as far as James himself. We do not have to admire this self-laceration, this option for unnecessary tragedy, or rather the conversion of genuine tragedy into self-pitying abdication. Historical distance gives us the means to "estrange" it and to deplore an ending that disfigures a great novel, for which a providential happy ending would have been much more suitable, as I argue elsewhere.

I have not forgotten that I still need to identify the second residue of melodrama, the second type of villainy to be found, equally characteristically for the whole epoch, in James's work. This is, if you like, not a hangover of the evil of a feudal past but rather the premonition of a revolutionary future: I discuss it elsewhere at some length,[9] this fearful contempt of the great bourgeois realists for the intellectual troublemakers who so ineffectually threaten the system. James does not know this (properly political) passion to the extent of the more worldly novelists, like Dickens or Dostoevsky, but there is one very privileged moment in this work in which he indulges it to his heart's content, and that is, of course, the venomous portrait of Olive Chancellor, the feminist radical, in *The Bostonians*, which thereby, far more than *The Princess Casamassima*, becomes his major political novel. Here, I think, we must really take our distance from Henry James: here, feminism is the stand-in for every other kind of political activism and the occasion for a *ressentiment* that runs the gamut. It is with mixed feelings that any radical reader must greet this triumph of the satiric vein: if you reproached liberalism with its lack of political feeling or engagement, then such a reactionary political gesture must be the object of at least a grudging admiration and acknowledgement. I myself think that any further psychoanalytic probes into the libidinal source of this hatred of feminism would be unproductive, but, wherever it is to be found, it certainly strengthens the anti-political politics that surfaces here in another one of James's novelistic triumphs.

Now it is time to disengage the allegorical levels of all this in a synthesis of differences that may well strike some readers as a familiar and quite undesirable gesture of totalization. I sympathize with the reaction but still believe that we must somehow sort out the mixed feelings this unique and extraordinary figure continues to inspire. The problem for

---

9 Fredric Jameson, *Postmodernism, or, the Cultural Logic of Late Capitalism* (Durham, NC: Duke University Press, 1991).

me personally (or theoretically) is the reconciliation between two schemes to which I find myself committed: one is the four-fold medieval schema of the allegorical levels; the other the Greimas semiotic square (which in fact goes back to Aristotle). But let's begin with a very provisional version of each of these schemata. The allegorical one might then look like this:

ANAGOGICAL: the diplomatic/melodramatic level—US versus Europe

MORAL: the subjective or psychoanalytic level—voyeurism, the dead girl

ALLEGORICAL: modernism and style, point of view theory, the sentence

LITERAL/HISTORICAL: the literary life, short story, métier, gossip

Each of these levels slants the interpretation in a specific thematic way, a thematic dominant, in terms of which the other levels are transcoded. There are two further observations about this ancient and theologically motivated allegorical scheme, devised to permit the assimilation of the Old Testament into a newer Christian historical narrative. The "literal" level, that of history or text, was then the object of this manipulation, which turned on the allegorical level or key—the life of Christ—to rewrite its events and its data accordingly. In modern times, the pre-eminence of that key falls away (save in specific worldviews such as the Marxian one), and the priority of the various levels then becomes optional, opening up what some might call a pluralism of interpretations. But it should be understood that the fundamental data remain the same and are merely rearranged and transcoded in whatever system of levels seems to impose itself.

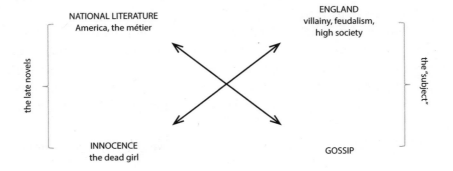

The other observation to make here is that my current suggestion bears on the oeuvre, the work of James as a whole, and not on any specific text. A choice of the latter would obviously take different forms, inasmuch as the "historical" or narrative level is given in advance and not merely hypothesized as we have done here for James's career. Now to our second schema, the square of binary oppositions. Their arrangement will seem a good deal more arbitrary, until we confront elements of the work that are not covered by the four terms that are our starting point.

It will, however, be clear that this structural arrangement of elements (semes) and basic oppositions is more analytical and microscopic than the terms of the levels, which turn out to be the various syntheses or combinations produced by the basic oppositions here. So, in a sense the semiotic square comes after the positing of the allegorical levels and serves to explain or at least to explicate it. It also presupposes an interaction between the terms that is absent from the rather static schema of the levels, in which each interpretive level is distinct from the others and lies parallel to them. The proposal is meant to be suggestive rather than "definitive" (whatever that might mean), methodological rather than genuinely interpretive. But, as these fine papers set out to deal with my own work as well as that of James, these concluding speculations may serve, for good or ill, to indicate the directions my current readings are tending to follow (and have for some time, I guess).

4

Language and Conspiracy in DeLillo and Yurick

These two novels by distinguished American writers underscore once again the spatial dilemma confronted by contemporary fiction in the "world system." That dilemma can be schematically described as the increasing incompatibility—or incommensurability—between individual experience, existential experience, as we go on looking for it in our individual biological bodies, and structural meaning, which can now ultimately derive only from the world system of multinational capitalism. This tension—which ought not too rapidly to be assimilated back to the old ideological opposition between the "individual" and "society"—has of course always been present in earlier periods, where, however, the social frame was nowhere near so vast, and was always somehow closer to individual perception. In the face-to-face situation of the village, the insertion of individual experience is achieved by way of the anecdote or the tale, the old-fashioned story. In the already more distant horizon of the industrial metropolis and the nation-state, the realistic novel has often been taken (e.g., by Lukács) as the classical moment of balance, in which the narrative of individual experience can still adequately map out larger social boundaries and institutions. In a latter moment, particularly when the apparent unity and intelligibility of the nation-state will be modified (and in many cases violently limited) by the new international system of imperialism itself, this earlier formal possibility will begin to disintegrate, making way for that explosion of

"The Names, and Richard A (review)", Minnesota Review (22), Spring 1984.

formal and narrative experiments we call modernism. In our own time, however—and the new slogan postmodernism may be taken as a symptom of this development—the older relations of imperialism and classical colonialism have been restructured into what must now be called the multinational or "world" system of late capitalism now grasped as a new stage in its own right. Here the principle of structural intelligibility is for the first time virtually completely invisible to the individual subjects whose lives it organizes: one may play with the terminology of the natural sciences, and suggest that the world system operates on a tonal or perceptual level beyond the capacity of the individual human body, or yet again, that it is a dimension of organization, in time and space, which is *experientially* as absent from our daily life as the ultimate laws of Einsteinian relativity are from our normal dealings with Newtonian gravity on this small planet.

This is then the situation in which enormously gifted writers—who wish for whatever reason to preserve the novel as a living form—confront the paradox, that where they still build their narratives out of pieces and bleeding chunks of raw experience, these last without meaning; and insofar as they venture into the area of socio-historical and economic explanation of what happens to people in our world, what comes out is abstract and nonnarrative.

Richard A. and *The Names* are particularly enlightening in this respect, since they adopt what are not only antithetical solutions, but ones which may perhaps be emblematic of the two fundamental logical choices in the face of this dilemma: totalization by fiat, in a situation in which lived totalization is impossible; and life among the unlinked fragments of the same untotalizable world. I will call Yurick and DeLillo "epistemological" writers, in the sense that for both the central "problem" to be solved formally is this ineradicable tension between fragmented, private experience and the "scientific" explanation of the world. Both, in other words, eschew the facile and conventional ways of ignoring the problem and the tension: continuing to tell individual stories and destinies (boy meets girl, etc.) in a world of billions of living beings for whom those individual stories are surely no longer very significant; or illustratively and "sociologically" offering this or that individual destiny as though it could still "represent" or be "typical" or "characteristic" of social laws in general.

Yurick's "epistemological" bent would seem to have derived from his fascination with collective actions and conspiracies. But for the author of

The Bag and *The Warriors*, inventing the conspiracy, dreaming it up, plotting it out, is the key moment of mediation between the objective action itself (the achieved conspiracy, whose narrative you now tell) and the subjective "inspiration" of the novelist himself, whose own moment of conspiring is not really different in kind from that of his characters. *Richard A.* marks a giant and ambitious step beyond the earlier books, not because it manages to "solve" anything either, but because it finally breaks through to the new myth, the new material totalization or totalizing machine, which is that of information flow. Indeed, on the level of content, in many garden-variety postmodernist works, the thematics of *reproductive technology* forms something like an omnipresent ground bass—the shift here from the late high modernism of Antonioni's *Blow-Up*, still an existential inquiry into "reality" by way of the older apparatus of the still camera, to De Palma's *Blow Out*, with its apparatus of film, video, tape recording, and its social expression of political assassination and pornography, is supremely emblematic. What was in Antonioni still a whole pathos of reality absence, becomes in De Palma a matter of doctoring tapes and editing film—"reality" has here resolved itself into little more than a stack of various kinds of texts to be modified at will. At the end of this particular figurative strategy—the attempt to "represent" the total system by way of iconic machinery or appliances that can grasp what our brains are much too simple to hold all together—there stands of course the computer, which then tends logically enough to become a new character in its own right in the science-fictional variants.

The message *Richard A.* seems to have for us on this figural level is that computers are better suited to film; in the novel, in order to ensure that the device still has some narrative content, it is the phone system which can most adequately "render" that untotalizable totality into which we are all longing to tap:

> Richard's system of taps and intercepts led, accidentally, into two realms, one visible, the other invisible. The New York Richard lived in was in the visible realm, the ordinary city of ordinary people. The other New York had everything to make it one of the great underground intelligence battlefields, right up there with London, Zurich, Moscow, Berlin, Istanbul, Washington, Athens, Paris, Teheran, Tokyo, Hong Kong. (16)

Yet if it is meritorious to want to keep on top of the system, and know how banks, multinationals, parties, presidents, and above all intelligence networks really function, there is also the little lower level of gossip and what one can only call voyeurism (in spite of the shift in senses):

> He thought it would be interesting to listen in to the rich and power-ful, see what they had to say to one another . . . sex, money, that kind of thing . . . Well, sir, you can imagine what he had to hear. Business, politics, intelligence, whores and whorehouses, sadism and maso-chism, homosexual arrangements, payoffs, bribes, state secrets, the great talking to the great, movie stars, both male and female. (411)

In short, a beginner's catalogue in yesterday's stale public curiosities: "you can imagine"—and indeed we can imagine; in that respect this book has no surprises for us and is not nearly perverse enough to gener-ate even a mild frisson.

Still, the two levels (power and sex, the "world system" and *National Enquirer* gossip) are plotted into the book by Richard's initial ambiva-lence: he likes technology and wants to learn the world's secrets; but he is also in love with a goddess who has been stolen from him by one of the world's great power brokers, and he is therefore also driven by *revenge*. Indeed, this is one of the more striking features of the novel, a reversion to what are virtually pre-capitalist plots in the form of the great revenge and vendetta motif. From Homer to the *Sagas* and reach-ing up to the dawn of the modern novel as we know it, in stories like Sir Walter Scott's "Two Drovers" (and in nostalgic forms like John Ford's westerns), the revenge motif is always linked to the clan system, the great landed family. Modern legality as well as modern social relations (and the "realistic" novels which explore and codify those) emerge from the breakup of the clans (and the penetration of a money economy). So the reappearance of this kind of plot (whose ultimate unity allows for the most episodic and picaresque meandering) is an interesting symp-tom of the formal or representational crisis just mentioned.

Richard A. has in fact not one but two enemies: the aging and myste-rious power broker Kelley, and his young male protégé Keats (we also get a little homosexual stuff here, as per the shopping list already quoted); but now the plot thickens—convergences are everywhere—and like *Spectre* in a more cartoon-type style, Kelley turns out to represent a mysterious Third World force called *Parvus* which is everywhere infil-trating both of the superpowers and is planning to use the impending missile crisis . . . but I can't quite remember for what. Meanwhile,

Richard's own parents—he thought they were immigrant small-business people on the verge of retirement—turn out to be espionage forces as well, and his mom is killed in a climactic shoot-out underneath Grand Central Station. In any case, have his parents not perhaps programmed him to be a time-bomb on the order of the hero of *The Manchurian Candidate* (to which explicit reference is made, but of course that has become part of our cultural fantasies also), or better still, on the order of the Golem? But I have to feel that this plot is more a matter of faith: that is, that as long as we are convinced that all these things hang together somehow, it doesn't matter how, and indeed the formal task of the narrative is to move so fast we have no time to wonder about any of that; a kind of perpetual present of conspiracy and intrigue, always aiming at a cataclysmic future, but always "present" in the form of feverish plotting dialogue about that future (which never comes).

At this point, one is tempted to make some conjectures about those formal pleasures, which involve the consolations of what is nowadays so often loosely called "paranoia." Far from being some ultimate nightmare state beyond simple forms of anxiety and delirium, "paranoia" in that sense strikes me as a pre-eminently reassuring thing, almost as good as a belief in God or providence. The point is that a paranoid world is the *opposite* of an "absurd" or meaningless one: in the former, every detail, every sparrow that falls, the make and model of every car that passes you, people's expressions—all that is programmed in advance and part of the basic conspiracy; the world is if anything too meaningful, and there is undoubtedly a deeper consolation here which translates itself into formal pleasures such as those of the theological spy story (good vs. evil) or of fantasies of sophistication and ultimate knowledge such as this one.

Still, modernist and "high literary" autoreferentiality is here retained: the very notion of the spy or intelligence network is just that, the book's way of referring back to itself and its own plot dynamic. Indeed, it occurs to me that a Weberian typology might be a useful way to interrogate plots like this: are they means-rational or end-rational, inner-worldly or other-worldly, or is there not in fact a basic seam or fault-line that runs down the middle of the narrative, which as in all forms of commodification tends now to break apart into means and ends, into plot ends (the "solution" of mystery stories or of this kind of political thriller, Hitchcock's McGuffins) which are little more than pretexts for the elaborate expansion and narrative unfolding of what were first only "means" to that end, namely the proliferation of the episodes themselves.

This is something that we can witness in a purer form in *The Names*, where the novel is at least implicitly a reflexion on this very problem, and where the two dimensions in question (means and ends) tend to resolve themselves each into positive and distinct phenomena and sources of formal pleasure in their own right. There is no great mystery about this, which happens in much of contemporary literature: it is simply the tension between the fragment, the writing on any given page, the quotable line or paragraph (and there are many, many of those in this splendidly written little work), and the overall drifting plot curiosity—here less a matter of solving the crime or finding out the facts (although there is a kind of crime—the cult murders—and maybe even a second one, having to do with, guess what? our old friend the intelligence network) than it is of finding out whether it is in fact those intrigues which are central in the book and which organize it, or whether they are mere episodes in a novel whose principal center of gravity is personal relations (a married couple in the process of separation). That is perhaps a healthier uncertainty than the excitement of commodification ("reading for the referent," eagerness to find out how it all turns out): where *Richard A.* sacrifices its detail and flings away page after page in the ultimate quest for the synchronic, for narrative unity (of the type of Borges's *El Aleph*), leaving nothing behind in the process, *The Names* prudently, even obsessively, collects the pages in spite of the risk they may disintegrate into that rubble of stone inscriptions from long-dead languages which give the novel its title.

For many of us, Don DeLillo has been the most interesting and talented of American postmodernist novelists (which is to say finally, I suppose, of current white male novelists, although the category may also include a few individuals of other gender or racial specifications). He has, like some of the newer movie-makers, tended to work in older genres, reviving them self-consciously across the distance of the pastiche. It is a patient kind of formal work you don't begin to notice until the titles begin to add up: a sports novel (*End Zone*), a rock novel (*Great Jones Street*), a Great American Novel (*Americana*), a science fiction novel (*Rainer's Star*), a couple of elegant, postmodern thrillers (*Players* and *Running Dog*)—the thriller is after all the easiest empty form to play with—and now this one, a tourist novel about innocents (i.e., Americans) abroad. Is this exactly what we were expecting from him? Probably not, if that was to have been the "major novel" and the great modernist statement (or Book of the World, à la Pynchon). But do postmodernists make major statements of that kind? Or rather, let me reverse the answer: *The Names* can be read as a book of that kind, a "modernist" major work, in which case it makes a statement on Language which looks metaphysical and profound but is bound to end up remaindered among all the other ideologies of language for sale on the current post-structuralist table. But you will be more satisfied if you read it as a determinedly minor work—something like a musical composition—"keyed" to the theme of proper names and their relationship to people and places, in which case it is a delicious experience (I read it twice).

But "naming" may not be the only thing *The Names* is "about." I've mentioned the narrator's marital difficulties—what this gives us above all is a marvelous, electrical, elliptic dialogue, witty in some new (and American) way, which makes you feel that Hemingway was good for something after all. This dialogue extends across the whole range of American businessmen and wives abroad to whom we are introduced here. They are nowhere near as vivid as, say, the characters in Malcolm Lowry with whom you are condemned to spend your entire life in exile, but they are certainly redeemed by their talk. There is a certain way in which this bright talk is a relief from customary (and generally well-deserved) American inferiority feelings and suggests the emergence of a culture, or at least a linguistic culture, which is commensurate with our technology, our business practices, and our sheer world power.

But if this is the newly emergent language (and culture) of some multinational American future, it is here starkly contrasted with the language of the potsherds and the inscriptions:

> No one can write Aramaic anymore. It only sounds. It traveled in history with the Jews. It was used by itself, it was mixed with other languages. Dog-Aramaic. It was carried by religion, and now it fades because of religion, because of Islam, Arabic. It is religion that carries a language. The river of language is God. (151–2)

What, we are supposed to wonder, will carry our nervous, intelligent, superficial version of English into the future? Names sacred and otherwise can at least be carved on stones, bits of signifier in the ebb arid flow of the signified. Repartee does not last in that way (although you could argue that the printed novel is the amber you preserve it in, or at least that this one is), but there are also other directions in which one can move. Towards the materiality of script itself and lettering:

"In my current infatuation I think I've abandoned scholarship and much of the interest I once had in earlier cultures. What the stones say, after all, is often routine stuff. Inventories, land sale contracts, grain payments, records of commodities, so many cows, so many sheep. I'm not an expert on the origin of writing but it seems to be the case that the first writing was motivated by a desire to keep accounts. Palace accounts, temple accounts. Bookkeeping."

"And now?"

"Now I've begun to see a mysterious importance in the letters as such, the blocks of characters. The tablet at Ras Shamrah said nothing. It was inscribed with the alphabet itself. I find this is all I want to know about the people who lived there. The shapes of their letters and the material they used." (35–6)

This, however, from the strange Wright Morris–type character, who abandons archeology for a mystical pilgrimage to an elaborate Sanskrit inscription in a local Indian shrine, yet whose Kansas childhood was deeply marked by religious revivalism and above all, the gift of tongues, which he himself was never able to acquire (and this is the point at which *The Names* ends, with a wonderful misspelled evocation by the narrator's nine-year-old boy of these alien experiences and stories by someone else—it is a prodigious stroke of timing!).

There are other languages in this book too, Kathryn's private language Ob, for example ("Fobuck yobou"), but above all, the *real* ones—the languages of the people who really live in these places, and which are not called American, Aramaic, hieroglyphic or glossolalic, but rather Greek, Arabic, Hindi. These languages (leaving aside some wonderful mimicry) mark the book the least, which is why we must now turn from the theme of language to the experience of space—no less remarkably realized here. The places are Greece—Athens and the islands—Jerusalem and Amman, the Empty Quarter, and finally a glimpse of India (not to speak of a second-hand and as it were posthumous glimpse of early twentieth-century Kansas). It seems right, in this allegedly shrinking global village, for the tourist or exile novel to be thus prodigiously shifted eastwards, away from Henry James's old Europe which we all know so well and which has no more mystery for us—or perhaps one should say that as Americans we no longer feel ourselves imprisoned in those European places and settings, we are not obliged any more to study those faces, houses, costumes, and gestures for dear life, in the way we still have to in

Cairo or Istanbul ("I was only there a day." "That's all it takes. Great cities take a day. This is the test of a great city. The traffic, the sewage, the heat, the telephones. Marvelous. Get David to tell you about the traffic in Tehran. Now there's traffic for you. There's a city" [95–6]). "Real languages," then—in other words, people's concrete social relations—are in *The Names* figured by way of space rather than by way of the themat- ics of words, something to which I will return in a moment. The point I am trying to make here is that in these concrete social settings, the cele- bration of language in fact has the intent of a celebration of those (for Americans, alien) social relations:

> People everywhere are absorbed in conversation. Seated under trees, under striped canopies in the squares, they bend together over food and drink, their voices darkly raveled in Oriental laments that flow from radios in basements and back kitchens. Conversation is life, language is the deepest being . . . It is talk as a definition of itself.
> . . . This is a way of speaking that takes such pure joy in its own open- ness and ardor that we begin to feel these people are discussing language itself. What pleasure in a simple greeting. It's as though one friend says to another, "How good it is to say, 'How are you?'" The other replying, "When I answer 'I am well and how are you,' what I really mean is that I'm delighted to have a chance to say these familiar things—they bridge the lonely distances." (52–3)

It is important to sense the difference between this development of the theme of language or talking and the poststructuralist thematics mentioned above. When for example the formal novel (that is, the narrator's novel) ends on the predictable note—not merely the long deferred visit to the Parthenon, but above all this: "This is what we bring to the temple, not prayer or chant or slaughtered rams. Our offering is language" (331)—the motif of Language has here been reified, turned into a pseudo-concept, one which is supposed to send religious vibra- tions through one if one is a believing poststructuralist. In the passage quoted above, however, the "concept" of language or talk is not some end in itself, some ultimate formal stopping place which then becomes closure and mandala, decoration and provisional metaphysic; rather, it here lives from a content it has drawn from another place and another thematics, namely that of social life proper. Indeed, from this vantage point one is tempted to return to the matter of jetset American talk and

to wonder whether that is not also a mediated, symptomal way of inter-
rogating the qualities of contemporary consumer-culture social life in
terms of its linguistic possibilities and losses. From this perspective,
then, the twin movements of the novel would be this reflexive return of
American social life today and its radical distance from more traditional
societies like Greece or the Mideast, and a very different impulse which
aims to run with the thematics of Language and to transform it into a
modernizing symbol.

But there are several other narrative motifs one would want to
mention before drawing that conclusion. Motifs or perhaps narrative
temptations, in the sense in which these recurrent yet extremely episodic
ongoing anecdotes seem on the point of offering themselves as the "real"
novel, as the central narrative on which we are to pin our readerly antici-
pations and satisfactions. The murder cult is obviously the central one of
these—a kind of sacrificial mysticism in which an ailing, dying or
severely handicapped or deficient person is killed in a place whose name
bears the same initials. This episode, the object of interest on the part of
a number of characters, is plotted in the conventional way, so that we
finally do track the surviving cultists down, in an Indian village, even
though we are not exactly filmically "present" at the final sacrifice. This
is skillfully done, with all the excitement of the quest and the detective
story reconstruction; but I must confess that it is absolutely meaningless
for me; even as some aberrant form of religion it seems artificial, made-
up and quite gratuitous, and I must therefore take this element as the
equivalent, in DeLillo's novel, to that formal compensatory process we
have already commented on in Yurick's. Here too, a formalistic play on
themes which have been for the most part—deliberately, one would
want to say—emptied of their content (most notably the theme of
Language) seems to demand the compensation of an external, imported
content of a different type. I would not want to make an absolute rule
out of it, but it strikes me that such compensatory reinjections are most
often religious in nature (Marx's own conception of commodity *fetish-
ism* underscores this explicitly), or perhaps one should say it the other
way around, that "religion" is generally to be defined as an effort to
smuggle or pump content back into various formalisms. At any rate,
DeLillo's cult plot does strike me very much as being a classical example
of the irrational "end" of an otherwise rational and intelligent, satisfying
process of "means" (which one would in this case identify as "emplot-
ment" itself).

It is, however, not the only such motif. One of the people interested in the cult is in fact a maverick filmmaker, so that the question of representation raised by this disparity in media (the narrator's prose, Volterra's film, the nine-year-old's novel) now lifts off the cult story and positions it in a new way; the comments on spectacle society, for instance ("You have to ask yourself if there's anything about us more important than the fact that we're constantly on film, constantly watching ourselves" [200]), feed back into the social thematics (America versus traditional societies) mentioned above, while the evocation of film *within* the language of the novel secretly reasserts the elastic superiority of this language over the immediacy of the visual. Volterra is, however, another traveler, another tourist, another American wandering across the alien spaces of this non-American real world.

Finally, in a Nabokovian reversal, the narrator's information-collection agency (risk insurance) is revealed to be a CIA-informant source group; a colleague who like him jogs in the nearby hills is shot at, in a seeming assassination attempt that may have been meant for the hero; and yet another dimension of the form suddenly reveals itself as the political passions generated by these American presences (a kind of indigenous or Third World resistance which is paradoxically never even evoked as a possibility in Yurick's lurid conspiratorial fantasy). This is a mild form of closure also (you think of the similar hesitations, in Naipaul's *Bend in the River*, to bring all this to a really suitable, bloody and melodramatic climax, as more bestselling novelists on Third World themes would have been wont to do), but it is hard to take any of these alternate narrative "isotopies" (A. J. Greimas' word for levels or continuities) seriously as the ultimate organizing sequence in this only apparently narrative novel.

We therefore return to its most authentic content, which is, as I've suggested above, a certain experience of space itself, or rather the peculiarly American experience of space through which substantive, culturally different and other spaces are perceived. *Our* optic is one of separation, suspension, rather than ontic or perceptual immersion—jetliners versus the Parthenon: "He wanted to know about my travels. I told him I was a traveler only in the sense that I covered distances. I travelled between places, never in them" (143).

This is clearly DeLillo's solution to the formal dilemma raised at the beginning of these notes: if a totalized world is finally unavailable for perception (not even in the most delirious computer-paranoia vision), then it seems best to hold to the fragments of place, but to mark those with a peculiar structural absence, to arrange the camera in such a way as to underscore its own vacancy, the placelessness of this peculiar multinational (American) subject as it wanders across such clusters of full space, clusters still vaguely warm from the evanescent presence of the sacred. We conclude with one of those moments, an interesting wrap-up on the relations between names, space, and storytelling:

> I'd last seen Hassan in Lahore . . . Case had come from Nairobi . . . All these places were one-sentence stories to us. Someone would turn up, utter a sentence about footlong lizards in his hotel room in Niamey, and this became the solid matter of the place, the means we used to fix it in our minds. The sentence was effective, overshadowing deeper fears, hesitancies, a rife disquiet. There was around us almost nothing we knew as familiar and safe . . . The one-sentence stories dealt with our passing grievances or small embarrassments. (94)

5

The Autonomous Work of Art: Utopian Plot-Formation in *The Wire*

Generic classifications are indispensable to mass or commercial culture at the same time that their practice in postmodernity grows more and more complex or hybrid. Is *The Wire* a police procedural, for example? No doubt, but it is also a version of the organized crime story. The majority of its actors and characters are black, which, nonetheless, does not exactly make it a black film (a film for black audiences). There is a political drama going on here, as well, but its nature as local politics reminds us that it is also very much a local series, one framed in Baltimore and very much about Baltimore (something not always to the liking of Baltimore's elites). It is, however, also the case that most detective or crime literature today (as well as its filmic offshoots or inspirations) is local and based on the consumption of a specific landscape (whether a foreign country—Swedish detective stories, Italian ones, even Chinese detective stories—or regional—Montana, Louisiana, Los Angeles, Toronto, etc.). The broadest categories would then be that of the thriller or that of the action film (although there are few chase scenes, no cliff-hangers, few enough mass action or carnage scenes).

Each of the five seasons of the TV series is a unit in terms of plot and theme; and there are at least a hundred characters deployed in each season, many of whom carry their own independent plotlines. It may be argued that there is a single major protagonist, the Irish American

"Realism and Utopia in *The Wire*," *Criticism* 52(3–4), Summer/Fall 2010.

detective Jimmy McNulty (Dominic West), even though his status fluctuates over the five seasons of the series and is often eclipsed by other characters. This is to say that a work of this kind challenges and problematizes the distinction between protagonists and "secondary characters" (or stars and "character actors"), in ways most often described, I guess, as "epic" (*War and Peace, Gone with the Wind*)—a characterization that does not help to underscore what may be a historical development in the evolution of this kind of plot (see Alexander Woloch on secondary characters).[1]

The episodes in each season are not separate and freestanding as they were in *Homicide* (screenwriter/producer David Simon's previous series, also set in Baltimore and using some of the same actors); so this is a series, or serial, like those by Dickens, and an inquiry into a specifically televisual aesthetic would want to interrogate the fascination with individual actor-characters (pleasures of recognition and repetition), alongside the development of a distinct plot, where frustration and the week-by-week postponement (even the sense of deliberate retardation and the impossibility of closure)—all of this put back into question by DVD rentals—work in the direction of a difference stamped with a unique temporality, whose rhythm is, however, then reorganized into a repetition. Repetition enhances the function of the television set as consolation and security: you are not alone when it is on in the house with you, and you are not lonely or isolated when your space is peopled by so many familiar faces and characters. On the other hand, since both these features can function as neurotic denial, television carries with it a permanent possibility of boredom and sterile or neurotic repetition or paralysis. The program must then have available a secondary ideological pretext, the window dressing of a "value": art or quality would be one of those, but also "entertainment" or relaxation-distraction (after a long day at work, for example)—a pseudoconcept if there ever was one. And there is also the alibi of the political or social message, and the "cultural capital" of the cable channel (HBO in this case, which, of course, claims to be something more than mere television). There could also be an artistic bonus, owing to the fact that each of the episodes is written and/ or directed by different people, some of them distinguished visitors (George Pelecanos, Agnieszka Holland).

1   Alex Woloch, *The One vs. the Many: Minor Characters and the Space of the Protagonist in the Novel* (Cambridge, MA: Princeton University Press, 2003).

But, initially, we approach *The Wire* as a crime story; that is, a struggle between two collectivities: the police and the crime gangs (for the
most part, the crime is drug trafficking). Each of these groups has its
representational history: it was not terribly long ago in popular culture
that the institutional police emerged from the tradition of the private
detective, while organized crime gradually became an object of representation during Prohibition (its ethnic identification with the "mafia,"
"cosa nostra," etc., comes later). Mass-cultural representation of this
kind is a kind of recognition: it confers something like an institutional
status on the group or entity in question, and such groups are accorded
objective social reality (and so we understand that real-life members
of the so-called mafia regularly watched *The Sopranos* [1999–2007];
the incidence of police watching procedurals is unrecorded). At any
rate, such recognition confirms a feeling that society is static and
stable; its neighborhoods have long since been mapped out, and, if
there are shifts or changes in this social geography, they will have been
well publicized, so everyone knows that Lexington Terrace is no longer
Polish but black, etc.

But mapping is not so simple: spatial it may be, but it does not inventory objects and substances but, rather, flows and energies. Yet the
essential raw material of any social representation is bound to be that of
social types, of stereotypes as well as generic types (like the "protagonist") or as psychological ones; and *The Wire* is no exception, multiplying its recognizable entities on all these levels. To what degree it is original and innovative will depend on the revisions it is able to bring to
these levels and perhaps even on the new types it is able to invent. A
certain modernism was able to deal with the problem of types by dissolving them into individualities and singularities, by approaching them so
microscopically that their basis in the general or the universal gradually
disappears; yet even this operation must take the familiar type as its
starting point and is menaced by the twin dangers of the emergence of
new and more subjective types, on the one hand, and of the ironic return
to the external social starting point, on the other. The word "type" is, of
course, inescapably associated with György Lukács's theory of realism,
but I think we do his immense culture and theoretical sophistication no
service by assuming that this was a conception of pre-given social or
class types rather than an attention to their historical emergence.

At any rate, *The Wire* dramatically unsettles our typological expectations and habits by at once drawing us into an epistemological exploration

that greatly transcends the usual whodunit formula. To be sure, the series begins with a banal murder whose principal novelty lies in the victim's race (white) and whose solution seems obviously enough related to his forthcoming testimony in another gangland murder trial. But what we are quickly made to understand is that the police themselves are almost wholly ignorant of the structure of the gangs and the very names of the people who control them, let alone the latter's faces and localities. The uniform cops simply know the neighborhoods and the corners on which the drugs are finally sold to customers by teams of juveniles, some of them too young to be prosecuted. But this is, as it were, simply the *appearance* of the reality, the empirical or sensory form it takes in daily life; it is the most superficial approach to this reality, whose ultimate structure (source, refinement, transportation, sales network, and bulk or wholesale distribution) must remain too abstract for any single observer to experience, although it may be known and studied—and also occasionally sensed in a representational way, as later on in *The Wire* in various forms and probes. But the intermediate reality—the so-called drug lords themselves, here Avon Barksdale (Wood Harris)—are certainly knowable but not yet known by the street cops, who learn his name in an early episode and finally manage to glimpse his face and person when he organizes a basketball game with a rival gang. Is this because his rise to power is so recent or simply because the police have not concentrated on this level of the organization before? Or perhaps, since the drug trade is a business, police observers have not attributed to it the forms and structure of legal businesses before and have therefore not asked the right questions. Whatever the reason, this ignorance of their own city suddenly opens up a space for realism: for seeing things, finding out things, that have not been registered before; and for investigation, for solving problems and tracking down causes as in scientific experiment or classical detective procedures. But, here, it is not an individual criminal responsible for an enigmatic crime, but rather a whole society that must be opened up to representation and tracked down, identified, explored, mapped like a new dimension or a foreign culture. "Barksdale" is only one component of that whole social complex, which now demands new instruments of detection and registration (just as ever-newer realisms constantly have to be invented to trace new social dynamics).

To what degree is this sociological mystery reducible to the standard plot forms of the detective search or the solving of a puzzle? I tend to think that the deeper motivation of such forms—or, it might be better to say, our pleasure in such forms—has something to do with Freud's primal scene (which also underpinned the scientist's passion at unveiling Nature). One would want to add that the Freudian-type satisfaction is never complete: just as no desire can ever really be satisfied, so also this one leaves a sense of disappointment. "Who cares who killed Roger Ackroyd?" famously cried Edmund Wilson in denouncing the detective story as a trivial genre (the reference is to Agatha Christie's ingenious breakthrough novel [*The Murder of Roger Ackroyd*, 1926]); and it is certain that there will also be a discrepancy between the passion of the chase and the contingency and triviality of the quarry. But this very discrepancy in the content plays into the form itself—the television serial—for its ultimate satisfactions must never be complete, and we must also be motivated to come back for more in hopes of greater ones. And perhaps the appropriation of these dissatisfactions for high culture or high literature would then consist in affirming that incompleteness: we never do catch the Greek, the ending remains unknown—save that, here, that incompleteness simply means the drug trade will rebound, start all over again, continue, no matter who is finally brought to justice. But *The Wire* inscribes this fatal recurrence in social history when it shows the passionate but superficial Barksdale eventually succeeded by the ruthless and dispassionate Marlo Stanfield (who finally, albeit awkwardly, becomes a bourgeois businessman).

There is necessarily a tension here between the mystery and the agon, since we also see things through the villains' eyes and thus know some solutions the police have not yet worked out. Still, what saves the mystery format is that the discoveries are made successively like links in a chain, knots on a cord: they lead us closer and closer, and so some of the suspense is displaced from the Who to the How along with the modalities of legal proof. And here we must remark on the other specificity of *The Wire*.

Not only is the "discovery" or solution a whole milieu, the world of a whole society or subsociety cordoned off from the peace-loving bourgeois civilian public (of whatever color), but the "detective" is also a group and a conspiratorial one at that. The police as a whole is an institution and, as such, moves in the direction of a properly political plot (networks, personal relations either of services rendered or of personal animosity, taking credit, passing the buck, ducking blame, etc.), and it is a political dimension that in the last seasons and episodes will come to the surface and be transformed into an official political campaign.

But this is that institutional police which has little capability of identifying its targets since, on the one hand, it does not even know their
names and, on the other, has not yet even grasped the nature of the
crimes it is investigating or their interrelationship. The lonely private
detective or committed police officer offers a familiar plot that goes back
to romantic heroes and rebels (beginning, I suppose, with Milton's
Satan). Here, in this increasingly socialized and collective historical
space, it slowly becomes clear that genuine revolt and resistance must
take the form of a conspiratorial group, of a true collective (Sartre would
call it the fused group forming within the serial mass society). Here,
Jimmy's own rebelliousness (his lack of respect for authority, alcoholism, sexual infidelities, along with his ineradicable idealism) meets an
unlikely set of comrades and coconspirators—a lesbian police officer, a
pair of smart but undependable cops, a lieutenant with a secret in his
past but with the hunch that only this unlikely venture can give him
advancement, a slow-witted nepotistic appointment who turns out to
have a remarkable gift for numbers, various judicial assistants, and
finally a quiet and unassuming fixer.

This last—the ultimate hero of *The Wire*—leads us to say something
about the title, which rarely means a wire you wear on your body, but, in
general, wiretapping as such. The older movies, seen today, make it clear
how the introduction of cell phones radically transformed the constructional problems involved in plotting a mystery or adventure film, as well
as in tracing calls and wiretapping as such—complexities that are here
explored in detail. But it is the genius of Lester Freamon (Clarke Peters)
not only to solve these problems in ingenious ways, but also to displace
some of the purely mystery and detective interest onto a fascination
with construction and physical or engineering problem solving—that is
to say, something much closer to handicraft than to abstract deduction.
In fact, when first discovered and invited to join the special investigative
unit, Freamon is a virtually unemployed officer who spends his spare
time making miniature copies of antique furniture (which he sells): it is
a parable of the waste of human and intelligence productivity and its
displacement—fortunate in this case—onto more trivial activities that
nonetheless absorb his energy and creative powers more productively
than crossword puzzles, say. But Lester is also the type of the archivist-
scholar capable of spending long hours on minutiae and in dusty files,
which ultimately cracks open financial conspiracies all over the city; and
he has deep, unostentatious, yet invaluable, roots in the community, as

when he first uncovers an old photo of the youthful Barksdale in an old boxing hangout not many of his fellow officers would be likely to have any knowledge of; and, to many of them, he is also an inestimable mentor. This is then the sense in which *The Wire* not only offers a representation of collective dynamics (on both sides) but also one of work and productivity, of praxis. In both instances, then, there is at work a virtual Utopianism, a Utopian impulse, even though that somewhat different thing, the Utopian project or program, has yet to declare itself.

But Lester's creativity may also be said to have a counterpart on the other side. We have not yet mentioned Barksdale's sidekick, Stringer Bell (Idris Elba), who is something like his executive officer or prime minister in the classic political situation: the police themselves also have a degraded version of this dual structure, where the second in command is, however, by no means as disinterested or as efficient as Bell. Stringer is, in fact, a real intellectual, and when the police (and the viewers) finally do penetrate his private apartment, they find modernist furniture and a décor of unexpectedly enlightened artistic taste. Yet, although this figure may thereby come to seem a positive one, he gives all the most lethal killing orders without a moment of remorse. Still, the interplay with Barksdale, to whom he is absolutely devoted, but who envies his intelligence and sometimes seems to resent it, is characteristic of the extraordinarily dense and minute interpersonal situations through which *The Wire* plays out its larger plot.

Obviously enough, not only do the police not initially even know who Barksdale is, they have no inkling of Stringer's existence, save in those rare moments in which he has to visit the corners and monitor the operation on the street personally. Then, one day, Jimmy takes it on himself to follow this so far unidentified figure (it will later on transpire that he is administering a whole expanding real estate investment development for Barksdale, something only gradually revealed by Lester's extraordinarily creative curiosity and know-how). At any rate, the car leads Jimmy to a university and thence to a classroom, in which, through the window, he can observe the drug kingpin and gangster taking a course in the business school and obediently answering questions and doing his homework. To be sure, the comparison of the mafia with a business enterprise is hardly metaphoric or figurative, although we sometimes omit to think historically and to identify those who actually reorganized the crime gangs in this way, along the lines of profitability (Lucky Luciano, I believe, for the mafia; but see Roberto Saviano's

Gomorrah [2007] for a vivid contemporary example). But, here, *sur le vif*, we see something of the same well-nigh aesthetic creativity: Stringer will gradually reorganize the Barksdale mob; he uses words like product, competition, investment; he brings the gangs together to eliminate the kind of internecine warfare that is always bad for business (*la douceur du commerce*: its historic taming of feudal savagery). I have deliberately used the word *creativity* several times in this context: how can this element not be seen as somehow proto-Utopian on both sides in a bureaucratic society for the most part static and content to run in the normal time-honored way, with all the old problems and malfunctions? At this early point already, *The Wire* can be observed to be ceasing to replicate a static reality or to be "realist" in the traditional mimetic and replicative sense. Here, society, on microlevels of various dimensions, is finding itself subject to deliberate processes of transformation, to human projects, to the working out of Utopian intentions that are not simply the forces of gravity of habit and tradition.

But I want first to situate this discussion of Utopianism within the context of plot construction, and to show that this is not only a purely academic matter (which it also is, of course). I want to situate both these issues within the even larger context of mass culture as a whole. Plot construction is obviously a matter of practical importance in mass culture, as witness all the books and seminars on writing a script or a scenario, but it clearly has a theoretical or philosophical dimension that is not exhausted by these technical recipes and handbooks on the matter.

The philosophical meaning of plot construction has to start from what stands in the way of constructing a plot or story; and that obviously also has its historical side. The literary past—particularly the past of theatrical spectacle but also the surviving popular literature of various bygone cultures—offers abundant examples of plots that would no longer work for us today. There is, for example, the history of feelings and their expression and evolution: Adorno remarks that the teleology of modernist literature was governed by taboo, by what you could no longer use in an artwork because it had become too sentimental and too familiar, too hackneyed and stereotypical; and that teleology no doubt also holds for the history of popular or mass culture, despite the far more central role within it of the pleasures of repetition. For, where the modernist novel sought to flee repetition, or at least to translate it into something more lofty and aesthetically worthy, mass culture thrives on what used to be called the *formulaic*: you want to see over and over again the same situations, the same plots, the same kinds of characters, with enough cosmetic modifications that you can reassure yourself you are no longer seeing the same thing all over again, that interesting twists and variations have freshened your interest. Yet a time comes when the paradigm succumbs under the sheer weight of the cumulative and the fatigue of the overfamiliar.

But I want to look for another kind of explanation for such formal exhaustion—and that is to be found in its raw material. If raw material can be readily adapted to older paradigms, its absence can also modify them in striking ways. We all know the variety of historical and social situations that have provided raw material in the past: country versus city, for one thing, and the growth of the new city as a consequence; industrialism, foreign travel and immigration, imperialism, new kinds of wars, colonization, the country house and the urban slum of the "lower depths," a "picturesque peasantry" as Henry James called it. (Indeed, his little book *Hawthorne* is a founding document on what the unavailability of certain kinds of raw material does to literary and formal possibility—he is thinking of the advantages of Europe over America.)

But let's turn to a less literary and more conventional mass-cultural genre or subgenre: the detective story. The absence of sleepy English towns and villages, of cloistered settings and vicarages, has obviously made the (older) practice of the English-type detective story difficult in the United States. But we must also enumerate the shrinkage of motives for that indispensable ingredient: the murder. Not only did there used to exist an interesting variety of motives, they could be investigated by an interesting variety of private detectives, a species that seems to have become extinct. Social respectability—that is, the possibility of scandal and its damages; family structure and dynastic or clan systems; passions and obsessions of all kinds, from hatred and revenge to other complex psychic mechanisms—these are only some of the interesting sources for motivation that have become increasingly irrelevant in the permissiveness of contemporary society, its rootless and restless movement and postregionalism, its loss of individualism and of bizarre eccentrics and obsessives—in short, its increasing one-dimensionality. Thus today, paradoxically, the multiplication of consumer niches and the differentiation of "lifestyles" go hand in hand with the reduction of everything to the price tag and the flattening out of motivations to the sheerly financial: money, which used to be interesting in the variety of its pursuits, now becoming supremely boring as the universal source of action. The omnipresence of the word *greed* in all national political vocabularies recently disguises the flatness of this motivation, which has none of the passionate or obsessive quality of older social drives and the older literature that drew on them as its source. Meanwhile, the psychic realm has also been drastically reduced, perhaps in part as a result of the omnipresence of money as an all-purpose motivation, perhaps also as a result of the familiarities of universal information and communication and the flattening of the individualisms. I have observed elsewhere that that universal communicational equality that Jürgen Habermas (in *The Theory of Communicative Action*, 1981) associates with the spread of a new kind of reason also makes for a widening of the acts we can now understand; what used to be thought of as pathology, as rarer mental states and acts beyond the pale—all these are now human, all too human, in such a way that the very category of evil or absolute otherness has drastically been reduced, as well. That the organizers of the Holocaust were mere bureaucrats certainly diminishes their chances of representing absolute evil; that most pathologies are pathetic and provincial rather than frightening is a triumph of reason and liberal tolerance but also a loss for those still clinging to some outmoded ethical binary of good and evil. I have elsewhere argued against this binary system: Nietzsche was perhaps only the most dramatic prophet to have demonstrated that it is little more than an afterimage of that otherness it also seeks to produce—the good is ourselves and the people like us, the evil is other people in their radical difference from us (of whatever type). But society today is one from which, for all kinds of reasons (and probably good ones), difference is vanishing and, along with it, evil itself.

This means that the melodramatic plot, the staple of mass culture (along with romance), becomes increasingly unsustainable. If there is no evil any longer, then villains become impossible too; and, for money to be interesting, it has to happen on some immense scale of robber barons or oligarchs, for whom, to be sure, there are fewer and fewer dramatic possibilities today, and whose presence in any case recasts traditional plots in political terms, where they are less suitable for a mass culture that seeks to ignore politics. (Or, when it turns to politics, then we may begin to wonder whether something has not also happened to politics itself: the reign of Cynical Reason is also the omnipresence of the disabused conviction about the corruption of the political generally, and its complicity with the financial system and its corruptions—so virtually, by definition, this universal cynical knowledge does not seem to project any political consequences any longer.)

We therefore have here two converging problems: on the one hand, the repetition of the older melodramatic plot form becomes more and more tiresome, and more difficult to sustain. On the other, the raw material or content for such a practice of form is becoming unidimensionalized: evil is vanishing socially, villains are few and far between, everybody is alike. The Utopian writers already had a problem with the possibility of literature in their perfect world; now we have a problem with it in our imperfect one.

This explains why villainy in mass culture has been reduced to two lone survivors of the category of evil: these two representations of the truly antisocial are, on the one hand, serial killers and, on the other, terrorists (mostly of the religious persuasion, as ethnicity has become identified with religion, and secular political protagonists like the communists and the anarchists no longer seem to be available). Everything else in sexuality or so-called passional motivation has long since been domesticated: we understand it all, from sadomasochists to homosexuals—pedophilia being a minor exception here, to be classed as a kind of subgroup or subpossibility within the larger category of serial killers (who are generally, but not always, understood as sexually motivated). It is true that, with mass murderers of the Columbine type, we begin to shade over towards the political and here terrorism reappears, but the latter organized in terms of the radical otherness of belief and religious fanaticism, since little else remains. If we really grasped terrorism as a purely political strategy, then somehow its frisson also evaporates, and we can consign it to debates on Machiavelli, on political strategy and tactics, or on history.

I need not add that these two staples—terrorists and serial killers—have become as boring as the villains driven by "greed." Alas, as with the disappearance of the spy novel after the end of the Cold War, that boredom would seem to betoken an end of melodrama, which threatens to become the end of mass culture itself.

It is in the context of these dilemmas of plot construction that we now turn to season 2 and the first nonvirtual appearance of a certain Utopianism in *The Wire*. This season deals with the port of Baltimore, with labor unions and corruption, and with a whole outside network of drug suppliers (the Greek!). The magnificent landscape of the increasingly obsolescent port and its container technology perhaps requires a detour through the whole question of place and scene (in Kenneth Burke's sense) in *The Wire*. The place is, to be sure, Baltimore; and anyone's first and quite understandable impulse would be to classify this series as part of the "postmodern" return to regionalism, and not only in "high literature" (Raymond Carver, etc.). I've already mentioned the now constitutive relationship of detective stories and procedurals all over the world to local or regional commitments; meanwhile, "world cinema" makes those commitments virtually by definition, however its works might strike local audiences, since globalized film festival culture is organized by national production.

But, in *The Wire*, there are some interesting distinctions to be made. For one thing, the regional is always implicitly comparative: not the corrupt old eastern big cities, but Montana or the South, where we live differently, and so forth, with an emphasis on the small town, or the desert landscape, or even the suburb. Here, in *The Wire*, nobody knows that other landscapes, other cities, exist: Baltimore is a complete world in itself; it is not a closed world but merely conveys the conviction that nothing exists outside it. (It is not provincial, no one feels isolated or far from this or that center where things are supposed to be really happening.) To be sure, Annapolis (the state capital) is a reference, since it is where budgetary decisions are made (especially for the police force); Philadelphia is a distant reference, since occasionally gang members have to make a drop-off there; New York City is the place you have to hire killers from, in very special instances where you need someone unfamiliar from the outside. Where the Greek gets his drugs is absolutely not a matter of conjecture (or of subjective mapping). Even nature (and the shoreline) does not exist, as witness the bewilderment of the one unhappy youngster (Wallace, played by Michael B. Jordan) shipped off to hide out with his grandmother for a while before going back to Baltimore to be killed. Baltimore is the corners—it is the police headquarters, occasionally the courts and city hall—and this is why the very name of Baltimore is irrelevant (except for local patriotism and the TV viewers) and also why the docks and the port come as a real spatial opening, even though they are as fully integrated into the web of interest and corruption as anything else, and even though the distant ports of call or whatever vessels still put in here are also absolutely unrecorded, unimagined, and so irrelevant as to be virtually nonexistent.

The labor leader is a Pole, and this is then also the moment to evoke the ethnic in *The Wire*. "Baltimore" is a nonexistent concept, but the ethnic still very much exists here, particularly if you include the police as an ethnic category, both in some figurative or moral sense, and also on account of the Irish tradition still very much in evidence among them. But are black people "ethnic" in any of these senses? We have already seen that the drug scene, run by Barksdale, is not only black, but exists like a foreign city within the official one: it is a whole other world, into which you do not go unless you have business there ("you" here standing for the officially dominant white culture). So here, in absolute geographical propinquity, two whole cultures exist without contact and without interaction, even without any knowledge of each other: like Harlem and the rest of Manhattan, like the West Bank and the Israeli cities that, once part of it, are now still a few miles away; even like East and West Berlin today, where older East Berliners are still reluctant to travel to the former West, with its opulent shops they have no tradition of, and with a whole capitalist culture alien to them for most of their lives.

Still, this might be considered essentially as a black series; the bulk of its cast is black, drawing on scores not only of underemployed black actors but also on local nonprofessionals, as well; just as Baltimore itself is a predominantly black city. But, as has been observed of its predecessor series, *Homicide: Life on the Street* (1993–99), this very preponderance means that you see so many different types of black people (social, professional, even physical) as to utterly dissolve the category. Here there is no longer any such thing as "black" people, and, by the same token, no such thing as black political or social solidarity. These former "black people" are now in the police; they can be criminals or prison inmates, educators, mayors and politicians; *The Wire* is in that sense what is now called *post-racial* (something that might be sure to have its political effect on the US viewing public at large, just as the presence on TV of so many black entertainment celebrities has had its own impact on racial stereotypes and on the unfamiliarity essential to racisms).

But the Poles are still an ethnic group, as witness the ferocious vendetta waged against the labor leader Frank Sobotka by a Polish police major, which is one of the causes of Frank's eventual downfall. His ethnicity is at some distance, however slight, from his role as labor leader; and it is around this last that a certain Utopianism begins to gather. For the demise of the port of Baltimore has to do with the postmodern technology of containerization (see Marc Levinson's *The Box*, 2006) and its impact on the labor movement (many fewer workers needed, leading to the fall of once immensely powerful unions like the longshoremen's), as well as on cities (the postcontainer development of the port of Newark, New Jersey, having suddenly rendered a host of other competing East Coast ports obsolete, very much including Baltimore), the old port now seemingly reserved for police boats, such as the one to which Jimmy has been demoted. This is then an interesting case where the destructive force of globalization has been, as it were, interiorized along with a more general deindustrialization: it is not only the movement of work to other, cheaper countries that has ruined Baltimore, but rather our own technology (which, of course, amplifies the impact of globalization generally, as containerization develops foreign ports and modifies industrial production and what can be shipped, as well). But this historical story is part of the background of *The Wire*, and not its primary lesson or message.

The message is in part elsewhere, and it lies in the recontextualization of Frank Sobotka's alleged corruption (stereotypically associated with labor unions today, at least since Jimmy Hoffa); and it is certain that Frank is deeply implicated in the drug trade and lets the Greek use his container traffic. But Frank is not interested in money (and I suppose you could argue that Stringer Bell is not interested in money either and, maybe beyond that, that the excitement of finance capital itself is not really about money, in its older sense of riches and wealth). Frank uses the money to build up his own contacts, in view of a supreme project, which is the rebuilding and revitalization of the port of Baltimore. He understands history and knows that the labor movement and the whole society organized around it cannot continue to exist unless the port comes back. This is then his Utopian project, Utopian even in the stereo-typical sense in which it is impractical and improbable—history never moving backwards in this way—and in fact an idle dream that will even-tually destroy him and his family.

But I mean something more than that, and this enlarged conception of Utopianism has to do with plot construction. Realism was always somehow a matter of necessity: why it had to happen like that and why reality itself is both the irresistible force and the unmovable obstacle. To include Frank's pipe dream in a purely realistic work, we would have to see it (as Balzac so often did) as a mania, a psychological obsession, a purely subjective drive and character peculiarity. But this dream is not like that; it is not only objective; it draws all of objectivity within itself such that, if the plot of *The Wire* were to show its success, the representation would imply the Utopian (or revolutionary) transformation and reconstruction of all of society itself. Nor is it political pleading, a political program cooked up by *The Wire*'s writers and producers and endorsed by the public as a desirable political and social improvement. It cannot be all that—no viewer will understand this episode in that practical light, because it involves not an individual reform but rather a collective and historical reversal—but it introduces a slight crack or rift into the seamless necessity of *The Wire* and its realism or reality. This season then adds something to *The Wire* that cannot be found in most other mass-cultural narratives: a plot in which Utopian elements are introduced, without fantasy or wish-fulfillment, into the construction of the fictive, yet utterly realistic, events.

Yet Sobotka's Utopianism would remain a mere fluke or idiosyncrasy if it did not have its equivalents in later seasons of *The Wire*. (We could write it off, for example, by observing that the creators of the show, in their local patriotism, had taken this occasion to add in some more purely local statement.) But, in fact, it does, and at this point I can only enumerate the later incidence of a Utopian dimension in succeeding seasons. In season 3, Utopianism is certainly present in Major Colvin's "legalization" of drugs; that is, his creation of an enclave of drug use closed to police intervention. In season 4, on education, it is to be found in Pryzbylewski's classroom experiments with computers and his repudiation of the exam evaluation system imposed by state and federal political entities. Finally, in season 5, the most problematic, it is to be located in Jimmy's invention of a secret source for funding real and serious police operations outside the bureaucracy and its budget—and this, despite the artificial crime panic he deliberately fosters, and also somewhat on the margins of what was to have been a series dominated by the newspaper and the media (for each season of *The Wire*, like Zola's great series, or like Sara Paretsky's Chicago crime novels, is also organized around a specific industry).

The future and future history have broken open both high- and mass-cultural narratives in the form of dystopian science fiction and future catastrophe narratives. But in *The Wire*, exceptionally, it is the Utopian future that here and there breaks through, before reality and the present again close it down.

6

Flashes of World War II

Third Reich detective stories are required to be politically correct. It is obligatory for the protagonist to register his distance from the regime somehow. Otherwise, on the reader's part, no identification, no complicity! Something in the fine print—anti-Bolshevism, perhaps, or indignation at the injustices of the Treaty of Versailles—must give us license to distinguish him from those who are National Socialists out of conviction. The historian Geoffrey Barraclough pointed out, long ago, that Hitler's was Germany's first genuine bourgeois revolution. So, perhaps it's a matter of class?

> The reason, Martin-Heinz Douglas *Freiherr* von Bora, is that you are all that we're striving to leave behind, the kind of Germany of lords and ladies and generals' sons and estates . . . I'm not even sure you are fighting for the same Germany I'm fighting for.

The quotation is from *The Road to Ithaca* (2014), one of thirteen novels published so far in the Martin Bora series by Ben Pastor, a pseudonym for the Italian-born author Maria Verbena Volpi. The man speaking is the son of a family working on Bora's ancestral estate (*Freiherr* means "baron"); and he himself is a "real" Nazi, that is, a proletarian thug driven by class *ressentiment*. Both men are in the army, but between them is all

"War as a Rhizome: On Ben Pastor's Martin Bora Novels," *London Review of Books* 44(15), August 4, 2022.

the difference there is between an NCO and an officer—which may remind us of Gottfried Benn's remark that, during the *Nazizeit*, joining the army was the only elegant form of "inner emigration." So it was that long after the war an aristocratic Wehrmacht clung to the self-serving myth that the crimes and excesses of the SS had nothing to do with them or their mission. Bora's own excuse is also a familiar one:

> My aggressiveness . . . is a reaction. Against the wrongs done to our Fatherland after the Great War, against those nations that smother our vital space, and against demands that we keep justifying ourselves to the world as Germans.

He omits his own most striking virtue: fidelity. (After 1934 the army pledge to the constitution was rewritten: Bora is thereby bound by an oath of allegiance to his Führer.)

In the end, however, our discomfort with this protagonist, who is not an antisemite, may lie elsewhere. Bora isn't merely a professional soldier, he loves war:

> Ever since Spain I've had seven years of great fighting. The *glory* of it, the bloody idea of it . . . Spain, Poland, Russia—I volunteered for all. Being in war is as much fun as being in love, when the want's in it.

And perhaps even more incriminating:

> I long to be the first one to see the Volga. I dream of it after dark, wide as a lake, an artery in the great body of Russia. Still, even at the gates of Stalingrad and its river, 3,200 kilometres away from Berlin, we Germans stand on a mere southwestern sliver of the endless Euro-Asiatic plain. It helps to consider that all of us, ancestrally, hail from here. We belong here more than we know, much more than the enemy wants to admit.

Before we deal further with the *Schuldfrage*, however, we should note that these novels are not only detective stories, they are also historical novels; and this suggests that Bora will have to play two distinct generic roles, occupy two distinct narrative agencies, simultaneously. The detective solves crimes; the protagonist of the historical novel, by contrast, passively receives and observes History. The sleuth who, operating in a tense wartime situation, is assigned by his superiors to ferret out the truth of this or that potentially scandalous mystery, must also assume the status of what György Lukács in his classic work on the historical novel called the average or "mediocre" (*mittelmässig*) hero, Waverley or Fabrice, who observes great historical collisions from the sidelines. Lukács recommends that the historical novelist never allow history's inevitable "world-historical individuals" to be central to a novel (although they must necessarily be so in the historical drama). Indeed, Tolstoy's caricature of Napoleon was not his most successful literary decision. Bora, though scarcely a mediocre hero, never interacts with world-historical figures directly—never sees Mussolini in the flesh in Salò, for example—but only registers his presence in a mediated way:

> He also read expected but unnerving details about the deep antipathy among fascist leaders and corps, of Denzo's antagonism towards the RNG and vice versa, of Marshal Graziani's outbursts and Mussolini's resentful silence with almost everyone.

It's true that another of the novels is concerned with the Duce's compromising letters, and his suicide attempt before the spectacular rescue from Gran Sasso; but these events too are mediated, given to us as a story within the story.

There is a more serious problem, and Aristotle supplies its formulation: "The unity of a plot does not consist, as some suppose, in its having one man as its subject. An infinity of things befall that one man, some of which it is impossible to reduce to unity; and in like manner there are many actions of one man which cannot be made to form one action." A biographical existence is not a complete action, not a single event; it does not have closure (although its conclusion may ultimately be considered a "destiny"). This excellent advice is, however, vitiated by a presupposition we may no longer share, namely that, on the collective or the individual level, there exist "events" which it is possible to "reduce to unity," or whose actions "can be made to form one action." In our present context, History itself is no longer a functional category of closure. The unity of "World War II," or "the Eastern Front," or even "the Battle of Stalingrad," must be constructed by the individual, in this case by Bora's existential experience, and is lent an appearance of geographical unity in the protagonist's displacements, from Civil War Spain to Barbarossa or an Italian peninsula invaded by Allied forces.

But, despite biographical logic, there remains a certain contingency in these displacements, as though the novelist had simply decided it would be useful to have Bora present at key sites and moments in the unfolding of the war, at places of atrocity (Katyn Forest, or Rome for the Ardeatine massacre) or crucial developments (such as the Republic of Salò or the Battle of Stalingrad). It is a contingency which haunts all representations of history.

Take, for example, Kubrick's splendid historical film *Barry Lyndon* (1975), an adaptation of Thackeray's not exactly famous novel. Its craftmanship and power aren't enough to rescue it from a lingering feeling of gratuitousness. Why this resurrection of an eighteenth-century battle now? Unlike World War II, we cannot say that it is an abiding subject of interest. A passionate denunciation of war in general? A veiled comment on Vietnam, then? An illustration of the techniques of pre-motorized warfare? An object lesson in the treatment of veterans? A rehearsal and finally a substitute for the Napoleon film Kubrick never made? None of these extra-artistic justifications takes us very far in accounting for the necessity of this artwork, though they do open onto fields of inquiry in their own right. And, in general, our interest in historical works always seems dependent on something extra-aesthetic: on the questions posed by the history books, for example (what were Hitler or Stalin really like?); on this or that current fad (Nazi materials, of course, exert a seemingly perennial fascination); on our historicity in general as it has developed since the French Revolution and been sated by offerings from Walter Scott to Ken Burns, Tolstoy to Margaret Mitchell, Hilary Mantel to Ben Pastor. Pastor seems to have invented a new way of combining the whole and the part in what TV producers might call the limited series.

Yet it might chasten us to remember that, as a result of our increased historicity today, all novels are historical (when not, indeed, sciencefictional): all carry with them the fatal chronological questions "Before what?" and "After what?" Perhaps, then, it might be preferable to shift from the horizontal to the vertical: to see what it is that Bora's "history" is made of, what it offers us. For novels are put together out of all kinds of raw material; they don't really have the purity of the older genres. Rather than thinking in terms of linear narrative, we might do better to imagine a pile of separate and uneven strata, geological layers, irregular laminates, each one like an encyclopedic relief map, tactile as braille: each novel is a unique conjuncture of these, momentarily coordinated as with a tacking nail, and just as easily disjoined into a scattered pile of themes waiting for the conjuncture of a new event, a new novel.

What we call the War, then, fans out into a set of geographical, institutional, chronological constellations which translate our general categories into specific perceptions and encounters. We stumble, to be sure, over a great deal of military hardware—weaponry, tanks, aircraft—about which we are given a degree of technical information above and beyond what the garden variety policeman needs to know. Landscapes, meanwhile, return Europe to a bewildering multiplicity of topographies:

> It took them close to forty minutes to negotiate the seamed, cleft terrain skirting the bottom of the cliff. Once out of the ravine they faced an incline in full sun, hairy with drying grass and like the hump of a great albino bison. It was from this north side that Agias Irinis could be reached, by a natural ramp that sloped gradually into baldness; its foot instead was bushy, filled with cicadas, pristine. A scent of wild thyme rode the breeze from it.

These are physical and not purely visual landscapes: they engage the straining body and its fatigue and sweat, but also arouse affect in its most unpredictable forms:

> Everything was blooming early this year. In the fields around the cavalry camp, sunflowers had begun opening up nearly a month in advance, bright yellow like mass-produced stars on an assembly line. Bora—who'd grown used to seeing endless expanses of them in the East—found them newly jarring, on the threshold of disgust.

But topography also means cities, even though, for this Wehrmacht, it is peasant villages that predominate. Still, there remains timeless Rome, a vivid presence in these novels at the moment of the Allied advance up the peninsula; and there is Berlin, whose rubble Bora does not care to contemplate from the air. There is even his native Leipzig, to which we are treated during a prewar visit from a Japanese delegation. But, above all, there is Stalingrad, the eternal Stalingrad of the grain elevator, the tractor factory, the landing ferry, the White House, the brick kiln, even the Unimag, that stubborn department store that hosted Paulus's surrender to the Soviets (one history having here effaced another, the celebrity of the tractor factory as the first great

monument to Stalin's collectivization drive some fifteen years before).
Nor are the ghosts to be dispelled from the rubble, the legendary snip-
ers for example:

> Only snipers, like deities of Olympus, see and monitor everyone . . .
> truly the sniper is god. Rarely does he miss a shot or cause only a
> wound . . . The sniper is aloof from the miseries of this earth; he
> chooses and is the dispenser of fate to anyone who enters the magical
> circle of his telescope.

Stalingrad pioneers a new kind of warfare:

> Inside the city, war has become like a sea battle on paper, of the sort
> we played as children, drawing our ships on a squared sheet and
> marking the edges with numbers and alphabet letters as it's done on
> maps. When we called out "M3" to the other player, if it turned out
> that at the intersection of M and 3 a two-square destroyer of his had
> been struck, we could try to finish it off by calling out L3, N3, M2 or
> M4. For us today the few surviving buildings and landmarks are like
> those paper ships on their squares.

It is also the word for a new kind of experience:

> They are obliterating everything around us . . . The mutilation of the
> last buildings is ongoing. For the common soldier, the *Landser* who in
> this and other regards resembles a house cat, this creates psychologi-
> cal problems . . . His geography is based on the reliability of land-
> marks . . . And to think that at the beginning of summer, we advanced
> as through a grassy ocean, confident, brazen, heedless. We had no
> need of smelling the fragrance of spices to know that on our exotic
> course lay the islands we sought.

In these landscapes, silence becomes not merely the language of nature
but also a sixth sense:

> Ever since Spain, and more so after the Polish campaign, Bora had
> been hyper-sensitive to sounds. The faintest noise, barely alive at the
> level of hearing, did not escape him, a plus for a soldier on reconnais-
> sance duty. It implied a predator-like quality of stillness, outwardly

stolid but in fact so keen that other senses were involved, as if he could
smell or touch the source of the sound.

They are also occupied landscapes, landscapes of alertness and suspicion; and we need another map, another overlay, to fit them out with
the networks of interpersonal tension, the geographies of vigilant
distrust, that extend from vulnerable peasant huts to the offices of
competing intelligence agencies and personal rivalries. It should be
remembered that besides the local police forces (the Gestapo started
out as one of these, in Göring's Prussian state), each of the services has
its own secret information bureau (not to speak of those of foreign
allies—Italy, Romania—as well as the local police forces of the occupied countries). None of these "sister organizations" are exempt from
the surveillance of the SS, whose most formidable rival, however, is
that still aristocratic Wehrmacht in which Bora is an officer. Indeed, he
comes under additional suspicion by virtue of his position in the
army's own independent intelligence service (yet another one), the
so-called Abwehr (which will be dissolved later in the war). The map
of these innumerable spy networks and their hostile intersections with
one another turns out to be more complex than the actual battles
themselves (of which, as we know, many maps exist). This makes for a
record of contacts between the characters which, besides being almost
exclusively male, is also a combination of competing and mutual
investigations.

Bora's professional duties are in fact those of an interrogator, an
ominous métier indeed, whose modulations range from torture to the
wiles of a Dostoevskian examiner, and are not always limited to enemy
officers or partisans. Here, as elsewhere, Bora's role is ambiguous, hover-
ing at the blurred boundary between detective and inquisitor. (A certain
generic tradition persists here, as Bora's resistance to his enemies in the
SS—he is, for the moment, protected by high-placed friends and
mentors—reproduces the classic fictional policeman's struggle with
obtuse or complicit superiors.)

In addition to these narrative strata, there is a further set of points of
concentration, which, although never wholly absorbed into the action,
is never far from our attention. Bora's religion of monogamy will strike
the reader, as it does Bora himself, as a matter apart from the rest, a kind
of momentary transcendence. I hesitate to quote any of these passages,
which are a kind of luminous pornography—Petrarchan evocations of

the carnal, out-of-body experiences as it were, in which the body itself, in these very physical books, is beyond materiality.

Bora's wife, Dikta, is a character in her own right, far more striking and self-willed, more unpredictable, than Bora himself. Rather than a wife, it seems preferable to think of her as a partner in a conspiracy:

> Deep down, he too regarded his marriage as an extended love affair; he and Dikta were each other's passionate bookmarks in life, looking for no one else as long as they had each other.

This last qualification is significant, especially if you read "had" in terms of physical proximity. Divorce in wartime is no small thing, particularly when, like one of Bora's unhappy comrades, you get a note that simply reads: "I found another, all good wishes."

But do such erotic interludes—obligatory today in most popular fiction and enhanced by the now permissible and explicit physical details—deserve a separate rubric in our list of the truly heterogeneous raw materials out of which the Bora novels are composed? If the question is strange, it is made stranger still by compounding it with a reference to the phenomenon of courtly love, which has been the esoteric interest of thinkers from Pound and Rougemont to Bataille, Klossowski and Lacan (not to speak of Dante and *il dolce stil novo*), where it is often linked with transgression. Courtly love has indeed always been associated with asceticism, continence, and abstention, things wholly absent from these books, which do, however, insist on the uniqueness and self-control of Bora's sexual experience ("Everything that had ever opened before him, or been answered, revealed, given, had been preparation for this"). These are techniques, not for satisfying desire but for intensifying and at the same time sublimating it; for approaching that material transcendence Lacan calls *jouissance*. The purity and intensity of these sexual interludes—containable in a detective or war story only as one layer within a heterogeneous *agencement*—transcend desire or love itself, and assail Bora from the stolen painting of Titian it is his task to locate:

> At once Bora's attention fastened on it. There, languidly twisted to one side, the slick female body emerged in fleshy half-seen surfaces from the shadow, as if pouring out of nothingness in order to bloom before him . . . The Venus stared out of the murkiness of the canvas . . . When

he stepped away from the Venus, blood drove hard through him, making him anxious for an ennoblement of desire and the impossibility to fulfil it—a solitary lucidity of want.

This effect isn't simply to be attributed to the gendered qualities of the text, the omnipresent male physicality of a landscape at war, which reminds one of the pre-mechanized topography of World War 1, in which the movement of the great armies was signaled by an immense smell of sweat preceding them for miles and miles. There is here certainly, from time to time, the disgust with same-sex physicality, but not the nausea of the male other to be found in Bloom's exposure to a crowded pub at lunchtime ("Men. Men. Men.") or the disgust of the Nabokovian hero at the evidence left behind by his rival (a cigarette butt floating in the urine of an unflushed toilet). Omnipresent here is, rather, the physicality of the soldier—heat, chills, fever, sweat, showers, hyper-alertness—whose unremitting vulnerability stands as an inescapable ground bass to the immense spatio-temporal phenomenology, from Spain to the Volga, which is World War II:

> Flies everywhere ... Skin food excrement wounds rubbish are to them all the same, all appetising. Chasing them makes no difference: they're like a noxious thought you can wave off but not eliminate. Not even cleanliness keeps them away, just like virtue isn't enough to keep away evil thoughts. I can see why Satan is called Lord of the Flies. This is, and always was, war. We are, in the year of Our Lord 1943, like our counterparts in the year 1943 before Christ was born, in Sumer or Egypt, chasing flies and killing lice.

But perhaps it is time to look at Bora himself, as yet another of these thematic bands or unities of which these books are composed, with a short detour through what is perhaps even somewhat extraneous to him, namely his class background. The family, descended from Martin Luther's wife (despite which it is firmly Roman Catholic) includes (like Kant's lineage) a Scottish heritage, with a military ancestor boasting the glory of having been killed alongside Gordon in the Battle of Khartoum. Although Saxon and raised in Leipzig, he knows holidays in Rome as well as summers in East Prussia. Martin's natural father had been a world-famous orchestra conductor (and sometime composer—in Proustian fashion, we owe the suite called the *Gypsy Synagogue* to him), with a glorious career that extended all the way to imperial St. Petersburg. The son seems just as gifted musically (he is a fine pianist until an injury prevents him from playing), but has instead devoted himself to the same career as his stepfather, a Prussian officer:

> How can I explain to my stepfather . . . that the reason I chose to attend university before army school was that I wasn't sure that Germany would commit to an army after all, and that the army would commit to *something*? Nation-building is well and good for some; but for those like myself who have heard nothing else but retribution and bitterness for Versailles, there has to be something more than nation-building. A holy goal, a course sanctified by necessity and God's own injunction that we must protect civilisation. As a German, I need to feel civilised, and civilising: wars provide a shortcut to that comfortable feeling of superiority. God keep me from being wrong about any of this, or else show me the way before it's too late.

Bora's relationship with his mother provides the most touching and tender moments in these works, something it is awkward to point out in our post-Freudian age. The aristocratic Almanach-de-Gotha family lines form a web that transects the whole of the Wehrmacht; their mirror-image is the party network that resists, subtends and extends far beyond them.

Bora's psychology is, however, another matter, as it involves us in literary-formal as well as phenomenological problems. From time to time, we can see him from the outside: Aryan, as handsome as Stauffenberg (a concession to political correctness which will be expunged by Bora's later intense dislike of the man), authoritarian, unpredictable, without friends and never fully revealing himself, whose very self-control is controlled; yet beloved of his troops, who appreciate his extraordinary luck in battle. Despite his nightly confessions (to us) in his journal, however, none of these external traits and forms of subjective confidence seem to cohere. Bora remains an enigma; we never completely identify with him, notwithstanding any number of exciting adventures and deductions.

There are ways of accounting for this lack of identification; though one hypothesis—an awkwardness in multiplying Bora's character traits—we can immediately discount. It is possible to entertain the illusion that these are, against all expectations, novels of ideas. In that case,

Bora becomes an exemplar or illustration of Ernst Jünger's "archon," the survivor in the midst of institutional repression, a true inner emigrant, the one available hero for totalitarian times. This is not to say that the philosophical interpretation is implausible; but it does tend to reduce the work to the status of a thesis novel, with those overtones of militarism with which, rightly or wrongly, Jünger's own work is associated ("war as an inner experience"). Jünger is himself a character in one of Pastor's novels.

It would perhaps be even more of a stretch to associate Bora's story with the teachings of his old professor Martin Heidegger. At best, this might clarify his relationship to death, for Heidegger's *Sein-zum-Tode* or being-unto-death is less a call to death anxiety than a way of grasping death, not as my disappearance but as that of my "world." "Capitano, surely you've thought out what you'd like to be watching when you die." In these novels, death is always a matter of place: in every wartime city or landscape Bora asks himself whether these will be his last surroundings, his final glimpses of the life world. (Meanwhile, it appears to be irrelevant that both Jünger and Heidegger ended their lives as Roman Catholics; but some readers may think otherwise.)

Character traits—of which Bora has so many excellent ones—are qualities observed from the outside and as it were reified; whether Bora's thoughts about himself (as narrated, for example, in his journals) are any more reliable, any less objictified, is a literary or psychological question. But there are other kinds of trait—the "control of his self-control," for example—which are more likely to seem regulative rather than substantive: what might normally be called "reserve." "By upbringing and from habit, physical contact was for him an extreme resort, necessarily aggressive or sexual." Is this a characteristic—related, for instance, to his athleticism as it manifests itself in horsemanship—or the repression of a characteristic?

> Ever since Spain, Bora had taken inordinate care in the practice of storing anxiety deeply within, as safely as an army trunk was organised, with the heaviest objects at the bottom, tucked away in the corners.

Nor is this the only way of dealing with potentially uncontrollable psychic reactions:

He remembered each instance of great fear as a precise scenario comprised of layers, circumscribed horizons, dimensions unforgiving and eternally set. The room where he stood was instantly transformed into a paradigm of itself, so that for ever—in the moment it took for an SS officer to dismount from his vehicle—this wall and doorway, that slice of winter light across the desk and flaws in the tile floor would be associated with fear.

Repression, aestheticization—if one cares to psychologize, these can clearly be thought of as defense mechanisms. But I continue to feel that Bora's "consciousness"—that black hole with which the reader is invited to identify—is a good deal more inscrutable and enigmatic than the adjectives psychology gives us, a good deal closer, in other words, to some phenomenological account of an empty ("purely intentional") consciousness than most novelists, intent on the business of producing "believable" yet idiosyncratic "characters," would be willing to endorse.

Yet, what if "character" were something like this:

His wholeness was scattered all over, as far as his mind could go—strands of him, loose ends, strange pieces, and he would need to pick them up and braid them back together to reshape his balance.

What used to be called the self is a heterogeneity about which it is best to take the stoic's advice: "But the parts which are beset by pain, allow them, if they can, to give their own opinion about it."

There is, finally, the matter of guilt:

A round-up was in progress there, Bora couldn't say he wasn't used to the scene. He wished he could say it troubled him; in fact nothing seemed to trouble him anymore. It was all already seen, done, experienced. Crowds lost individuality; it came down to shoves and rifle butts pushing or dividing or striking, quick turns on the feet as someone sprinted to get away and the weapon was righted, aimed and fired without missing. Everyone played their role perfectly, victims included. Bodies lay around, blood pooled under them. Only his anger (which was something other than a feeling of pity) was stirred, like a thick liquid that needed mixing and scooping but in the end agitated on its own. Principle, not people; not feeling what he didn't feel. Virtue had nothing to do with it.

This visceral disgust should not, I think, be read as moral indignation, but as some more immediate perception of the stupidity and brutality of just such programmed killings. Bora's mind does not move on the level of policy or philosophical ethics—a level, for example, on which the Reich's official antisemitism takes the form of a state religion, whose true believers are, in Jonathan Littell's *The Kindly Ones* (2006), characterized as "idealists." No doubt he has arguments with his eminent teachers on these subjects; but we do better to see them in terms of narrative and behavioral concreteness than abstract moral theses. His relations with the SS are not ideological but rather the precautions one takes with respect to the danger posed by a variety of malevolent officials ranging from the brutal to the efficiently hostile.

The War is a rhizome, striated by encyclopedic information, and delivered in intelligent sentences, the like of which, as Chandler observed long ago, always exasperate the readers of airport paperbacks: boundaries expanding and contracting and the series delivering unpredictable spots of time. There is, of course, a satisfaction in the solution of the local problem—the disappearance of two Italian physicists in a Ukrainian battlefield; the murder of a celebrated Weimar performer and confidence man; Mussolini's missing letters; the theft of a priceless Titian Venus—whose conclusion is timed to coincide with this or that world-historical event or battle. But the series is neither a chronology nor a *Bildungsroman*. Each novel affords a glimpse into a unique and heterogeneous intensity in the stream of time.

Bora is carried forward in it like the War itself, and the jumbled chronology of the publications—Salò followed by Barbarossa, the attempt on Hitler by the battle of Stalingrad—distracts us from any question about his ultimate fate. Perhaps, indeed, as we have grown attached to him over this seemingly immense period of time and space, we would rather not know; and it is as hard to imagine him in the rubble of Germany year zero as to think of his corpse on the Eastern Front (or in the prisons of the SS). Best, then, to let his fate remain as indeterminate for us as it is for him. Meanwhile, Maria Verbena Volpi is to be credited with having invented him; but perhaps, even more, to be congratulated on her creation of his author, "Bèn Pastor," whose imagination seems indeed to have invented World War II itself.

7

Germany's Double Plots

Can there be literature after reunification? It strikes one as something of a science-fictional question. Philip K. Dick, indeed, posited a future world in which the Axis powers had won World War II, and proceeded to divide the United States down the middle into two zones with two decidedly different regimes of military occupation. In *Fire on the Mountain*, Terry Bissell posits a world in which a successful John Brown's raid sets off a black revolution in the American South which leads to the formation of a socialist state, ultra-modern and prosperous, in contrast with the shabby private-enterprise North that limps along on the crumbs of world trade. But what if the Allies *had* won World War II, and divided Germany itself into two occupation zones dominated by two different modes of production? And what if—for the science-fictional fantasy has the peculiar property that its conceits refuse to remain static or fixed, but suddenly convulse, change and grow with the dynamics of History itself—what if, eventually, after several generations, these two different German-speaking nations somehow rejoin? Is one to imagine the coming into being of some undreamt of new third entity, distinct from each of its constitutive halves (assuming the post-national dimensions of a European federation don't deprive secession and reunification alike of anything other than local significance)? Or does the one half appropriate the other and subject it to its own specific forms of exploitation,

"Prussian Blues: On *Ein weites Feld* by Günter Grass," *London Review of Books* 18(20), October 17, 1996.

as the North did to the conquered South after the real Civil War, sending
in the various tribes of carpetbagger, from the academic to the financial,
from land speculators to the police force (with their newly repainted
vehicles), in order to teach the errant member its true subalternity and
to endow it with conformity to the law and custom, the property rights,
of the allegedly consanguine state that has taken its poorer cousin in out
of charity . . .

As for literature after reunification, George Steiner thought there
could be none anyway after Hitler; but he had in mind the bureaucratic
degeneration of the language. The question reactivates the matter of
tradition, and of the framework in which the new text—any new text—
is to be received and evaluated. For it is not clear, first of all, which
Germany the present one continues, except that it is surely not that of
Hitler's Reich. But Weimar, to which so much radical German literature
still appeals, was—besides being a victim of that West of which the
successor state is the hegemonic power—a failure that it might be
unlucky to be identified with; while the second Empire, the Wilhelminian
period, combining the Victorian harmonies of a bourgeois golden age
with the grisly overtones of the trenches of World War 1, also offers little
in the way of imaginary satisfaction and genealogical pride and fulfilment. Beyond that, we lose ourselves in a well-nigh medieval night: the
Holy Roman Empire? Wallenstein and some putative South German/
Bohemian Catholic kingdom? The two Fredericks? And why not Tacitus'
Germania, while we are at it, and the Teutoburger Wald? There are good
reasons for the solution that seems to have been arrived at, without any
particular planning or forethought: the new Germany will be a larger
version of the Federal Republic; that is to say, of a provincial West
Germany with which very few of its writers wished to identify in the first
place, preferring to live in West Berlin outside that dispensation, when
not in outright exile.

Günter Grass's new novel, *Eine weites Feld*, proposes another solution, a more radical and scandalous one. The scandal, predictably,
aroused the outrage of all those (and they were and are many) who
thought that politics could now be abandoned once and for all, and that,
in Germany, as elsewhere in the world, after the alleged triumph of capitalism, we could return to the untroubled cultivation of the aesthetic as
such, to Literature, and to an appreciation of *belles lettres* apt to adorn
and distinguish a prosperous bourgeoisie ready to take up its duties and
privileges where they had been broken off when class struggle and

fascism reared their ugly heads. Not the least entertaining response to the novel was the attempt of the well-known reviewer and television critic, Reich-Ranicki, to tear it up (literally as well as figuratively) on the small screen. Bourgeois aesthetics and culture as an unfinished project: so might run the ironic Habermasian judgment on this new mood, this new task for no longer committed intellectuals. It accounts for the opprobrium called down on Grass himself, who, just when we thought we had got rid of the postwar and of the boring "critical" and would-be subversive writing associated with it, produced this 800-page monstrosity about a pair of old men in East Berlin, the former East Berlin: pages whose very sterility allegedly attests to the drying up of his own (only too political) talent and to the end of an era now best forgotten, whether in the East or the West.

His enemies and critics clearly understood the project: for the positing of a tradition—even a "merely" literary one—is a utopian and political act. Thus, the universalism of *Finnegans Wake* projected a transfigured Ireland that was at one with some new world culture to this day not realized. *Ein weites Feld* more modestly rewrites the German past on the basis of a Prussia of which East Germany (the German Democratic Republic) was the rightful heir: the new Germany, therefore, is here asked to assume the legacy of the socialist and Prussian Germany as its imaginary other. A few strong but isolated voices have long been telling us that the identification of Prussia (let alone Berlin) with the Nazi side of the "German character" is based on the sheerest misinformation about this tolerant Protestant culture, so different from what one encounters in a Catholic and provincial West Germany, or in a reactionary Bavaria or Austria (see, for example, the seductive arguments for Prussia pursued by that marvelous historian Sebastian Haffner). Yet the suggestion cannot rest on historical opinion; it must be demonstrated to be possible, in other words, to be concretely imaginable: and this is the vocation of Grass's novel.

His protagonist (there are really two of them, perhaps even three) is a seventy-six-year-old eccentric with an emblematically checkered career: a wartime aide in Göring's Air Force Ministry (and a courier on the Western Front, captured and imprisoned at the end of the war); after the founding of the GDR, a messenger in the Ministries Building (by a useful coincidence, the very same edifice, the only one to have survived the wartime razing of central Berlin), as well as an occasional lecturer on literary and cultural subjects, associated with the Fontane archive in

Potsdam (whose co-workers form a kind of inconspicuous Greek chorus to this interminable tale); kept on after reunification by the so-called Treuhand Anstalt, the institute charged with the privatization of East German industry and housed in the very same building on the corner of the Leipzigerstrasse and the Wilhelmstrasse; finally, in his later years (our present), vanishing into the Cévennes in the company of his long-lost (illegitimate) French granddaughter. Theo Wuttke's destiny is promising in the same way as the destiny of those characters in Balzac who lived through the Revolution and the Napoleonic era, the Restoration, and the July Monarchy, is promising: their lifelines serve as Geiger counters or electrocardiograms of History at its most hectic.

I have, however, omitted the essential about this character, also known as "Fonty" to his larger circle of acquaintances in the East German bureaucracy (and beyond): this is his mania, an imaginary identification with the great Berlin and Brandenburg novelist Theodor Fontane (1819–98), the "Immortal" (or *Unsterbliche*) as he is here described, whose complete works and letters Fonty knows by heart and quotes extensively on appropriate occasions. But are not all occasions appropriate for the quotation of this writer, whose wit and freshness have earned him a devotion comparable only to the cults of Balzac or Galdós, or Dickens, among their respective national readerships? Unlike the early or mid-century novelists, Galdós and Fontane are distinguished by the slippage of their narratives away from "reference" towards a running commentary on people and events: the witty aperçu, the unforgettable formula or characterization, spring as much from the dialogue as from the authorial voice itself. The language of Fontane's great books—all written after the former apothecary's fifty-fifth year, and after the "first" unification of Germany in 1871—is delicious and unmistakable, mixing the Prussian-aristocratic with Berliner big-city wit, often dropping pronominal subjects in favor of a kind of telegraphic style, allowing the sentences to turn ironically on their own content and figures of speech, on the choice of words imposed on them by the German language. For those for whom Berlin is Germany, Fontane is the greatest German novelist; for those with some feeling for the relationship between narrative possibility and social order, there is unique satisfaction to be derived from the meeting, in Fontane himself, between sympathy with a landed tradition not unrelated to that of the Russian gentry, an amused disdain for the *nouveaux riches* of the Gründerzeit (those decades of feverish industrial and financial development after

1870), and a fellow-travelling ideological weakness for revolution (he fought in 1848) and, later on, for the nascent socialist movement and the naturalist literature related to it. It is an unbeatable combination, which the contemporary reader, no longer accustomed to nineteenth-century narrative longueurs, can skim and savor in the pages of this second-degree Fontane novel, in which Fonty's twentieth-century life collapses back into Fontane's nineteenth-century one, to the point where the protagonist himself (let alone the reader) is sometimes unable to tell the two apart. Nor is it always clear which is the tenor and which the vehicle. Devotees of Grass (of that fine Joycean book, *The Flounder*, for example, whose eternal return runs from the primal swamp of prehistoric Danzig all the way to West Berlin at the height of the sixties) will relish these confusions: Fonty and Fontane have the same birth date, give or take a hundred years, and the same birthplace; they have both had to sacrifice their literary interests to years of clerical drudgery; both wrote war dispatches; both travelled in France; both participated in revolutionary events (1848, June 17, 1953) and then worked for repressive regimes; they had the same number of children and the same kind of wife. Last but not least, they said the same things, literally; but this is less surprising in view of the fact that Fonty had already existing texts to quote.

The conceit affords us extraordinary set-pieces: the wedding of Fonty's daughter to a West German businessman, in particular, is a true comic anthology-piece. Meanwhile, the previous biography, the already-lived life of the great predecessor, hangs ominously over the enormous exposition of the first part without dimming our curiosity as to how the parallels are to be demonstrated. The official political project is clear: as Grass has said, it is "to replay the current process of German unity against the background of the first unity of 1870–71"; or in other words, to discredit the new reunification, which passes itself off as a novel historical event, by identifying it with the older one, itself estranged and retroactively compromised by this latest annexation. This will be the meaning of the book for a West German (or formerly West German) public, who could not be expected to like it very much; and did not. But this political project conceals another one, of even more momentous consequence, which explains the novel's relatively greater success with East German readers: the acknowledgment of a properly East German daily life, the very conception of which has been obliterated by the Anschluss and by Western propaganda—a more subtle form of anti-communism than simple sacrifice in the name of a socialist construction that is swept away from one day to the next, the factories sold and then shut down, the institutions condemned as you might condemn an old building.

Perhaps we need a new word for this last activity, which the West calls "privatization." (Towards the end of the novel, Fonty is given the task of finding a substitute for the official West German euphemism *abwickeln*, which might sound something like "de-development" in Western bureaucratese. But he is not confident that his plot-motivated solution—*umtopfen*, "to re-plant" or "re-pot"—will catch on either.) A far more subtle censorship governs our imagination of socialism, when it is reduced to repression and resistance, and the other qualities we attribute to a genuine daily life are "de-developed," and, if not privatized, then subject to systematic evaporation. I'm not sure that we can have a direct intuition of our own daily life: it is par excellence what others have, and what we acknowledge in a kind of productive and generous envy (or what a "living literature" is sometimes capable of disclosing to us about ourselves). To deprive other humans of the acknowledgment of their lived time as daily life is a fundamental form of alienation too little recognized, and perhaps a more basic form of discrimination than any more commonly named and identified as such. But the representation of a daily life is itself a complicated task, to be achieved only by indirection, and as it were out of the corner of the eye: it is this kind of representation that Grass supremely achieves for the citizenry of East Berlin, through the medium of his unrepresentative hero. Nor is it limited to the time before reunification: for after the familiar strains of "Ode to Joy" had died away, "daily life began. In its calendar-determined succession there once again predominated the cares of actually existing immortality." One may well find this second section episodic, and something of an indulgence on Grass's part, his own license to comment on a variety of topical events, from television culture to the assassination of the Treuhand chief Rohwedder: repetitive as well, since we tend to get everything in multiple forms, recapitulated by Fonty's own letters on these subjects and then sentimentalized by the idyllic reunion with the granddaughter. But something similar happens in the later part of Thomas Mann's *Doctor Faustus*, a work whose peculiar status in this half-century Grass's novel may well occupy in the next.

There is also a kind of devil figure, but without any of Mann's medical or musical, let alone theological, overtones: there are, indeed, two kinds of doubling here, two distinct sets of mirror-images, the symmetrical and the asymmetrical. Fontane and Fonty echo each other across two centuries: closer to home, a pseudo-couple is formed, in which Fonty is linked to a character virtually his opposite, and no less indebted to a literary precedent. This is his Stasi alter ego or guardian angel, a jovial police spy whose name is a tribute to a novel by someone else, as Grass's concluding credits indicate: "the figure of Tallhover, who lives on as the character Hoftaller in the present work, is derived from Hans Joachim Schädlich's eponymous novel of 1986." The benevolent protection and discreet "advice" extended by Hoftaller to his eccentric old friend outlive the Wall and the "peasant-and-worker's state" itself (as is fitting in the new world situation where the various Cold War espionage services meet to compare old times on television).

Yet the historical Tallhover (I mean by that designation Schädlich's fictional character rather than any real person) had an even longer career: as immortal as Fontane himself, he served the Prussian state from the Holy Alliance well up into contemporary times. Tallhover's extended lifetime underscores the principal point to be made by Schädlich's estimable novel: namely, that surveillance is itself immortal, under all forms of state power (an anti-bureaucratic position evidently shared by Grass himself: see his Kafka essay). At the end of his long existence, the Schädlich character finds it in himself to lament bitterly the ingratitude and short-sightedness of state power as such and in general, never funding us enough, and never listening to our advice (we could have seized Lenin in Berlin in 1917, and we should certainly have taken him off the famous train).

It is a fact that both Fonty and Fontane have had their troubled relationships with the secret police and with the state in its various avatars. For Fontane was also arrested as a spy during the Franco-Prussian War (and was saved, perhaps, although the case is unclear, by his archenemy Bismarck); nor is it improbable that he was kept under surveillance during the period immediately preceding and following the abortive revolution of 1848, at which point he broke off his enthusiastic militancy to accept a journalistic sinecure in the most reactionary Prussian government of the century (a position he held for the next twenty years).

Tallhover's surveillance of Theodor Fontane is not recorded in Schädlich's novel; and, in any case, Grass's Hoftaller is a far jollier figure, who intervenes fully as much to protect the sometimes naive Fonty as he does to "repress" him. Or better still, in *Ein weites Feld*, these two things seem to go together, and the squat figure with the baseball cap (whom one must imagine in tandem with Fonty's tall and mustachioed Fontane-like silhouette) reappears in order to enforce prudence by way of black-mail, and to threaten our hero with the disclosure of various early scan-dals and indiscretions, such as the affair in France. Prudence is counseled at all those moments when Fonty is tempted to cut himself loose, to travel to Fontane's beloved Scotland, or even to take an unauthorized outing to the North Sea or to the Immortal's birthplace. As with all such counsels of wisdom and renunciation, from the Grand Inquisitor down to the various modern secret service agencies, the reasons for this enforced restraint remain mysterious: a Fromm-like "escape from free-dom," a preventive brake on permissiveness and the proliferation of Desire? But Grass is a Salvationist writer, who transmutes dystopian accents like these in spite of himself, and his Mephistopheles, like Goethe's, "always wills the Bad and wreaks the Good."

Or perhaps the philosophical questions are implicit in the representa-tion itself, whose more passionate commitment lies in its visual and narrative delight in the pseudo-couple: Fonty and Hoftaller henceforth joining Vladimir and Estragon, or Don Quixote and Sancho, if not Mutt and Jeff, as classic embodiments of this archetype, which has its own testimony to offer on subjective autonomy and neurotic dependency, on freedom and the choice of subalternity. "Was Fonty imaginable without his shadow?" Grass has his intermittent-chorus narrator disingenuously cry. "Would not the latter's absence have put an end to a story whose effects fed on echo and demanded to be sung in two voices more or less out of tune?" But such questions are themselves part of the effects Grass wishes to produce, along with a visual multiplication of two joined figures across the landscape and through time, like the surcharged images of a film.

The pseudo-couple is, in one fundamental sense, a denial of the Jamesian point of view, of the aesthetic that aims to represent the fullest possible richness of the bourgeois monad, of the individual conscious-ness. It denies James's attempt to make the most private recesses of the mind (and sensibility) enter language and the public sphere; but, if the failure of this strategy (along with the bankruptcy of bourgeois indi-vidualism) is thought to be catastrophic, another evaluation is open to us: the Habermasian one, where that rich privacy is superseded by inter-personality, where the pseudo-couple can stand as the emblem of communication and intersubjectivity. Surely Holmes's remarks to Watson are worth reams of "internal monologues" recording the detective's more private thoughts and fantasies? On the other hand, is not Fonty himself something like a biographical spy or literary Stasi, who shadows his own chosen target and longs to know everything there is to know about his object of study? And is not "immortality," in that sense, simply the fact of being wholly given over, as Sartre might say, into the hands of other people: and henceforth to be nothing but what they read and write down? Do we not want to know everything about such figures, the smallest detail of daily life, the contents of the garbage bag, the secrets, the mechanism of their double lives?

It is certain that we have here, if not a celebration of the Stasi's mode of existence, then at the very least a tone very different from that of Cold War literature, of *1984* or even of Christa Wolf, who (in *Was bleibt?*) still tries to register the historical and psychic peculiarities of an existence under surveillance, producing as it does endless reveries:

> which all too often ended with the absurd question, What do you want anyway? . . . addressing an institution as if it were a person . . . One day I had understood that there was no addressee for protestations and attempts at explanation; I had to assume that which I had balked at for such a long time, that the young gentlemen out there were not accessible to me. They were not my kind. They were the messengers of the other.

But perhaps the phenomenon of the Stasi—in which I wish to include the popular fascination with the phenomenon of the Stasi, since, in the form of a collective fantasy-delirium, it has played so great a part in German politics—is only the anticipation of a worldwide transformation that includes capitalism as well as communism and has a more universal significance than can be deduced from its more parochial, Kafkaesque cultural forms. I refer to the process of informatization itself, which some have gone so far as to theorize into a whole new mode of production, and which is celebrated in David Lindsay's detective story, *An Absence of Light*, a product of American mass culture, in the following terms:

> The age of the personal computer had brought about a sea-change in the private investigation and intelligence business. Now anyone who could afford a modem could enter the voyeuristic world of "databanking" where a subterranean network of information resellers, known as

superbureaux, had assembled in a limitless number of categories every fact imaginable about most American citizens . . . The fact was, in the United States today, the individual had no way of controlling information about himself. For a price, everybody's privacy was for sale . . . Now that the Computer Age suddenly had given private investigation the means to be enormously profitable, the budgets of literally hundreds of agencies—and corporations who had their own competitor intelligence divisions—outstripped those of many budget-stressed law enforcement agencies . . . Now, more than at any other time in world history, "private" information was in danger of becoming only a nominal concept.

It is a development which allows the older spy novel to be conflated with the domestic mystery thriller, as a generic bonus of the globalization process. But it also warns us to re-evaluate the Stasi system, since we can, presumably, no longer indulge the pathos and the terror of a breach of privacy in a world in which it is the private which has become unimaginable—if it has not ceased to exist altogether.

Grass's own fabulation is probably best situated in a different lineage from either the mass-cultural or the dissident one: indeed, of all contemporary European writers, Grass is probably the closest to the magic realism of the Latin Americans and above all of García Márquez, whose own breakthrough novel *The Tin Drum* preceded by eight years (just as it broke the spell of Steiner's prediction of only a year before). The Latin Americans, however, trace their lineage back to a not-yet-magic-realist Faulkner (followed by a Commonwealth third generation of which Salman Rushdie is only the most illustrious). Grass's would be a magic realism which descends from Döblin rather than the chronicler of Yoknapatawpha County; and which at best shares the marginality of the Southern and Third World novelists by virtue of the off-center position of Danzig and the omnipresence of a Slavic East in his narrative framework (in that sense, Berlin, or even East Berlin, in the twentieth century is a kind of "capital of the East" rather than the "capital of a reunited Germany"). This suggests (and the influence and authority of Faulkner confirms the hypothesis) that a true magic realism must always spring from defeat—that is, it must always somehow be post-colonial—and work on the materials of an essentially subaltern history. Does this account for its absence in Western Europe or augur its disappearance in a reunited Germany?

I don't really mean to argue for the magic-realist status of *Ein weites Feld*: the ostentatiously, even aggressively, drab cannot be deployed in folds of mesmerizing color. The kinship can more easily be uncovered in a technique for producing artificial events, which, instructively enough, goes back to Faulkner. Repetition is the crucial mode of inscription here, returning over and over again to images and effects which were initially only "poetic" and produced as "conceits" by the ingenuity of the author, in order, in some deeper self-indulgence, to admire them and celebrate their unexpectedness as "realities." Thus, an external referent—the contingency of the inspiration (or *Einfall*)—is drawn inside the work and made to seem organic and inevitable. We have already seen Grass doing something like this with his multiplication of the silhouettes of his pseudo-couple (the starting point of his text, and not its incidental bonus or supplement). I would cite two other images (there are many others): the whooping crane of the Tiergarten, which vicariously illustrates a process of submerging and resurfacing, of reappearing unexpectedly at the crucial moments, and disappearing at others (perhaps equally crucial), which is gradually generalized, not merely into Fonty's own existential "method," but also to the persistence of the past in the novel. It is an image which complements Benjamin's related idea of "blasting open the continuum of history" with a more graceful combination of evasion and persistence.

Then there is the *Paternoster*: I do not know whether English has an equivalent for this word, whose referent I have only confronted in Germany: a kind of open elevator in which a linked chain of cages rises and falls uninterruptedly, and onto which you must step with a certain address. Fonty's plea for the preservation of this characteristic piece of old-German technology is celebrated in terms of the "eternal return," while in the climactic history lesson of this endless reiteration of historical cycles, the masters of German destiny are caught, descending in the *Paternoster* feet first until the all too familiar features are reached: the Reichsmarshall, first of all; then the "Goatee" (Ulbricht); finally the surrogate for the bulky Chancellor of unification himself—it is a vision in which reification and sheer process are pleasantly (if not dialectically) harmonized.

I can well imagine the complaints of non-Germans about this enormous brick of a novel (whose narrative, in the image of the *Paternoster*, combines the static with interminable repetition): isn't the novel supposed to be the celebration or even the invention of the Event, rather

than this catalogue of paths and little walks through Berlin, this anecdotal travelogue? But perhaps a privileged function of the novel as such
(not the only one, to be sure) is here rediscovered: was not the *Odyssey*
such a travelogue (its interpretation as a virtual map of the Mediterranean
gave Joyce aid and comfort in his readaptation of it as a guidebook to
Dublin)? Wasn't the classical (or Byzantine) novel more generally just
such a guidebook, a grand tour of the ancient world for the sedentary?
And how about *Tom Jones?* (Franco Moretti has recently argued for the
structural function of the underlying geographical map as a narrative
mechanism in Balzac and Jane Austen.) So now, slowly and sublimi-
nally, by way of the appropriation of imaginary footpaths, the older
Prussia is drawn back into the so-called West, with effects as yet
unforeseeable.

It is a subject that could tempt one into further broad and untrodden
fields, but best to take the advice of the novel's title, itself an allusion to
the evasive formula of Effi Briest's father, when confronted, as Grass is
here by the history of Germany, with a topic that presents an only too
great variety of embarrassments: "Ach, das ist ein zu weites Feld" ("It's
too broad a field").

8

An Eastern Waiting Room

Anyone with a commitment to socialism needs to take an interest in the history and fate of the German Democratic Republic (DDR), up to now the object of systematic neglect by West-of-the-Rhine liberal and radical intellectuals alike, who have scant knowledge of its achievements in painting and film, and assume its economic and political lessons to be exclusively negative. This is yet another instance in which Cold War dismissals in the name of Stalinism and totalitarianism—essentially political judgments—continue to be tacitly accepted by today's lefts in embarrassed silence. To be sure, the Soviet Union is another matter, and its rise and fall is as respectable a historical topic as the life and death of the Roman Empire; but, at the same time, it is widely assumed that the evolution of its "satellites" is necessarily a secondary matter.

Yet Germany was the very heartland of Marxism, with the largest party in Europe, its leaders and intellectuals the most enlightened and committed of such formations anywhere, comparable to the prestige of the Italian Communist Party after World War II. It is not to be assumed that the German survivors who returned from Moscow after the war to found a new socialist state were mere puppets of the Russians (however unattractive we may find Ulbricht's character). On the contrary, there were probably proportionately fewer opportunists among these believers than in the minority parties of the other Eastern states. As the only

"Dresden's Clocks: On *Der Turm* by Uwe Tellkamp," *New Left Review* 71, September/October 2011.

socialist country besides Korea to share a border and a language with a
capitalist counterpart, and as the object of the most intensive Western
strategy of obstruction and sabotage outside Cuba, East Germany—
virtually levelled to the ground and its own diminished population
drowned in German-speaking refugees from further east—faced problems unparalleled in other socialist experiments since the early years of
the Soviet Union itself.

Meanwhile, the disgrace of the wholesale privatization of collective
assets after "the fall" was matched only by the crimes of the oligarchs in
the soon-to-be ex-Soviet Union. As for culture, after Brecht, only literature in which "dissidence" (a late '70s term) could be detected was of any
interest abroad, the daily life of the DDR constituting for the West little
more than one long life sentence or waste of time. The absorption of this
aberrant entity back into the Bundesrepublik was thereby seen as a
simple return to normality, with the exception, to be sure, of economic
normality—production, employment, and the like.

This is the situation in which we may well wish to take note of the
appearance of what has seemed to some the most considerable work of
East German literature, Uwe Tellkamp's massive novel *Der Turm* (The
Tower). The book appeared three years ago in what I am still tempted to
call West Germany to enormous acclaim, winning all the literary prizes
and catapulting its author at once to the summit of the current German
pantheon. The scandalous unfamiliarity of this author's name is only
partly due to the absence of an English translation (as far as I know, it
has only been translated into Dutch and Italian); probably the lack of
interest in the DDR is just as significant, and—despite Susan Sontag's
naive questioning of the very existence of a "second-world literature"—
publishers have understood that, after the end of the Cold War, there is
little enough public demand here for accounts of everyday socialism.
Still, I call this work by a forty-year-old writer who grew up in the DDR
an "East German novel" because it is saturated by that daily life, so
different from our own, and has an authenticity unavailable even in the
finest imaginative descriptions by outsiders, such as Günther Grass's
remarkable *Ein weites Feld*; let alone the punk literature of younger
Eastern writers who have never lived in the system that formed their
elders. Meanwhile, to be sure, Tellkamp's is an extraordinary and
demanding art with a sentence-density comparable only to Thomas
Mann or Grass himself (in German; in other languages Proust or
Faulkner might be distant reference points); while his narrative

experimentation, although by no means as complex as that of earlier East German writers such as Uwe Johnson or Heiner Müller, has all the maturity of traditional modernist virtuosity.

Even German readers, however, have complained of the length (a thousand pages), of which, as one critic put it, only the last one-fifth—the disintegration of the East German state—has any genuine, if muffled, narrative excitement. And it is certain that the temporal focus of this work, which begins with Marx's centenary (and Brezhnev's death) in 1983 and ends in November 1989, demands a painstaking and detailed laying in place of the daily life of its protagonists in order all the more accurately to show its dissolution.

So, the first part of the book is necessarily iterative, in Genette's sense of specifically situated scenes which are, nevertheless, designed to show how it always was, what they always did (Combray on a Saturday or Sunday morning). This makes for an episodic series of sketches of apartment life, school, publishers' meetings, and official encounters with the ideological "central committee" of the region; of parties and of vacations at Party establishments on the Baltic Coast; glimpses of *Haushaltungstag* (when bachelors are given time off to do the cleaning), hospital routines, the brief East–West contact of the Leipziger Buchmesse, and so forth. "Only the exhaustive is truly interesting," said Thomas Mann; and it will be a central question for us whether such loving detail constitutes what is today identified as *Ostalgie*—nostalgia for an "actually existing socialism" that has vanished.

But we must be careful not to grasp Genette's technical concept in any oversimplified way; to be sure, on the one hand, the iterative constitutes a solution to the older way of summarizing past events and their "uneventful" continuities. But it is not necessarily—or at least, not in this novel—the opposite number to the Event, the vivid representation of things finally happening; or to the real time of change and history as we might be tempted to imagine it emerging from the breakdown of a seemingly rather static system. "There is no misfortune other than that of not being alive," cries Christa Wolf at the conclusion of her Stasi-novella *Was bleibt*. "And in the end, no desperation other than that of not having lived." But that is not my impression of living in *Der Turm*; and we will have to wait for its sequel to know what "real life" lies beyond it.

At any rate, events here—and on their presence turns the very status of *Der Turm* as a historical novel—take place off stage; and, in a society as yet uncolonized by the modern media, they are transmitted in gossip and as rumor, as what takes place outside and beyond daily life, but also as what requires no explanation: Bitterfeld 1959, Chernobyl, the meaning of the presence of both German leaders at the reopening of the rebuilt Dresden opera house, Andropov's death, Father Popieliuszko, the Central Committee's suspicions of the new Soviet leadership, etc. Nor are the usual ingredients of the dissident novel present: no mention of the Wall or of the shooting of escapees, no Stasi informers, no secret police visits at three in the morning; only the most distant reminiscences of the suave and smiling villains, familiar since Dostoevsky. No Big Brother; in short, none of the conventional trappings of literary totalitarianism, or of the pity and fear it is designed to arouse. The shortage of consumer goods, which looms so large in Western visions of Eastern unfreedom, is here simply a fact of life, as are the infuriating insolences of a bureaucracy identified by the West as the repressive state.

Of the dissidents themselves, heroically celebrated in the West, little trace is to be found until the final pages, when hitherto unfrequented preachers suddenly begin to attract followings—and to alter their language accordingly; samizdat groups spring up, organized around previously unknown or insignificant figures; massed crowds in the railway stations begin to impede traffic and the packed trains heading for the Czech and Hungarian borders begin to disrupt the protagonists' daily lives. Christian's hitherto apolitical mother becomes a demonstrator and would obviously be the heroine of an officially dissident novel; here, even the "event" of her political conversion takes place off stage and never becomes part of the novel's narrative representation.

The ordeal of Christian himself—the youngest of the three protagonists and the one of whom it can be said that *Der Turm* is at least his *Bildungsroman*—thus remains the principal exhibit for a political—that is to say, an anti-communist—interpretation of this novel, which is certainly no apologia for socialism either. The regimentation of his military service (in this country, for all practical purposes it lasts six years!), his moment of revolt (at the accidental death of a fellow draftee), and his condemnation to hard labor—these experiences, which seem to have been at least partially autobiographical, are ambiguous to the degree to which they can also be accounted for by his rebellious temperament; not necessarily the best argument for political heroism. In any case, the oppressiveness of military service is no more unpleasant than what one finds in Western war novels, though no less, either; while Christian's labor in the mines (he will, in fact, eventually be reinstated in the army) gives the novelist a brief opportunity to convey the true proletarian underside of what remains an essentially bourgeois existence and indeed a privileged one at that.

Indeed, the very title of *Der Turm* designated a relatively affluent section of Dresden, whose spatial disposition—on an elevation reached by way of an antiquated funicular—and distinctive buildings play no small part in Tellkamp's story. The old saw, that this or that (generally non-Western) city is really a small world in which everyone—that is to say, the intelligentsia—knows everyone else, is certainly true of *Der Turm* and its narrative. (The inhabitants of the most important apartment houses are listed inside the back cover.) The novel is organized around three such inhabitants, related, but dwelling in different buildings: the teenager Christian; his father Richard, a hand surgeon with a short fuse but many high-placed contacts; and Christian's Uncle Meno, in some respects the central protagonist. A zoologist by training, he now occupies a significant position in a prestigious publishing house; which is to say that he is also professionally part of the state censorship system, even when he resists it.

Richard's dilemmas are the most familiar: he has to deal, in secret, with a second family (there is occasional half-hearted talk about "fleeing" to the West). His position in the hospital is a vantage point from which we can observe the process of promotion in this system, as well as the ways in which hierarchy is felt in collegiality and in treatment. Richard's bluster is also capable of expressing itself in all kinds of aberrant adventures, from stealing a Christmas tree in a state-protected forest to the rebuilding in secret of a rare Hispano-Suiza car. These amount to a pushing of the envelope without serious consequences, since allowance has already been made for his character in his evaluation by the system. On the other hand, a series of futile attempts to appeal or at least to reduce his son's sentence testifies to the limits of influence of even so essential and valued a skilled professional. At least he escapes the fate of his superior, Dr. Müller, a Party member and disciplinarian whom we first observe at Richard's birthday party, warning his colleagues (and Christian) against telling jokes against the regime. But Müller—head of the entire hospital system—has indulged himself privately in amassing an impressive (and expensive) collection of glass sculptures and artworks; on the day after his retirement, he receives a summons to the police station and notification of a house search and confiscation of unlawful property. Müller destroys the collection before committing suicide, leaving a note whose final sentence reads: "This is not the socialism we dreamed of."

Richard is not, to be sure, unlike his other brother-in-law, a Party member; but it may still not be inappropriate to range him among a kind of cultural *Nomenklatura* (the Germans say *Bildungsbürgertum*, to distinguish them from the more secular garden-variety petty bourgeoisie), and to observe that, as is the case in so much of Lukács's "critical realist" tradition, there is not much proletarian presence in this particular realism either. Still, one must note that as a hand surgeon, Richard's activity does lay a kind of manual labor in place; and his hobby of carpentry underscores a utopian handicraft tradition, explicitly related to the construction of *Dichtung*: "As in the operating room here also [in his workshop] there reigned, not the speech of words, but rather that of the hands—a speech familiar to him, in which he felt at home." In one of those lyric digressions which so frequently enrich and interrupt this lengthy novel, to our delight or annoyance, the hand itself is celebrated (the occasion is an operation on his own wife, injured after a domestic accident—or argument):

> He loved hands. Hands belonged to those living forms that gave him joy. He had studied hands: the lily-like femininity of Botticelli's women's fingers (and did these fingers not make up the hands themselves?); hands stubbornly convinced of something; hands in despair both about their failure to grow and their emergence from childhood; hands creamed and uncreamed; cooing hands, as unfathomable as moss; lady gardeners' tanned by the sap of plants, and male stokers' so devoured by coal dust as to be unwashable ... *Reading* hands had already given him satisfaction in his internship, challenges that might have seemed chafing or bothersome to others for him were sources of excitement, that you approached carefully and willingly, shyly, fearful of a nakedness that was however there, throbbing softly, in the lust to be known.

Richard's fascinations are here the very locus of a central ambiguity in praxis as such: they can express Sohn-Rethel's sense of the emergence of ideology from the split between manual and intellectual labor; or a phenomenon akin to those discoveries by Michael Fried, of the embodied auto-referentiality of the act of painting itself in the presence of the hand in a Menzel or a Caravaggio. And, in fact, this celebration of the "hand" in *Der Turm* means both and faces both ways: as the shadow of a fundamental production process in this socialist state, in which it has slowly begun to deteriorate; and as the mirage of art and its objects and traditions, by which so many of its protagonists are mesmerized and, as it were, immobilized, under a timeless spell.

As for Christian, we have already observed that this otherwise unremarkable protagonist of the *Bildungsroman*—a shy, musically gifted boy, attentive to his uncle's lessons and experiencing the first bewildering approaches of love and sexuality, as well as the confusion of the unpolitical soul (this side inherited from his maternal uncle); reacting to the approach of the political with rebellious anger (his inheritance from his father)—this story is the place to which the representation of the peculiar oppressions of the DDR is centrally consigned.

But it is important to note that Christian's transgression is one of language, and that indeed, in this elitist version of DDR life and politics, it is language which is, from literature to politics, the crucial space in which the relationship to the state is tested: "The problem is not what you did but what you said," explains the interrogator to Christian. "You damaged trust. This is not a matter of comrade junior officer Burre's death, which is of course regrettable. We will naturally investigate that, it goes without saying. But that's not the debate at present! That's a wholly different case. No, Hoffman, you and your buddy Kretschmar, whom we know very well, you made observations. You slandered us. You openly attacked our state."

Our own first lesson in language sensitivity is, in fact, administered by the very same Dr. Müller, who observes, at Richard's birthday party, "Not a very good joke, gentlemen . . . we have responsibilities, gentlemen; and it is easy to take part in cheap denigrations of our country . . ." (the alternation between the words *Land* and *Staat* is a crucial clue; Müller here uses the former). Only the *Nomenklatura*, whose fidelity to the state can for the most part be taken for granted, are allowed to permit themselves the occasional political pleasantry, as we shall see. But, as far as Christian is concerned, his lessons began much earlier, and in a rather surprising form:

Erik Orré [an actor] had been a patient of Richard and wanted to show his thanks in an unusual way, namely to demonstrate the art of effective and professional lying to the boys, Richard estimating that this was something Christian in particular needed to learn; so the mime ... practiced enthusiastic expressions of praise and flattery with them in front of a mirror, corrected their gestures, showed them how one could blush and grow pale at will, and how one could toady with dignity, emit stupidities with a straight face, using these as a mask over one's true thoughts, thresh out empty and yet intelligently flattering compliments, dissipate distrust in others and even in a pinch recognize other liars.

It is obviously not a lesson Christian has assimilated, despite his Uncle Meno's maxim: "A wise man walks with his head down, almost invisible, like dust."

Meno Rohde is by far the most interesting character in *Der Turm*, as well as being the most reserved, despite the political ambiguity that has led a number of (West) German reviewers to charge him with the kind of apathy and submissiveness which not only kept the regime in power, but can even be read as a form of active support, by virtue of its very passivity. As the reader for Hermes–Verlag and its prestige series of classic authors, he is part and parcel of the censorship apparatus, as we have noted, however often he seems to argue against its decisions; and we may well wonder why it is always to his chapters that one looks forward and with his reticences and withdrawals that one feels sympathy. One of those rare people for whom silence is not shyness, nor indifference either, but rather some genuine distance from things, an almost Buddhist disengagement from personal action, coupled with an equally genuine passion and detached curiosity for observing it in others, Meno is a genuine intellectual—even though mostly patronized by the novel's official intellectuals, inasmuch as he is not a professional writer (save for his book reports and a private diary of which only the reader is given installments).

Yet there exists a more positive way of celebrating Meno's passivity and that is as scientific observation. His formation was in zoology, and it is this active detailing of the outside world and, in particular, of its life forms that Christian learns from his uncle, "and is not troubled by Meno's demands, not angry when Meno in a friendly but implacable fashion gives him to understand that he had observed poorly and had not couched his impressions precisely enough in his language." For it is also a training in *le mot juste*, in the fashion in which Flaubert corrected the descriptions and observations of the young Maupassant; and much of the ensuing discussion (in the passage just quoted) turns on the characterization of the kind of green to be identified on the wings of the Urania moth. (Veronese green? They finally settle on "powder-green," which elicits not enthusiasm but the slightest nod of assent from his teacher.)

The professional hunt for bad punctuation and incorrect grammar in his authors' manuscripts therefore has its creative dimension in such observations, which are verbal as well as visual (let's also remember Nabokov's lepidopterology); but perhaps its social equivalent is something rather different. Meno himself observes a young writer, Judith Schevola, scrutinizing her fellows like "a researcher on insects": "her face distorted and twisted . . . only the eyes belonging to her . . . seeming to register everything with hostile curiosity." But that drive is the motor impulse of great satire, as in Proust's portraits; and as for the smaller details, Meno's characterization might well come from the Thomas Mann of *Doctor Faustus*: "These are the orchestral parts to which the composer devoted his most painstaking labour, even though the public will scarcely hear them."

It is to Meno then that we owe the most painstaking reconstruction of this seemingly timeless world, its antique objects rescued and stored up in the apartments of this once-prosperous quarter, the memory of the goods of yesteryear, marked with forgotten brand-names ("a Fortuna typewriter as bulky as an old 'Konsum' cash-register," etc.). Sometimes indeed it seems as though the life world of these characters were little more than one immense collection of prewar objects and furniture, with the proviso that they are threatened at every moment by the coal dust that also saturates this novel, by its odor when not by smears and coatings, or its literal omnipresence in Christian's life in the mines.

But it is to Meno also that we owe the extraordinary and well-nigh zoological tableau of the intellectual flora and fauna of the late DDR, in portraits in which German scholars and historians have identified historical DDR celebrities (not always known in the West). I will say a little about those portraits before returning in conclusion to the issue of the temporality (or timelessness) of the Dresden of this novel. Nothing here is indeed quite so delicious as these portraits, whose mimicry—as in Proust—expresses malice and sympathy in equal parts. Here we truly have a kind of intellectual and artistic *Nomenklatura* of the regime, at one and the same time believers and cynics; and the central proving ground for *Der Turm*'s insistent foregrounding of language. Stalinist dandies, with their theatrical delight in outright affirmation: "I was and remain an avowed defender of Stalin's order and have never concealed it . . . The murders were necessary, on the whole. Urgent times cannot have recourse to less-than-urgent measures. Desperate times cannot have recourse to less-than-desperate measures. The Soviet Union was surrounded, what else was he supposed to do?" Others are more resigned: "We are a part of the Soviet Union, without it we couldn't exist [*waren nichtlebensfähig*]." There are hatreds and passionate exchanges in the official meetings, particularly when exclusions are debated (that of Judith Schevola in particular); but the regional boss (Hans Modrow) deals with such decisions and the people they affect in a jovial yet matter-of-fact way. What goes without saying on this level—what the writers ought not to say in the first place—is rather different from the more standard ideological arguments of the everyday; as in the defense of the demands on professionals by Christian's girlfriend: "This country gives you a free education and free healthcare, isn't that something? Don't you think we have to give something back?"

Characteristically, the sons of both *Nomenklatura* speakers above violently disagree with their positions, from the right and the left, respectively; thereby underscoring the generational dynamics that also run through this novel. (Indeed, in my opinion, this theme is allegorical of socialism's most fundamental political problem, which is that of generational succession, or if you prefer the technical term, of social reproduction.) Still, it is important to realize that the apparent cynicism of this cultural *Nomenklatura*, at least in East Germany, in fact expresses a more complex psychological and political disposition, namely the tension between a believer's commitment to socialism and an insider's embarrassed distance from the Party's public decisions and rules (whose political necessity—the presence of the USSR—these intellectuals fully grasp). Irony is the expression of that embarrassment, and it is quite different from the cynicism of the characteristic West German talking points. I cannot resist quoting virtually the only sample of the latter (since these characters have so little contact with the West or indeed interest in it): this one we owe to a West German publisher visiting the Leipzig book fair, who in feigned astonishment at the continuing partic-ipation of the DDR writers in their state, places the following "devastat-ing" question: "Would you be capable of killing a dolphin?"

Meno's presence in the novel then also affords an opening onto the question of temporality in what is, at least from one perspective, a lovingly detailed recreation of the space and objects, the daily life, of the DDR, with an intensity of feeling that might well be identified as nostalgia, or even *Ostalgie*—were it not for the obviously critical stance on the political administration of these realities, summed up in Christian's rash outburst after his accident: "*So was ist nur in diesem Scheissstaat möglich!*" To the degree to which the "timelessness" of this moment of DDR history is identified as stagnation (*zastol*, in the Russian characterization of the Brezhnev years), and attributed to late socialism in general, the two perspectives are paradoxically one and the same.

On one level, to be sure, that of the *Bildungsroman*, the nostalgia is most easily explained as Christian's vision of his own childhood, brought abruptly to an end by military service. For Meno, the past is Dresden itself, virtually destroyed in the notorious firebombing of February 15, 1945: its geography, scarcely disguised by the cosmetic substitution of street names, the recognizable monuments and surviving buildings; even the very objects themselves which—as we have said and in the absence of investments in the production of consumer goods—resemble the artefacts in an immense museum of a past in which prewar, Weimar and Wilhelminian Germany are virtually indistinguishable. Indeed, in this sense, nostalgia is an unstable contagion, an existential contamination whose objects are interminably substitutable. So it is that the writing of a novel about the nostalgia of the people of the 1980s for some older world before the war becomes itself effortlessly transferable to the later years of the DDR in which that nostalgia was experienced.

Still, the seemingly timeless atmosphere of the first part of the novel— a timelessness which the title of Alexei Yurchak's study of the comparable period of Soviet history formulates as "Everything was Forever until it was No More"—demands closer attention. The matter of consumer goods clearly enough marks a crucial objective misunderstanding and interference with Western perspectives on the situation, as when we experience traffic in Cuba as a delightful return to 1950s America, when it is, in fact, the result of the half-century-long blockade of the communist island. Here, the seeming transformation of commodities into antiques may itself be taken as an allegory of a non-commodity-producing society, in which books, artworks and musical instruments are cherished, and each rare item—the von Arbogasts' *Granatapfelsaft* from the Black Sea—is the object of heightened perception and intensified appreciation, as though the modernist "make it new, make it strange" had been reversed in the direction of the past.

Meno's own peculiar "ten-minute clock" might well be an example of this heightened perception, were it not for the fact that Richard's father had been an actual clock manufacturer, thus suggesting an older and more archaic state of production which we ourselves are tempted to confuse with handicraft work; and, above all, the fact that the novel is punctuated insistently by the tolling of bells, whose irreversible temporality itself foretells the impending intrusion of History into this seemingly arrested, timeless world. Yet timelessness is also a political issue in a different sense, and we may pause to observe the way in which so much of left politics today—unlike Marx's own passionate commitment to a streamlined technological future—seems to have adopted as its slogan Benjamin's odd idea that revolution means pulling the emergency brake on the runaway train of History, as though an admittedly runaway capitalism itself had the monopoly on change and futurity. It may well be that it is the gradual supersession of time by space in postmodernity which has released the very concept of temporality to a bewildering variety of speculative forms today. Thus, Freud's notion of *Nachträglichkeit* (retroaction), in which the effect precedes the cause—a paradoxical, subordinate, and pathological concept in its own period, governed by a now old-fashioned chronological time scheme—has become one of the dominant contenders for theoretical hegemony (in Lacan, Derrida, and Deleuze alike); while older forms of succession associated with Hegel are dismissed as teleological.

But perhaps here too, in this experience of the East, some new lessons on time are available to us by way of the temporalities of *Der Turm*. Heiner Müller has characterized time in the DDR as a kind of waiting-room situation, in which the train is announced but never arrives—a novel version of the locomotive of History. As Charity Scribner noted in *New Left Review* in 1999: "While the delays in the East allowed people to accumulate experience, Müller claims, the imperative to travel forward destroyed any such potential in the West."[1] This is another version of Benjamin's critique of progress, but perhaps it suggests some new possibilities for imagining what a different present of time and of history might look like.

At any rate, the temporality with which *Der Turm* concludes, and with which it represents the dissolution of the DDR, is not at all a heroic

---

1   Charity Scribner, "From the Collective to the Collection: Curating Post-Communist Germany", *New Left Review* I/237 (Sept/Oct 1999)

narrative of resistance and freedom. This is not, in other words, a political narrative at all: what we glimpse here is the breakdown of the infrastructure itself, rather than that of the political system. It is foreshadowed in Richard's experience of the power blackout in the hospital, and the desperate measures with which the staff attempt to keep the patients alive; in the heating crises, as well, in which the bitter cold of the German winter demands all kinds of black-market ingenuities; in the breakdown of the little funicular, which normally lifts the privileged inhabitants of the *Turm* suburb to their quaint dwellings; in the stalled railway stations of the city, finally, in which the whole transportation system of the region comes to a halt. This is, in other words, "the material base" on which superstructural collapse is predicated; and appropriately it breaks into the characters' existential experience with all the intermittent confusion of unconscious causation generally, whether physical or mental.

Meanwhile, in an odd and somehow impersonal montage, these events and experiences in the late DDR present are juxtaposed and punctuated with what appear to be long extracts from a seemingly autobiographical narrative of World War II and atrocities on the Eastern Front (presumably, the work of the writer here named Altberg, but who seems to represent Franz Fühmann; on this interesting figure, see Benjamin Robinson's 2009 *The Skin of the System*). We have had very little information about the past of any of these characters—Richard's experience of the Dresden firebombing, for example, or Meno's involuntary change of profession. Now, suddenly, this historical disaster, as it were an East German year zero, seems to summon up overwhelming memories of the older one, in a flash flood of returning temporality. *Der Turm*, however, ends, as befits a novel whose main character is much concerned with punctuation, with a colon, leaving the whole matter of political futures very much open. The author has projected a sequel, about the year 1990, entitled *Lava2*. Perhaps, as 1983 took 500 pages of the present work, it will not be necessary to repeat that *tour de force* for this next even more interesting year. But one is certainly curious to learn the reactions to it of intellectuals and inner Party circles, as well as of Meno himself and his family.

---

2 The sequel has since appeared: *Der Schlaf in den Uhren* (Berline: Suhrkamp, 2022).

9
Immortal Stalingrad

To claim that *Life and Fate* is a war novel is to reawaken all the old comparisons with *War and Peace*, as well as to confine Vasily Grossman's great book to the limits of a genre, and a predictably repetitive one at that: Stalingrad, here, means something else, as I will try to show.[1] Nor is it satisfactory to add it to the burgeoning list of holocaust literature, a genre of which much the same could be said but which is historically anachronistic as a label for a book written in the 1950s. Meanwhile, the translator has taken innumerable diatribes on freedom in the novel to justify the characterization of Grossman as a dissident, forgetting Adorno's maxim that the ideas in a work are its raw material and not its meaning, and also ignoring the historical emergence of this term only later, in the 1960s, when it was borrowed from the Western languages. It would be desirable, if possible, to dissolve such inevitable Cold War accretions by taking a more formalist approach to this historical novel about the years 1942–43. For now, let us note that the crematoria at Auschwitz entered into operation in September 1941, some three months after the German invasion of the Soviet Union. The Soviet government was evacuated to Kuibyshev in October of that year—Stalin

"On Re-reading Life and Fate by Vasily Grossman," *New Left Review* 95, September/October 2015.

1   Vasily Grossman, *Zhizn' i sud'ba* (Lausanne: Editions l'Age d'Homme, 1980); *Life and Fate* (1985), translated and introduced by Robert Chandler (London: Collins Harvill, 2006). Hereafter cited as LF in the text.

himself remaining behind and sleeping at night in the deepest level of the Moscow metro. The German army, on its way to new sources of energy in the oilfields of the Caucasus, arrived at the Volga city of Stalingrad on August 23, 1942. The action of the novel takes place within these three coordinates.[2]

In contradiction with narrative stands metaphor, which is a kind of denarrativization, and, within the novel as a form, there is always a tension—and a dilemma for the novelist—between poetic perception and narrative interest and attention. Grossman squares this circle by inserting the stray "poetic" sentence in passing, where you might not notice it at all. So it is that "the gravestones stood there like a crowd of unloved, unwanted old men." So also the body of a soldier, "so full of his own death," and the war knocking "obstinately at the door of the bunker"; or "the heavy male looks that bear down" on Katya, the only female in House 6/1; let alone the landscapes: "from the pines rose a sharp note of turpentine, an octave higher"; "now and then a tree would shake, frightened by a bad dream" (LF 136, 404, 414, 226, 143, 157). However, these heightened perceptions are not mere aesthetic decoration or adornment; they are there to remind us that the entire narrative is not a matter of action and the notation of facts and "realistic" events, but, rather, the organization of so many perceptual and thereby potentially poetic unities. Hosts of short chapters are organized into larger sequences, each of which is a kind of small world in its own right, with its own tonalities and rhythm, its own temporality and affective logic, distinct, and different from all the others. Bravura pieces: yes, we can only do justice to Grossman by grasping the way in which his whole novel is composed of just such pieces bound together inextricably by the war and by a network of characters themselves bound together by life and fate.

Lyudmila Shaposhnikova's doomed mission to her wounded son, Tolya, is only the most seemingly distinctive of these narrative monads. (Auschwitz is another, and House 6/1 in Stalingrad yet another.) She bears within herself an undying resentment at her husband's indifference to this son of an earlier marriage, to whose hospital she must take the Volga steamer, surrounded by the fur coats and white fur stoles of the wives of important bureaucrats. Tolya, who is a pleasant boy,

---

2   Tamara Deutscher gives an excellent account of the historical situation in her original review of the translation in *New Left Review* I/163, May/June 1987.

well-liked by all the nurses and staff, dies after his third operation, before his mother arrives. The hospital is not prepared for this headstrong, formidable woman, who does not, however, waste her time in recriminations but gives herself to the delirium of her own grief, lying overnight on his grave. This extended episode is both a meeting place of a host of sharply individualized characters, and the long, subjective, well-nigh surrealist nightmare of a single central protagonist.

Sometimes, indeed, this enclave-form shrinks temporality into a present that is wholly self-sufficient: not the present without a future of the gas chambers, or the empty one of waiting, fear, isolation, and uncertainty, but a full present, a full temporality of battle as such, in which everything in the world, materiality and force, your own body, contracts into an intensity properly beyond time itself, insofar as you have no idea how long it lasts, whether the words short and long have any meaning any more. But this happens by alternation rather than by some mysterious or mystical intensification:

> One sense almost entirely lost during combat is that of time. After dancing all night at a New Year's ball, a girl will be unable to say whether time passed quickly or slowly . . . The night at the ball is full of looks, smiles, caresses, snatches of music, each of which takes place so swiftly as to leave no sense of duration in the girl's consciousness. Taken together, however, these moments engender the sense of a long interval of time that contains all the joys of human existence . . . The distortion of the sense of time during combat is something still more complex. Here there is a distortion even in the individual, primary sensations. One second can stretch out for eternity, and long hours can crumple together. The sense of duration is linked to such fleeting events as the whistle of shells and bombs, the flashes of shots and explosions. The sense of quickness on the other hand is linked to protracted events: crossing a ploughed field under fire, crawling from one shelter to another. And as for hand-to-hand fighting, that takes place quite outside time. (LF 32)

Yet this nameless dialectical distinctiveness of combat is only one of the unique ground-tones with which Grossman must endow each of his narrative enclaves.

It is this inseparability of the objective and the subjective that we must admire in Grossman, the extraordinary skill with which a network of fully realized personalities is endowed with the unity of affect—what Heidegger might have called *Stimmung*—that is at one and the same time the mimesis of an action. I would want to insist that we find the same formal mastery in the long political or scientific discussions, which may seem like so many pages from some standard "novel of ideas" until we appreciate to what degree the moment of awkwardness, the political gaffe, the embarrassing mention of a forbidden topic or personality, transforms the whole exchange into an event in its own right, a whole, or a mimesis of a completed action, as Aristotle might have put it.

Notions of realism and modernism are not particularly useful here; nor does Lukács's account of the historical novel and its "average" hero and witness seem particularly relevant—for one thing, there are no "world-historical figures" in the distance, even though Stalin and Hitler both make appearances. What does loom as a central absent presence is "fate" itself, the "mysterious force" that governs everything and everyone: sometimes called "the will of Stalin," without any particularly personal reference. It is against that absent totality, that all-encompassing necessity, that the authorial digressions on freedom must be read. The 1987 paperback edition of this translation exhibits an obscene testimonial from the *Wall Street Journal*, to the effect that to read the book "is to have some sense of how it feels not to be free." To which it might be well to add that Grossman shows no interest in the free-market system or in the West in general; most of his characters are old Bolsheviks, and, as paradoxical as it may sound, what holds his novel together as a unified narrative is also what holds the Soviet Union together in this period, the unfreedom that allowed it, improbably, to defeat Hitler's Wehrmacht and win World War II.

New kinds of collectivity

Let me develop this scandalous paradox further, until it turns into the dialectic as such. What is here most dramatically represented as the loss of freedom are, to be sure, the prison scenes—the camps, the Gulag, the Lubyanka; but also Stalingrad itself, which means imprisonment for both sides, a mutual siege, until the final pincer movement of the Russian tanks that seals the German army's fate. But these historical places and emplacements are then replicated in a variety of shapes and forms and sizes. Thus, Stalingrad itself is epitomized in miniature in the legendary

House 6/1, in which a handful of Soviet troops are isolated from the rest of an army they are connected to only by a tunnel. Here we are, as it were, beyond official society, and in a new kind of informal collectivity which may or may not be the authentic kind. "I can't make head or tail of what goes on there," says one of the visitors, "they all seem terrified of this Grekov, but he just pretends to be one of the lads. They all go to sleep in a heap on the floor, Grekov included, and they call him Vanya. Forgive me for saying so, but it's more like some kind of Paris Commune than a military unit" (LF 224). Another visit by a key protagonist, the commissar Krymov, an old Bolshevik and the first husband of Lyudmila's sister Zhenya, ends badly: the inhabitants of House 6/1 fail to appreciate his quite sincere lectures on socialism and the meaning of Stalingrad, while he fails to appreciate their "informal" fraternity as well as the mystery of Grekov's personal authority, which the sociologists would, no doubt, name charisma without understanding it in the least. Grossman conveys the shocking contingencies of war later on by noting in passing the eventual obliteration of this enclave by the Germans.

But something of the same closure is evidenced in Kuibyshev, where the government has been evacuated:

Kuibyshev at this time was the location of many of the Moscow People's Commissariats, newspaper offices and other establishments. It was the temporary capital, and here had come much of the life of Moscow—diplomats, the Bolshoi ballet, famous writers, impresarios and foreign journalists.

All these thousands of people lived in cramped little rooms and hotels, and yet carried on with their usual activities. People's commissars and the heads of important enterprises planned the economy and gave orders to their subordinates; extraordinary and plenipotentiary ambassadors drove in luxurious cars to receptions with the architects of Soviet foreign policy; Ulanova, Lemeshev and Mikhailov delighted the audiences at the ballet and the opera; Mr Shapiro, the representative of the United Press Agency, asked the head of the Soviet Information Bureau, Solomon Abramovich Lozovsky, awkward questions at press conferences; writers wrote radio broadcasts or articles for national and foreign newspapers; journalists wrote up material gathered from hospitals into articles on the war.

But the everyday life of these people from Moscow was quite transformed ... the editors of the most important Soviet newspapers

received visitors at tables where, after office hours, children prepared
their lessons and women did their sewing. There was something
strangely attractive in this coming together of the weighty apparatus
of State with the bohemianism of the evacuation. (LF 105)

Here, that nameless thing called the government—not exactly the state,
as we shall see—has been turned back into a ragtag population of individuals of all classes, in that respect little different socially from the
heterogeneous groups at first walled up in their ghettoes and then
herded onto the trains. In structure the two sets of evacuees are similar:
both are driven together by external force, but where one is on its way to
an unspeakable fate, the other strikes Zhenya as somehow liberated
from the constraints of official society. It is only by way of a sense of the
fundamental ambivalence of the dialectic that we can grasp this duality,
which lies at the very heart of the novel's form.

But, to articulate this feature of the dialectic, which is, in many ways,
its very essence, is a delicate process, which will confirm its enemies in
their feeling that the dialectic is fundamentally immoral; it is certain
that it is "beyond good and evil," insofar as the latter constitute very
precisely one of the fundamental oppositions it claims to transcend and
to overcome, in the process situating those same critics in the space of a
purely moralizing or ethical dogmatics. For it is not only in the logical
realm that the dialectic claims to transcend the law of non-contradic-
tion: in history, in politics, in ethics as well, its impersonal and painfully
indifferent view maintains an identity of good and evil, which can
perhaps best be dramatized by the opening of the *Communist Manifesto*,
in which Marx simultaneously affirms the extraordinary productivity of
capital and its illimitable power of harm and injury. This argument is
not to be taken in the sense that capital achieves some good things and
has other features which are destructive: rather, it posits the identity of
good and evil simultaneously, within a single phenomenon. That identity will hopefully seem less scandalous when examined in the context
of formal phenomena; still, I want to stress the necessity of a dialectical
perspective here, in order to forestall the conclusion that Grossman's
novel simply equates socialism and totalitarianism. This is a question of
form and, above all, of the form of totality, of the social preconditions
for narrative coherence, and, ultimately, of the paradoxical relationship
between the two fundamental categories of closure and collectivity
which preside over *Life and Fate* and which presuppose each other, no

matter how distasteful that might seem for readers from an affluent Western bourgeois society.

We may pursue this thread with the help of yet another miniature analogue, familiar from any number of war movies: it is the collective kitchen omnipresent in such cramped quarters:

> Yevgenia found it strange, after Stalingrad, to be sharing a small, quiet room with an old woman who never ceased marvelling at how a little girl with plaits could have turned into a grown woman.
>
> Jenny Genrikhovna's gloomy little cubby-hole had once been part of the servants' quarters of a spacious merchant's flat. Now each room was inhabited by a whole family and was divided up by screens, curtains, rugs and the backs of sofas into little nooks and corners— one for eating, one for sleeping, one for receiving guests, another for the nurse to give injections to a paralysed old man . . .
>
> In the evening the kitchen fairly hummed with the voices of all the inmates.
>
> Yevgenia Nikolaevna liked this kitchen with its sooty ceiling and the dark red flames of the oil-stoves. People in dressing-gowns, padded jackets and soldiers' tunics bustled about below clothes that had been hung up to dry. Knives gleamed. Clouds of steam rose from tubs and bowls full of washing. The ample stove was no longer in use; the Dutch tiles lining its sides seemed cold and white—like the snow-covered slopes of some long-extinct volcano.
>
> The tenants of the flat included the family of a docker who was now at the front, a gynaecologist, an engineer from an armaments factory, a single mother who worked as a cashier in a store, the widow of a hairdresser who had been killed at the front, the manager of a post-office, and—in what had once been the large dining-room—the director of a surgery.
>
> The flat was as extensive as a town; it even had room in it for its own madman, a quiet little old man with the eyes of a sweet, good-natured puppy (LF 100).

This promiscuity can be attractive ("Yevgenia would have liked to draw this flat [she is an artist]—not so much the objects and people themselves as the feelings they aroused in her"), but a few instances of meanness, resentment, and petty cruelty are enough to expose its unescapably negative side as well.

Conversations

Such imprisonment, such enclave existence, need not be merely spatial, however: is not that of conversation itself an instantiation of much the same form? So it is that an idle word dropped in passing (it might concern a rumor about the capture by the Germans of Stalin's older son Yakov—or the ambiguous remark about Krymov's alleged association "with all kinds of Trotskyists and Bukharinites" [LF 107–8, 106]) suddenly reveals the limits of talk even among friends:

> He spoke straightforwardly and openly, seemingly as straightforwardly as the manager of a knitwear factory or a teacher at a technical institute might talk about their work. But they all understood that this openness and freedom were only apparent—he knew better than any of them what could, and what could not, be talked about ... the depths concealed beneath the surface of this animated and spontaneous conversation ... Galina's brother understood that this stupid, trivial incident would be forgotten; he also understood that it would not be forgotten entirely. (LF 90)

But it is also pleasant to report that such self-censorship or limits on "free speech"—the staple of Western denunciations of totalitarianism—can also call out unexpected resources of inventiveness and ingenuity, as when a commissar, himself a Jew, confronted with an antisemitic attack on a Jewish member of the platoon, turns the antisemitism into an anti-nationalist correction of the victim himself ("I'm surprised to find the mentality of the *shtetl* in a member of the Komsomol"):

> Berman's words always had a strange, hypnotic effect on people. Everyone knew that Solomatin had deliberately offended Korol—and yet there was Berman confidently explaining that Korol had failed to overcome his nationalist prejudices and that his behaviour evinced a contempt for the friendship of peoples. And Korol should remember that it was the Fascists who exploited nationalist prejudices ... Everyone settled down again in their chairs, sensing that the affair had now been resolved. (LF 153)

But antisemitism is not always so easily deflected. Just as the inescapable yet invisible lines that bind an entire population together in a situation of siege inevitably project betrayal and suspicion as the negative side of forced solidarity, so also a permanent possibility of antisemitism suffuses the social relations of this society: "forgotten, but not forgotten entirely" . . .

This is the drama of Lyudmila's husband (and Zhenya's brother-in-law), the Jewish physicist Viktor Shtrum, who suddenly makes a fundamental discovery in his exile in Kazan. The evacuation of his Institute produces yet another enclave situation, in which—presumably—it is atomic energy that is at stake. Viktor's mood swings are among the most vivid effects of Grossman's psychological notations, alienating Lyudmila by his indifference to the fate of her son and the reader by his self-pity and narcissism. The Institute returns to Moscow after the victory at Stalingrad and, at the height of Viktor's personal triumph, he begins to sense betrayal and hostility, by way of the deprecation of so-called Western science—that is to say "Jewish science," the science of Einstein. However, a bleak period of depression and isolation is interrupted by a phone call: "Good day, comrade Shtrum." The well-known voice inquires benevolently about his laboratory working conditions and his research needs, and then concludes, "I wish you success in your work" (LF 746). But this momentous phone call, with the reversal of fortune it guarantees, has the unwanted consequence that Viktor is called on to sign a denunciation of one of his colleagues: do as you are done to. His agonized acquiescence scarcely guarantees his future, for the reader is aware of the Doctors' Plot that lies over the horizon at the end of the war.

"Stalin's will"

This is, then, the moment to speak of "the will of Stalin" and the centrality of the state. Krymov, rearrested after his mission in Stalingrad, is well aware as an old Bolshevik, a communist of the first generation, of the

> new type of Party official . . . those who had replaced the Old Bolsheviks liquidated or dismissed from their posts in 1937. They were people of a very different stamp. They read new books and they read them in a different way: they didn't read them, they "mugged them up" . . . Krymov could understand that both the new and the old cadres were bound together by a great common goal, that this gave rise to many solidarities . . . nevertheless, he had always been

conscious of his own superiority over these new people, the superiority that was his as an Old Bolshevik . . . Krymov hadn't noticed how it
happened, but now it was his investigator's self-assurance that was the
assurance of a true Communist. (LF 761)

Always running through the work, as through the historical reality, is
the tension between officers and commissars, that uneasy duplication of
powers inherited from the French Revolution and expressive of the
revolutionaries' suspicion of experts: indeed, Krymov himself is a political commissar, and we have seen this tension run the other way in the
hostility of the real combatants of House 6/1 faced with his intrusion.
But now he is himself the target of a new kind of commissar, the faceless
young "new men" of 1937 who have replaced the revolutionary comrades
Stalin then began systematically to liquidate.

But we must not call them a new bureaucracy, exactly, for they do not
administer anything but terror; just as we must not, in this novel, substitute psychological explanations of Stalin (his paranoia, his lust for
power, and so on) for what seems to me Grossman's deeper view here, as
over and over again he detects a mysterious force at work on all the characters, pulling and driving them against their own wills. Yet this force,
sometimes also named—by the Russians—"Stalin's will," is not personal,
it is the state as such. "Stalin! The great Stalin! Perhaps this man with the
iron will had less will than any of them. He was the slave of his time and
circumstances, a dutiful, submissive servant of the present day, flinging
open the doors before the new age" (LF 826). This omnipresence in *Life
and Fate* of the mysterious new power of the state as such is the secret of
Grossman's view of some convergence of Stalin and Hitler—the latter
glimpsed only once, in a lonely stroll through a nature that bewilders
and frightens him. What they both represent as allegorical figures is not
the "totalitarianism" of liberal Cold War ideology, but, rather, the historical emergence of some new kind of all-powerful industrial state;
Grossman is neither a Trotskyist nor a dissident but an anarchist, and it
is an aesthetic as well as a political offence to enlist him for "free-world"
anti-communism.

Likewise, the omnipresent word "freedom" characterizes something
rather more complex than the usual anti-Stalinist rhetoric, something
indeed a little closer to Tolstoy (and his master Stendhal), a psychology in
which the deeper, more truly human personality is submerged and
repressed by the deadening effects of the state. In Tolstoy this repression is

that of society and of its artificial sociability, from which only the peasants, in their proximity to the earth, are exempt. Here, however, a more
invisible, unpresentable pressure is only indirectly to be detected in the
reawakening from it. In the past, the revolution itself is remembered as an
immense explosion of human vitality, which is then tamed and overcome
by obedience—an obedience that "bears witness to a new force acting on
human beings. The extreme violence of totalitarian social systems proved
able to paralyse the human spirit throughout whole continents" (LF 198).

It is a doctrine of authenticity, but one different from that of Stendhal's
genuine feelings, or Tolstoy's opposition of the artificial to the natural:
closer perhaps to modern, more Sartrean notions of a slumbering and
unconscious freedom, above all in this sense, that the layers of inauthen-
ticity must first be painfully broken through and destroyed.

> There were also [Grossman is speaking of the German army] the
> beginnings of other, deeper changes, in the hearts and minds of the
> soldiers who until now had been spellbound by the inhuman power
> of the nation-state. These changes took place in the subsoil of human
> life and mostly went unnoticed. This process was as difficult to pin
> down as the work of time itself. The torments of fear and hunger, the
> awareness of impending disaster slowly and gradually humanized
> men, liberating their core of freedom. (LF 715)

Becoming human: this is the bitter secret of Grossman's vision. For not
only is it profoundly ambiguous: Paulus's officers recover their idiosyn-
crasies and their personal characteristics and selfishness after the
surrender—"these officers had indeed become human again, but not in
the most admirable manner" (LF 785). The process inevitably also
means suffering, it is only suffering that brings a painful life back into
the numb members, that allows those paralyzed by the deadening power
of the state to revive, to become human again. This conviction—it was
clearly Grossman's experience of people in that period—is not some
remnant of a traditional notion of redemption. It is far more medical
and therapeutic; and the cure—tragically enough—is the war itself. It is
the torment of war on both sides that makes the surface of an artificial
and bureaucratic society begin to crack, and to free these people to their
authenticity, to their personal agonies and the genuine feelings that lie
beneath their ambitions, their obedience, their cowardliness, their fear
and consent to the state.

War into form

So much for Grossman's vision of history, and of the greatest war history has seen. But we also need to be analytical about all this, and heartlessly formalistic: for the interesting questions not only concern the content of the book, or Grossman's immense talent; they want to probe the matter of historical possibility and to get some idea of how a book like this could be written in the first place. And the answer is the same, of course: it is the war; but it is the war now seen from a peculiar and perhaps even unpleasantly inhuman angle. For only the content enables the possibility of form; the Western writers were not able to write like this, through no lack of talent of their own; nor did Tolstoy achieve this narrative totality, however extraordinary he was in so many other ways.

Let's think back to the communal kitchen, and to the seventeenth-century neoclassical unities. Reality itself must be compressed, and uncomfortably thrust back on itself, living on top of itself, in order for genuine relations to exist: our own parks and surveillance cameras, the gated communities of the isolated rich, only give us a handful of separate individuals, at a distance even from themselves. The bourgeois world gives us families in apartments and cars, in intermittent juxtaposition; even their wars are little more than deadly vacations. In the Soviet war, however, superimposing the implacable web of socialist economic relations upon that, redoubled, of the war effort itself, and from that macrocosm to the microcosm of Stalingrad itself, the other is omnipresent; there is no privacy, let alone solitude, and everyone is bound by the ligatures of unspoken gossip, betrayal and the Cause itself, not excluding its joyous energies and the pride of its achievements. It is this human raw material that alone enables the new unities, not merely of plot, but of the totality itself: totality of relations, totality of a social locked in on itself, totality of narrative and of the novel as a form. If everyone is related here, in the most banal sense of kinship and marriage, of soldiers and commanders, of people and *vozhd'*, there is nothing to surprise us or to make us uncomfortable with arbitrary cross-cutting or unnecessary, contingent chance, with improbable additions or unbelievable solutions or coincidences—everything coheres, from Poland to the Urals, it is all one single experience, sublime or sickening, a doom or a chance liberation, life and fate, Spinoza's god.

Like all the populations surviving until the war's end, whether Axis or Allied, with or without their ration books and their residence permits, and only gradually prepared to shed their habits of obedience, if only to search for food, these people know a historical moment of collective hope, quickly dashed. The liberation of Paris, Labour Britain, the emergence of the partisans all over Europe, the 8th Road Army, the return home of many different kinds of soldiers—here Stalingrad means something like that:

> Three different strata of life lay exposed in the ruins: life before the war, life during the fighting, and life today. One building had started out as a tailor's and dry-cleaner's; then the windows had been bricked up, leaving small loopholes where the German machine-guns had been mounted; now women queued at these loopholes to receive their bread ration . . . "What's this?" she asked, pointing to a blackened wall with gaping windows.
>
> "Just various offices. What they should do is let people live here."
>
> "And what was it before?"
>
> "This was the headquarters of Paulus himself. It was here he was taken prisoner."
>
> "And before that?"
>
> "The department store. Don't you recognize it?" (LF 842–3)

But, here, the short-lived euphoria of war's end is the end of a task, of a superhuman one that absorbs everyone's breath and waking hours on all sides. Now there is no longer anything to do but survive; and the immense historical social totality of the war itself begins to falter and to dissolve. It is appropriate that the novel should dissolve with it.

10

The USSR That Wasn't

In general, in the novel, youth is riding for a fall; something in the very form of the novel itself warns us obscurely that things will not turn out—indeed, it is in the very nature of things that they can never turn out. So it is refreshing to come upon *Red Plenty*, in which youth and its hopes and excitements—forever enthusiastic even in its minor disappointments—are preserved as in a time capsule; as if under a spell, or enclosed within a fairy tale, as the author, Francis Spufford, tells us. And this, in a historical novel—one of those new so-called postmodern historical novels that are springing up all around us—in which we all know very pertinently that it never did turn out in the first place. This youth, in which the world was new, and very bliss it was, is the youth of the Soviet Union; but not the 1920s, the world of revolutionary hopes, but, rather, the youth of Khrushchev's '60s, a whole new generation of Soviets who have put Stalin and the War, deprivation and the secret police, behind them. A generation, indeed, who have never known any of those things, whose emblem is Sputnik and education, and whose hope is "red plenty," in a distinctly different sense from the consumerism of the American postwar. Spufford has done well, first to stock and bury his time capsule, and then to dig it up and open it for us. He has his own lessons to draw from its contents, but there may also be others he has not thought of.

"In Soviet Arcadia: On *Red Plenty* by Francis Spufford," *New Left Review* 75, May/June 2012.

But what a wonderfully and formally unusual novel: the docudramas on TV to which it presumably corresponds generically are really nothing like this, and not only because they keep encouraging us to compare the actors with the originals. Nor is this exactly a historical novel, even though it deals with a specific historical period—the Soviet 1960s—and includes real people as characters, most notably Nikita Khrushchev himself, alongside fictional characters, as well as "fictionalized" characters "standing roughly where real people stood," as Spufford puts it in an explanatory "Note on the Characters" that follows the sixty-strong Cast List. Why this is not, then, simply a historical novel is an important theoretical question, which transcends the merely technical and classificatory one of genre.

It can be sharpened, however, by a few more classificatory questions: why is it not a non-fiction novel, for example (in some more meaningful sense than the fact that this generic category no longer exists or never really caught on in the first place)? And what about what might be called the new "narrative journalism"—big books which purport to tell the story of a given crisis? I quote the beginning of one, perhaps the "biggest" and best; certainly the most famous—Andrew Sorkin's 2009 *Too Big to Fail*:

> The morning air was frigid in Greenwich, Connecticut. At 5:00 am on March 17, 2008, it was still dark, save for the headlights of the black Mercedes idling in the driveway, the beams illuminating patches of slush that were scattered across the lawns of the twelve-acre estate. The driver heard the stones of the walkway crackle as Richard S. Fuld Jr shuffled out the front door and into the backseat of the car.

Now, every detail of this paragraph could be true (and probably was) and that would not make it any less fictional. Barthes called this kind of writing "novelistic," I believe, without thereby implying that it had to be part of a novel; only that it gives off the signals a novel is supposed to give in order to instruct its readers to shift into the novel-reading mode.

Red Plenty is not like that either, despite its equally novelistic opening sentence: "A tram was coming, squealing metal against metal, throwing blue-white sparks into the winter dark." It includes, for example, fifty-four pages of endnotes, many of which are long and readable, in explanatory prose; Sorkin has forty pages of one-line references, plus the "five hundred hours of interviews" he was able to draw on. To be sure, novels have included notes before—as in *Finnegans Wake* or *Infinite Jest*—but not for reference purposes; and both Spufford and Sorkin include lengthy bibliographies. Thus, both books are based on research, but what is the (generic) difference between journalism and history? Neither is supposed to include fictional characters, after all.

Spufford tries to clarify all this, and the uniqueness of his own text, by framing it as a fairy tale. I will say later on what I think this means and why it is not wrong. For the moment, I think we need to return to the uniqueness, not of the form, but of the content, and to the strangeness of the fresh start, the new age, the new beginnings. This is not exactly "the sixties," which is a periodizing concept rather than a date, and which happens at different times in different countries: Spain's *movida* begins after Franco's death, or better still, after the failed coup; China's starts in the Deng era, etc. Nor is it exactly the same as "the Thaw" or *perestroika*, let alone the Cultural Revolution; but it is certainly a generational event and a youth movement, which breaks with the attitudes (both moral and political) and authority of an older generation and a ruling class; "anti-bourgeois" captures something of this revolt, even where we are dealing with non-bourgeois societies.

But the Soviet '60s dealt with here is not that kind of period (which probably began in the late Brezhnev era). For one thing, the young still believe in socialism, as do their elders; for another, the objective situation has itself changed, not merely by the disappearance of something—Stalin and his programs and methods—but with the emergence of something new, which is not only the technologies of the dawning computer age but also the release of older heavy industry to produce consumer goods for the first time; this is the first and, as it were, literal meaning of the title. So, we might call this new age "the postwar," as it happened in non-Soviet reconstruction as well—the Labour Party's National Health Service, the US highway system, MacArthur's agrarian reform in Japan, decolonization in Africa. In that case, *Red Plenty* can be seen as an analysis, not of reconstruction itself, so much as of its ideology. In the Soviet case, however, the ideology of reconstruction, the ethos of the "new beginning" and the "fresh start," is not framed, as in the West, as the invention of something new and the call for a whole new mentality, but rather as a continuation: the restoration of the original Soviet revolution, the starting up again of the original aims of Soviet communism, as they were before foreign intervention and the Hitlerian war. As for the Cold War itself, Khrushchev's trip to the US, whose story is again told here, is enough to reassure those Soviets alarmed by Truman's invective (and then again by Reagan's after the end of this book).

The characters are mostly scientists, young and old, real and invented; and the principal new beginning staged here is a scientific one—or, to be even more precise about it, an informational one, involving the use of computer technology. But we are also given enough of a sampling of daily life to understand that the scientific excitement and enthusiasms of the students are representative (allegorical) of a much more general feeling. The visit to the 1959 US pavilion in Sokolniki Park, the life of peasants and racketeers, natural childbirth, popular crooners, the factories and their suppliers and contracts; with all of this—although it does not seem to follow a laundry list of the topics any thorough sociologist might want to cover in a totalizing picture of everyday life in a modern or modernizing society; indeed, what would such a list look like?—we somehow feel that the novel has covered enough of its subject, and that its non-technological or non-political sections are not mere examples of something, nor relief from the more serious historiographic parts (which can, as I will show, be taken as steps in an argument), but that they end up giving a complete picture. (This is to be sure a miserable capitulation on my part, inasmuch as the account of how and why a work of art feels complete and seems to stand as a totality is probably the first and most difficult task any critic has to confront.) To put it another way, Spufford's artistry lies in his ability to make us forget, while we are reading his novel, all the things that have been left out: the areas in Soviet life as well in which people do not have renewed hope, the realities that do not fit into the fairy tale. Yet papering over the necessary exclusions is also part of the writer's métier.

But it is not fair to mention exclusions without commenting on some of the more surprising inclusions, starting with the endnotes, where we find information on open-air markets, viscose production, Soviet cars, the psychology of middle-men, types of apartments furnished to officials according to rank, popular music, and much more. To be sure, all this information is referred back to (probably non-primary) sources, but the point is not only that it functions like local color in the old-fashioned *costumbrista* or exotic historical novels, but also that the novel as a form is today in competition with popular non-fictional genres, such as economic or sociological texts, popular biography and so on. These genres scarcely existed in the nineteenth century, when novelists like Balzac themselves functioned as experts and sourcebooks on the various social strata and their customs. Indeed, the naturalists understood their vocation as the supplying of just such information: Zola's notebooks and fieldwork testify to how seriously he took the responsibility of reporting on the structure of mines, for example, or the functioning of the stock market; something that occasionally returns today in bestsellers—it is a generic term—about airports (Arthur Hailey) or architecture (Ayn Rand), where however this knowledge also has a secondary novelistic or ideological function. But that is precisely the point about the naturalists' descriptions: they could not, in the framework of the novel or of literature in general, consist in the communication of technical information for its own sake. All the objective material had also to be endowed with a symbolic or metaphorical function; thus, Zola's mine *devours* human beings.

It is not until the collapse of the aesthetic systems of the modern that postmodern works such as this one can shamelessly include information as such and briefly function like textbooks. Whether this is the result of the aestheticization of information in an informational society or of the informationalization of aesthetics in a spectacular or image-saturated one I do not decide, except to underscore the ideological significance of the answer settled on and to note the availability of yet a third solution, which is the dedifferentiation of specialized fields in the postmodern. This is a kind of response to the problem of historical information as such in *Red Plenty*, and it is a kind of return to Brecht's defense of the didactic—learning facts and skills is a pleasure in itself, which the work of art need never renounce.

Still, this is supposed to be a fairy tale, and at its very center is set a real utopia (or "paradise," if you follow the Persian etymology of a walled or gated garden). This is Akademgorodok, founded by Khrushchev in 1958, and gathering together all kinds of scientists and Academicians, including graduate students and even some artists, musicians and the like:

> The path she was following turned in among a denser group of trees, and delivered her, only a hundred metres on, into forest hush. Suddenly the path beneath her feet was carpeted with dry pine needles; suddenly, the world was roofed with a speckled canopy of leaf and sky through which the sinking sun filtered only as a focus of greater brightness. Sounds were filtered too. Now and again she could

still hear the grinding of construction machinery, but it had become as tiny and unimportant as the buzz of the occasional bees that cruised between the tree trunks. The wood was a mix of pine and silver birch.

The love of nature also comes with national characteristics, and this whole settlement is a collective *dacha* in the industrializing Siberian waste, a *dacha* for Russian intellectuals and mushroom hunters; and we may well recall the charmed surprise of Europeans on first encountering American college campuses. Something of that, and even something of the American freshmen arriving on campus for the first time in their family-sheltered lives, is captured here in the disembarkment of Zoya Vaynshteyn (a fictional analogue for geneticist Raissa Berg) in this socialist campus, which, like the other kind, will combine the excitement of learning and discovery with the toxins of academic politics.

This is, then, the moment to admit that *Red Plenty* is essentially about intellectuals, however wide it seems to cast its net. In fact, the "totality" of Soviet life it presents is a totality seen from the point of view of intellectuals: even the political crisis it will face will be a kind of academic crisis; and this is, no doubt, what will make the novel so attractive for a certain kind of reader. It is not a historical novel about "the Thaw": these people have for the most part not even known Stalin, any more than students today know the Jim Crow laws or the anti-communist witch-hunts. It is not a novel about "hope" in the sense in which great revolutionary periods live that out and determine genuine collective struggle, as in the China of the 1950s or the Spain of the early Civil War years. No, it is, rather, a novel about activity, having a chance not only to do things but to do new things, in fields that have never existed before. No one here is passive, suffering a kind of forced objective paralysis or the onslaught of terrible waves of subjectivity: neither unemployment nor depression. Even Khrushchev's first thought, when deposed, is "No one needs me now . . . What am I going to do without work? How am I going to live?" Defeat here means not existential anguish, but the melancholy of the unemployed, and it is a pity that more Western writers do not understand that what they are tempted to denounce as greed, the lust for power and ambition, also has as its secret driving force the delight in activity.

Yet as the very event of Khrushchev's fall testifies, this lively period—and *Red Plenty* itself—must come to its end in something it would be too hasty to call disillusionment. (It is significant, in its hindsight, that the Brezhnev years were universally characterized as the "period of stag-nation.") Many theories have been advanced to explain the collapse of the Soviet Union, including the failure to implement computer technol-ogy, to which I will return in a moment. But many have agreed that the Khrushchev moment was the last one in which any genuine rebirth of socialism in the USSR was possible. Spufford has his own theory, and this novel is in that sense a thesis novel, which has a point to make. The author's own (genuine) "disillusionment," as distinct from that of his characters, may be detected in his remark in an endnote about Galina's painful experience of "natural childbirth" (the Lamaze method, of course, originated in the Soviet Union): "another piece of mangled Soviet idealism, another genuinely promising idea ruined by the magic combination of compulsion and neglect."

The word "magic" nonetheless inconspicuously underscores some-thing unique about this situation, something like the Strugatsky Brothers' mixture of spaceships and Baba Yaga which is alluded to in the endnotes. It is time, then, to come back to this whimsical, seemingly generic question of fairy tales, and in particular Russian fairy tales, and their relevance for what is, assuredly, a seriously researched and schol-arly historical novel. Spufford's thesis has to do with that age-old left question of the market (and market socialism), a topic seemingly rendered extinct by the triumph of "free market" ideology, despite the contradictory evidence that in our situation free market means not competition, but, rather, monopoly, and on a world scale; or, perhaps, feudal capitalism, as Veblen and Horkheimer thought. Yet funny-money theories, the abolition of markets altogether, the elimination of the commodity form, and so on—these heady visions, along with their often disastrous consequences, do now seem a thing of the past. Consumer society is not a propitious environment in which to dream of the aboli-tion of money, however easy it may be to dream of the abolition of finan-cial markets, which is not the issue here.

But the novel's hero—its world-historical figure, mostly glimpsed in the distance by the book's more "average" protagonists, as Lukács might put it—is a real-life mathematical economist, Leonid Vitalevich Kantorovich, whose revolutionary discoveries of the late 1930s, in their isolation, mirror and anticipate the intellectual excitement of this gener-ation of the dawning 1960s. Exceptionally, in the darkest days of Stalinism, his aloofness from every form of political consideration and the specialized character of his field meant that Leonid Vitalevich prospered, his theories were put into practice and, far from suffering the by now stereotypical fate of all Soviet innovators (or of all postwar Soviet Jewish innovators), he reached the heights of Soviet academic glory and also won the USSR's only Nobel Economics Prize.

His mathematical analysis of production—it seems to be a kind of Taylorization of industrial production processes, as opposed to Taylor's own analysis of the industrial exploitation of human labor—then feeds directly into the exploration of cybernetics and information technology by the generation of the '60s, in Akademgorodok and elsewhere. The idea that computers can solve the dilemmas of a planned society, and that a computerized information system can serve as the material foundation for some future socialism, is not a new one: we find it in both of Ursula Le Guin's utopias, *The Dispossessed* and *Always Coming Home*, as well as in all kinds of theoretical projects. Yet the very sensitivity of the topic is also reflected negatively in the fact that there are no great utopian texts after the widespread introduction of computers (the last being Ernest Callenbach's *Ecotopia* of 1975, where computers are not yet in service). Instead, we have the free-market deliria of cyberpunk, which assumes that capitalism is itself a kind of utopia of difference and variety. I think this failure of imagination on the left can be attributed to the assumption that computers are enough to "take care" of totalization: that the well-nigh infinite complexities of production on a global scale, which the mind can scarcely accommodate, are mysteriously—Spufford might say, magically—resolvable inside the computer's black box and thus no longer need to be dealt with conceptually or representationally.

The term "market socialism" is, to be sure, carefully avoided by the Soviet economists, probably because it is generally thought to be the first step on the road back to capitalism (Spufford points to some who argue strenuously against such a presupposition, and to others whose language prudently veils their ultimate opinions on the topic). But perhaps the matter can be sorted out by distinguishing the perspectives of production and consumption. From the latter standpoint, that of consumer society, everyone wants the same thing—the standardized product, labelled by whatever different brand-name you may prefer— and it is a question of polling those desires and then making sure there are enough items to go around, in the proper places (how advertising intervenes into the consumers' unconscious is yet another factor, which can presumably itself be measured). For the Soviet economists it is a question of computerizing the costs of production, and the sources of its various ingredients: totalization is here a matter not only of the networks of raw materials, but of the way in which each source itself becomes a new center whose restructuration by the outflow of such basic ingredients then must be recomputed in its turn. Notoriously, the managers defend their own production sites against any attempt to integrate them into a larger system, which is of course just what the computer people want to do.

At any rate, it is a question of returning politics to the primacy of economics and putting the actual costs back into the plans, which only now begin to show mathematical accuracy. The intellectuals are predictably jubilant when these new ideas are adopted by their superiors and then by the state itself; for them, this is the climax of the new era, the moment in which "actually existing socialism" (a later expression) is on the point of rising to the level of its own concept, as Hegel would have put it. But the moment at which costs are adequately reflected in their mathematical formulations is also the moment at which prices are made to rise: prices are indeed the cost of the concept, and the results are bread riots and the one (relatively unintentional) massacre of the Khrushchev era, the little-known repression of Novocherkassk on June 3, 1962. As in the ironies of misrecognition in the Victorian novel, our protagonists evidently know nothing of this carefully censored event, and are thus astonished to find, in the much-heralded Kosygin reforms of 1965, that everything but the essential corresponds to their own recommendations and calculations. In the same way, the Great Innovator himself is presumably astonished when he is quietly packed off into retirement in a grade-B limousine. All downhill from there!

This fairy tale is, then, in reality, the novelistic working-out of a rather different genre, which the historians know under the term counterfactuality, whose simplest exercise has to do with the turning of a crucial battle in warfare, or the unexpected death of a leader. Thus, Arnold Toynbee speculated that, had Alexander the Great not died at the Christological age of thirty-three, a world empire of lasting peace would have emerged. So also, Philip K. Dick allows us to glimpse a world in which the Germans and the Japanese won World War II; while Niall Ferguson adumbrates the blessings (no Soviet revolution!) that would have accrued to mankind had Germany won World War I. Spufford's fairy tale counterfactuality does not undertake to represent his alternate universe with science-fictional speculation; but the point of his wonderful novel is certainly to flex the mind's long-numb faculty of wondering, what if?, and to restore the freshness of an era in which for a long moment still, everything was possible. As for the future of this past which scarcely existed, it is worth concluding with the author's somber reflexions on it, typically consigned to an endnote:

> On the face of it, one of the great historical mysteries of the twentieth century should be the question of why the Soviet reformers of the 1980s didn't even consider following the pragmatic Chinese path, and dismantling the economic structure of state socialism while keeping its political framework intact. Instead, the Soviet government dismantled the Leninist political structure while trying with increasing desperation to make the planned economy work. But the mystery resolves rather easily if it is posited that Gorbachev and the intellectuals around him, all children of the 1930s and young adults under Khrushchev, might strange to say have been really and truly socialists, guarding a loyal glimmer of belief right through the Brezhnevite "years of stagnation," and seizing the chance after two decades of delay to return to their generational project of making a socialism that was prosperous, humane, and intelligent. With disastrous results. This whole book is, in fact, a prehistory of perestroika.

Red Plenty thereby lapses into conventional wisdom: why did the Party not simply "dismantle the economic structure of state socialism" like the Chinese? Spufford reads his own fairy tale, like its originals, as a wish-fulfilment falling to the hard earth of reality and succumbing to the peasant common sense of traditional wisdom. But is the market really a common-sense reality, except in fairy tales? What Spufford gives us here is an unrealized utopia; not necessarily an unrealizable one.

11

Faith and Conspiracy in Japan

It is necessary to study precisely how permanent collective wills are formed, and how such wills set themselves concrete short and long-term ends—i.e. a line of collective action.

Gramsci

Nobel Prize-winners seem to fall into two categories: those whom the prize honors, and those who honor the prize. And then there are those assumed to be in the first category, who turn out to have been in the second all along. Such was, for example, "the author of a dirty book called *Sanctuary*," who proved, unexpectedly, to be the greatest novelist in the world. Such also, I believe, is Kenzaburo Oe, whose latest novel shows how mistaken American stereotypes of him were (and perhaps how mistaken his own stereotype of himself was).

At least two things were thought to have been known about this writer when Grove gradually began to introduce his work in English in the late 1960s (Oe was born in 1935). The first is that he was a committed anti-nuclear activist (the West probably not knowing enough about Japanese politics to grasp the complexities of the ANPO, or New Left, movement of 1960). The second is that he is the father of a handicapped son, born with a strange protuberance on his head, who has grown up to be a musician and a composer. Anyone unaware of the first of these

"Pseudo-Couples: On *Somersault* by Kenzaburn Oe," *London Review of Books* 25(22), November 20, 2003.

features is much less likely to have remained unaware of the second, since it appears in virtually every book Oe has written.

But it appears with variations, as do all of Oe's themes or obsessions. This is not to be understood psychologically, as a pretext for deducing the primal fantasy or archetype repeating itself like the eternal return of some endless murmur. I prefer to think of the process as one of never-ending construction and reconstruction with a finite number of building blocks, which you put together in all kinds of different ways: tragically, comically, mythically, and, in the case of *Somersault*, with a kind of "late-style" simplicity, like the architectonics of a Bruckner symphony.

Still, it would seem that something is new here (the "somersault" of the title suggests renunciation and rebirth). Oe himself has announced that what he calls the "idiot son" cycle of his narratives is over. That is not quite true; but the father-son motif, withdrawing into the background, does seem here to be transformed almost beyond recognition, giving way to an urgent preoccupation with group formation which was always present in Oe's earlier work, but never posed so directly. *Somersault* (*Ch⁻ugaeri*, published in Japan in 1999) tells the story of the attempt by its founder to resurrect a religious cult he has himself discredited and virtually destroyed. It is an oddly formalistic exercise, in which the mechanics of group formation—assembling mailing lists, scheduling meetings, renting meeting places and deciding the order of business—seem to take precedence over the content of the particular religion. Not that such a focus would be altogether without interest: one imagines the naturalist novelists taking this social phenomenon apart like a machine, and describing all the steps and pitfalls with gusto, while disregarding the spirituality altogether. Oe's novel has little in common with naturalism, but it is also resolutely non-spiritual and non-psychological; what Oe has in common with Dostoevsky (the comparison is often made) are the endless philosophical conversations which allowed the latter's novels to escape the "monologic" perspective of the ideology or set of opinions or beliefs the author may have held in real life. With Oe, too, it might be preferable to dissociate the author from ideas he merely seems to endorse (I will touch on the "sacrificial" and on religion itself later on); and where the naturalists might have offered us a sociologically rich cast of character types—organizers and bureaucrats, fanatics, groupies, secretaries, fellow travelers etc.—the supporting cast here is larger than life, and, at the same time, formulaic (the building-block system) and existential or unique.

We shouldn't, however, neglect the shadow presence of *The Devils* behind all this; or the equally Dostoevskian abjection, in which grotesque characters wallow in their shame and inferiority (Oe's greatest novel, *The Silent Cry*, published in 1967, begins with the narrator squatting in a muddy pit destined to become a new septic system, and holding a stinking dog in his arms as he evacuates). Victorianism didn't permit Dostoevsky to indulge in the outbursts of obscenity recurrent in Oe's work and very much in evidence in *Somersault* (Judge Woolsey might have pronounced them "emetic" rather than "aphrodisiac"); I doubt whether they reflect the hatred of the body often implicit in such passages, but I also want to exclude culturalism and its myths (such as the idea of some "Japanese" sexuality).

Contingency seems to me a better way of understanding all this: it presides over the grotesque detail fully as much as the various bodily functions, and re-places Oe squarely in the existential tradition, to which, as a French scholar, he remains indebted (Japanese critics, however, also make much of his American-style narratives, including the "Americanisms" of his Japanese). If he is not exactly a realist, he is not really a modernist either (despite the fireworks of his earlier writing: "his woollen jacket striped with light and dark brown was worn with an air of reverent care, though the odds were that it would soon deteriorate into a crumpled, baggy heap like a large dead cat"—*The Silent Cry*). His work avoids standard modernist devices such as autoreferentiality; and, although it is often a question of art in Oe—the great Jonah triptych here, the Tantric Buddhist painting of hell in *The Silent Cry*—my sense is that, as in Hegel, the aesthetic center of gravity has shifted imperceptibly towards ritual rather than in the direction of the autonomous work of art. Yet *Somersault* is scarcely postmodern either, save perhaps for that interest in small groups which parallels a Western ethnic or identity politics.

Indeed, it now seems best to grasp the "idiot son" motif as being itself a first attempt at group formation. It is a failed attempt, although it is not "a personal matter" (the title of Oe's most famous version of the subject) and is thus not to be interpreted according to the usual humanist misreadings, such as guilt, or even the existential ones, such as the "life sore" of Paule Marshall or Sartre's ineradicable past act. Rather, the multiple permutations of this relationship end up revealing it as that sad and comic dramatic structure Beckett called the pseudo-couple, a vaudevillesque situation of neurotic dependency in which two differentially maimed and underdeveloped subjectivities provisionally complete each other. Nor is this a family structure exactly: sometimes a wife is introduced, vengeful and aggressive (as in *The Pinch Runner Memorandum*, 1976) or alcoholic, lachrymose, and catatonic (as in *The Silent Cry*), but we could equally well see this pseudo-couple as a fraternal pair, and indeed in *The Silent Cry* the deformed baby is very much upstaged by the central struggle between the two enemy brothers, while in *The Pinch Runner Memorandum*, a galloping and comic nightmare more reminiscent of Lem's *Futurological Congress* than of anything in Philip K. Dick, the father and son actually change places (it might have been called "The Switchover"), the former becoming a teenager while the latter assumes the advanced age of the father (thirty-eight), the whole being projected onto an analogous father-handicapped-son pair whose "story" the narrator (presumably Oe himself) relates in the voice of the alternate progenitor, who has become the son and teenage buddy of his wiser son-father.

The pseudo-couple has not disappeared altogether from *Somersault*, where the handicapped boy (who has, like Oe's own son, become a musician and begun to compose in his own right) is a minor character, accompanied by a "normal" sister; but it can be rediscovered in the central narrative frame, where it is compelled by outright homoeroticism in the person of the cancer-ridden arts teacher (Kizu) fascinated by the "dog-faced boy" (Ikuo), a taciturn and stubborn youth he had observed long ago as a small child awkwardly carrying an enormous model building (they will years later be unexpectedly united around the reorganization of the sect). Yet, even this idiosyncratic adolescent figure was foreshadowed in a completely different narrative context in *The Silent Cry*, where he turns out to be the leader of a children's group in Oe's native Shikoku forest valley (a role Ikuo reassumes in *Somersault* when the sect moves to that same valley, itself a constant throughout Oe's work).

What to do with these multiple permutations, in which the return of the same is always different? The pseudo-couple, to be sure, traces an august (if ridiculous) lineage all the way back (via Flaubert) to *Don Quixote*; but Beckett, who was the first to name this structure (in *Mercier and Camier*, I believe), gives us what is perhaps a more productive clue in *Waiting for Godot*. The Beckett play involves two pseudo-couples, the relatively egalitarian team of the two clochards (differentiated only by their physical ailments) being episodically juxtaposed with a very different and decidedly unegalitarian pair in the persons of Pozzo—the master, presumably signifying England—and Lucky, the slave, presumably signifying Ireland and its intellectuals. The first pseudo-couple offers the interminable repetitions of everyday life and existential experience and boredom; the second brings power and history into the matter (the conflation of the two pairs into one in *Endgame* does not overcome this mysterious incommensurability, even though we are told that Beckett came to loathe his first, allegorical and world-historical effort).

This kind of doubling is also to be found in *Somersault*, where the first pseudo-couple of the sickly painter and the adolescent rebel (itself harboring, as I have said, echoes of the primal pseudo-couple of father and handicapped son) is confronted with what may be called a political pseudo-couple, in the twin direction of the sect and the persons of the peculiarly named Patron and Guide. But these nicknames (invented by a journalist) are modest euphemisms for their fundamental roles as Savior and Prophet respectively. A spiritual division of labor of this kind is not uncommon in the history of religious movements: Moses and Aaron, Jesus and St. Paul, Sabbatai Sevi and Nathan of Gaza, are only a few of the joint religious leaderships that come to mind. (In an article in the *London Review of Books*, Perry Anderson has suggested that, at least in Latin American politics, the reverse is frequent, with the public leader being shadowed by his decidedly unpublicized éminence grise: perhaps a theory is to be concocted on the basis of this interesting inversion?)

Again, something of the catastrophic reversal of *Waiting for Godot* is to be found in *Somersault*: for, early in the revival, Guide is murdered by the so-called radical faction of the older followers. His disappearance serves to lay Patron's fundamental helplessness bare: not only has the Savior had no new visions since the end of the older cult, but the public interpretations of those visions turn out to have been fabrications on Guide's part, flights of fancy engineered according to Guide's own view of the direction the movement is to take (indeed, the sub-faction of scientists and technicians responsible for the group's dissolution, and later on for Guide's death, is very much his own operation).

The disappearance of Guide clarifies Patron's decision to start the group up again: *Somersault* is centrally concerned with the possibility of forming groups—a political movement, an active collectivity, a return to the communal in some new form after the ravages of modern or modernist individualism—which do not posit violence as a necessary accompaniment or outcome. This is a fundamental dilemma in what is, despite appearances, a political rather than a religious novel: religion being, in an apolitical age like ours, the privileged form of the Ruse of History. But politics or political theory is here not a matter of empirical interests or even ideologies and parties, of class struggle as such: it constitutes an ontological inquiry into the very possibility for biologically isolated human beings to form groups which can function as historical agencies. Nor is Patron's preoccupation with violence to be grasped as a merely pacifist or humanist "value," as Oe's early history as an anti-nuclear activist has been thought of in the West: rather, it addresses a fundamental dilemma in the existence of groups as such. The philosophical confrontation with these issues has been at best sporadic; in modern times one thinks of Carl Schmitt or the Sartre of the *Critique*, while, earlier, it was mainly around the founding of religions (and their subsequent schisms) that group formation was presented as a problem that eludes the visual field of liberalism or humanism and their various forms of repressive tolerance. For the conceptualization of the group or collective always comes up short against the unhappy fact (if it has to be a fact!) that in order to differentiate itself and to achieve that mode of praxis which is today loosely and ideologically called its "identity," the nascent collectivity seems necessarily to have to define itself by way of frontiers and borders, by way of a kind of secession: it must always, in other words, following Schmitt's remarkable formulation, posit an enemy. Thus, in order for humanity as a whole to experience the perpetual peace and harmony fantasized by the humanists, to enjoy one great collective identity all across the globe, we would need, as Sartre observed, the unifying intervention of an enemy in outer space (it is a logical corollary beautifully imagined by Ursula Le Guin in her novel *The Lathe of Heaven*).

The issue is not only philosophical or ontological, however, and the recent history of Japan is there to account for the way Oe dramatizes it in *Somersault*, and also for the relative formalism of its staging. For Japan—that simultaneously violent and very well-behaved place—having had its own experience of the great mass movements of communism and fascism, came to the contemporary forms of collective action somewhat earlier than Europe or the US, in the great ANPO anti-treaty demonstrations of 1960, from which both an anti-nuclear mobilization and the Narita Airport movement emerged, the latter enjoying perhaps the longest lifespan (some twenty years) of any

radical action of the postwar period. The displacement and supersession of the Communist Party by New Left or extraparliamentary left
movements—what the France of 1968 called "groupuscules"—meant
not merely a draining away of the central ideological conflict of the
Cold War (particularly since most of these small groups were more
passionately anti-communist than anti-capitalist in the first place); it
also meant the emergence of the new political dynamic epitomized by
the fraternal conflicts of Oe's *Pinch Runner Memorandum*, where it is
difficult to distinguish between the revolutionary group and the counter-revolutionary group attacking it.

This is not to suggest that Oe, himself the target of right-wing and
nationalist, pro-Emperor violence, believes in some hypothetical
convergence between Left and Right, even less is it to compare skin-
heads with multiple left groupuscules, perfectly capable of killing each
other off without the help of the Right. He is indeed anti-nationalist and
anti-Emperor, but he may also be seen as a political regionalist, substituting the problematic of space for the reprehensible rhetoric of the
nation and of patriotism. In *Somersault*, warring factions coexist uneas-
ily within the overarching religious framework of the movement. It is
important, however, not to characterize this kind of religious politics as
conservative or reactionary, as one would for the most part be entitled
to do for similar movements in the US or Europe. Oe's religion could
probably be described as Blakean (see above all *Rouse up, O Young Men
of the New Age*, 1983), Blake being, along with Sartre and Dostoevsky,
the central literary reference point of his work (always accompanied by
a host of minor allusions: in the present novel there is a lengthy appreciation of the poetry of R. S. Thomas and his doctrine of "quiet
emergence").

We have learned in recent times that religion emerges (quietly or not)
as the ideological form of political content whenever the openly political or socio-economic has been discredited or withdrawn: as it was by
the long history of Stalinism, or, in the Middle East, by the wholesale
massacre of one national Communist Party after another, which left
only Islam as an available framework for revolt and resistance.

All this is complicated by a peculiar turn in recent Japanese history
which must be taken into account for the proper intelligence of
Somersault. In Japan, the September 11 experience, the shattering of a
First World complacency with political results as yet incompletely
known, took place on a fateful date which will not generally be

recognized in the West: namely, March 20, 1995. This was the day on which Aum Shinrikyo spread sarin gas in the Tokyo subway system, killing twelve people and injuring thousands. It is only after al-Qaida that the West has been able to appreciate the collective trauma inflicted on Japan, one different in kind from its earlier political violence. For the long-lasting experience of the Narita Airport movement was not only geographically contained, confined to the "solidarity huts" ringing the airport then under construction; it was also repressed by the Japanese public sphere, which ceased to report or to discuss it, and at the same time made to seem antiquated by the multiple left ideological slogans which still decorated its banners. The invasive power of Aum's intervention could not be muffled or disguised in the same way. This is how *Somersault* summarizes the movement, on which its narrative is a more than implicit commentary:

> The founder of the group called Aum Shinrikyo was trained in India, and at the point where he first declared himself to be the Final Liberated One he had only 35 followers. By the next year this had grown to 1500. Later, a core leadership joined that committed several terrorist acts. The following year, the year their Mount Fuji headquarters was completed, they reached 3500 followers and became a religious corporation. Two years later they ran candidates in a national election, and even the one billion yen they spent in the effort didn't seem to faze them, so great were their financial resources by this time. Finally, they made contacts with sources in the collapsing Soviet Union and purchased some large helicopters, all the while developing the capability to produce 70 tons of sarin.
>
> So they started with 35 people and got to this point in less than ten years. If they'd really been able to carry out their Armageddon battle, the 4000 people killed and injured in the sarin attack on the subway would have been nothing in comparison.

Patron's Church of the New Man also preached the end of the world, the dystopian collapse of late capitalism in ecological disaster, mass starvation and internecine violence. Predictably, it also included a "radical faction" bent on Aum-style violence, a strategy to which *Somersault*, and Patron in his revised movement, propose an alternative.

Both movements, however, the real one as well as its fictive analogue, will necessarily startle Western observers by the presence in them of

highly educated scientists and technicians (as attested by Aum's formidable arsenal). We are accustomed to learning that Militia sympathizers
in the US study the internet for their technological recipes, but not that
such fringe groups include a significant population of trained doctors
and university researchers attracted to their aims and beliefs. Patron's
Church includes scientists (among them the "radical faction" which
killed Guide), along with many other kinds of social combination: a
feminist collective, for example (the "Quiet Women"), who meditate a
Jonestown-style solution at the end of the novel; a group of teenage or
pre-teen boys, the "Young Fireflies," ultimately led by Ikuo (but already
foreshadowed in Oe's first novel, *Nip the Buds Shoot the Kids*, published
in 1958, a Solzhenitsyn-like novel about so-called juvenile delinquents);
the significantly named Moosbrugger Committee (after the serial killer
in Musil's *Man without Qualities*, one of the most remarkable portraits
of psychopathic consciousness in all literature); groups of surviving
followers from the earlier Church, who had turned away from Patron
after his "somersault" and gone their own independent way; and, in the
foreground, various oddball, handicapped or misfit protagonists. This
multiplicity of social backgrounds serves, in my opinion, to displace
standard Western diagnoses of alienation and anomie with the more
positive appeal of collective practice and group participation; the novel,
in other words, is more interested in the construction of the group than
in psychosocial theories about its motivation.

That same ignorant liberal Western reader who has been such a
convenient straw man throughout this piece provides yet another
misreading for instructive denunciation: viz. the impression that Patron's
"somersault" is designed to avoid the pitfalls of tyranny and totalitarianism, the personality cult, and charismatic authority of all kinds; but I
don't think that such liberal or anarchist preoccupations with egalitarian
or radical democracy are much of an issue here. Both Patron and Guide
are flawed characters with seriously doubtful pasts (although neither
quite so horrendous as the 1976 anticipation of Patron in *The Pinch
Runner Memorandum*, where he is the very caricature of corrupt power,
pulling all possible strings behind all possible scenes, and worthy of
every imaginable political protest, including assassination). The novel
faithfully lays the facts before us, without debunking the mission or
vocation to which these not very successful people have suddenly found
themselves called: perhaps psychoanalysis has defused the critical
impact of such revelations (or perhaps the current regime of cynical

reason takes them for granted). At any rate, Patron's qualifications as a prospective savior seem to lie exclusively in his vaguely schizophrenic visions of the cosmos, to which I prefer the more science-fictional one of *The Pinch Runner Memorandum*:

> My personal speculation is this: Earth is part of a gigantic cosmic construct, and it is being pulled along, like on a conveyor belt, towards its proper place in that construct! And our Milky Way is the conveyor belt carrying Earth to its designated point on the blueprint; at the last stage of this journey, the Milky Way functions both as the launch pad, and as the energy source providing the correct vector and thrust for Earth's lift-off. This near-perfect spherical unit, humankind's abode for so long, will fit into place with a snap, and complete the preplanned cosmic construct! However, back in the preparatory stages, when all the units for assembling *were first being created*, a minute defect was found on the sphere called Earth. In the end, to correct that defect, beasts, birds, fish and insects, as well as humans—all infinitesimal on the cosmic scale—had to be introduced ... I think those nuclear explosions that have occurred—on deserts or coral atolls—are Earth's finishing touches, the polishing up or corrections of the defect— whatever you want to call it. The next targets are big cities, excluding of course the two already devastated. When Earth is a perfectly sized sphere meeting cosmic specs, it will blast off from the Milky Way launch pad, and snap into its proper place in the ultimate structure!

Patron's visions are perhaps little more than the necessary but not sufficient qualifications for group formation: Guide was always there to give them the appropriate content. Indeed, one has the sense that in this novel it would be enough for someone publicly to announce the intention to form a new group or sect for people to flock to it. But poor Fourier advertised in vain (he remained at home faithfully every day at noon, waiting for a Maecenas who never appeared); and Americans will be more familiar with the process whereby an existing group fragments into smaller and smaller ones, in never-ending schism and sectarianism.

But what was the "somersault" in the first place if not just such a schism in which (as with Mao or Lacan) former devotees are invited to "bombard the headquarters"? With this radical act, Patron moved to disarm his militant faction (intent on bringing about the long-prophesied end of the world by the nuclear destruction of Tokyo) by publicly renouncing his own doctrine and confessing that he and Guide were both charlatans who never had any authentic visions and whose prophecies were little more than an elaborate hoax. With this, the movement for the most part collapses, the radical scientists are rounded up by the police, and Patron and Guide "enter hell," where they remain for ten years until re-emerging (at the beginning of this novel) to found a new movement on the ashes of the old one. The somersault was thus a form of self-destruction all along, anticipating the suicide whereby Patron removes himself from his own regenerated movement at the novel's conclusion. But I would rather not characterize it as sacrificial, any more than I would like to lapse into culturalism by suggesting something quintessentially Japanese about the suicides which run through Oe's work and culminate in this one. Sacrifice is here seen as the momentum of history and of the repetitions of revolt, but we cannot understand that properly without coming (in conclusion) to the "power of place," the "power of the land."

I have already touched on the return, in almost all Oe's novels, to his native valley in Shikoku. This new regionalism is no surprise in the era of globalization, where the local tends to constitute an inevitable protest against urban standardization and the destruction of nature and the peasantry (or farmers) by agribusiness: it also tends to organize itself into an ideology and a compensatory fantasy rather than a political program. *The Silent Cry*, however, teaches us that we must grasp "the power of the land" as the recovery of history; and even Patron's last, sacrificial act is explicitly linked to a similar episode on the same spot a generation earlier (an incident celebrated in the as yet untranslated epic *Burning Green Tree* trilogy of 1993). But Oe's work contains many more historical levels than this: and *Somersault* merely adds a new post-Aum layer to a series of historical strata which reach all the way back to a pre-Meiji Shikoku peasant uprising, proceeding from there through the new imperial dispensation down to the village turmoil at the end of World War II. The 1960s looting of the new capitalist supermarket (in *The Silent Cry*) once again recapitulates the cycle of revolt that resonates through Oe's novels, now in mythical form (in *M/T and the Marvels of the Forest*, 1986) and now in the grim and bloody desperation of *The Silent Cry. Somersault*, in yet a new way, continues to make accessible to us "these madmen, who like kings, come one at a time."

12

History as a Family Novel

The first centennial of the Soviet revolution, indeed the fifth centennial of Luther's, risks distracting us from a literary earthquake which happened just fifty years ago and marked the cultural emergence of Latin America onto that new and larger stage we call globalization—itself a space that, ultimately, proves to be well beyond the separate categories of the cultural or the political, the economic or the national. I mean the publication of Gabriel García Márquez's *One Hundred Years of Solitude* in 1967, which not only unleashed a Latin American "boom" on an unsuspecting outside world but also introduced a host of distinct national literary publics to a new kind of novelizing. Influence is not a kind of copying, it is permission unexpectedly received to do things in new ways, to broach new content, to tell stories by way of forms you never knew you were allowed to use. What is it, then, that García Márquez did to the readers and writers of a still relatively conventional postwar world?

He began his productive life as a movie reviewer and a writer of movie scenarios nobody wanted to film. Is it so outrageous to consider *One Hundred Years of Solitude* as a mingling, an intertwining and shuffling together of failed movie scripts, so many fantastic episodes that could never be filmed and so must be consigned to Melquíades's Sanskrit manuscript (from which the novel has been "translated")? Or, perhaps,

"No Magic, No Metaphor: On *One Hundred Years of Solitude* by Gabriel García Márquez," *London Review of Books* 39(12), June 15, 2017.

it may be permitted to note the astonishing simultaneity of the beginning of his literary career with the so-called Bogotazo, the assassination
in 1948 of the great populist leader Jorge Eliécer Gaitán (and the beginning of the seventy-year long *Violencia* in Colombia), just as García
Márquez was having lunch down the street and, not much further away,
the twenty-one-year-old Fidel Castro was waiting in his hotel room for
an afternoon meeting with Gaitán about the youth conference he had
been sent to organize in Bogota that summer.

The solitude of the title should not at first be taken to mean the affective pathos it becomes at the end of the book: first and foremost, in the
novel's founding or refounding of the world itself, it signifies autonomy.
Macondo is a place away from the world, a new world with no relation
to an old one we never see. Its inhabitants are a family and a dynasty,
albeit accompanied by their fellows on a failed expedition which just
happened to come to rest at this point. The initial solitude of Macondo
is a purity and an innocence, a freedom from whatever worldly miseries
have been forgotten at this opening moment, this moment of a new
creation. If we insist on seeing this as a Latin American work, then we
can say that Macondo is unsullied by the Spanish conquest as also by
indigenous cultures: neither bureaucratic not archaic, neither colonial
nor Indian. But, if you insist on an allegorical dimension, then it also
signifies the uniqueness of Latin America itself in the global system,
and, at another level, the distinctness of Colombia from the rest of Latin
America, and even of García Márquez's native (coastal, Caribbean)
region from the rest of Colombia and the Andes. All these perspectives
mark the freshness of the novel's starting point, its utopian laboratory
experiment.

But, as we know, the form-problem of utopia is that of narrative itself:
what stories remain to be told if life is perfect and society is perfected?
Or, to turn the question inside out and rephrase the problem of content
in terms of novelistic form, what narrative paradigms survive to provide
the raw material for that destruction or deconstruction which is the
work of the novel itself as a kind of meta-genre or anti-genre? This was
the deeper truth of Lukács's pathbreaking *Theory of the Novel*. The
genres, the narrative stereotypes or paradigms, belong to older, traditional societies: the novel is then the anti-form proper to modernity
itself (which is to say, of capitalism and its cultural and epistemological
categories, its daily life). This means, as Schumpeter put it in an immortal phrase, that the novel is also a vehicle of creative destruction. Its

function, in some properly capitalist "cultural revolution," is the perpetual undoing of traditional narrative paradigms and their replacement,
not by new paradigms, but by something radically different. To use
Deleuzean language for a moment, modernity, capitalist modernity, is
the moment of passage from codes to axioms, from meaningful
sequences, or indeed, if you prefer, from meaning itself, to operational
categories, to functions and rules; or, in yet another language, this time
more historical and philosophical, it is the transition from metaphysics
to epistemologies and pragmatisms, we might even say from content to
form, if the use of this second term did not risk confusion.

The form-problem of the novel is that it isn't easy to find sequences to
replace those traditional narrative paradigms; the replacements inevitably tend to reform into new narrative paradigms and genres in their own
right (as witness the emergence of the *Bildungsroman* as a meaningful
narrative genre, based as it is on conceptions of life, career, pedagogy,
and spiritual or material development which are all essentially ideological and thereby historical). These newly created yet soon familiar and
old-fashioned paradigms must be destroyed in turn, in a perpetual
innovation of the form. Even then, it is rare enough for a novelist to
invent wholly original replacement paradigms (paradigm change is as
momentous an event in the history of narrative as elsewhere), let alone
to replace narrative itself, something modernism can be seen everywhere to strive for, unsuccessfully I might add: for what is here demanded
is a new kind of novelistic narrative which replaces narrative altogether,
something obviously a contradiction in terms.

The perpetual resurrection of newer narrative paradigms and subgenres out of the still warm ashes of their destruction is a process I
would attribute to commodification, as the primary law of our kind of
society: it isn't only objects that are subject to commodification, it is
anything capable of being named. Many are the philosophical examples
of this seemingly fatal process, and the philosophers who—like
Wittgenstein or Derrida in their very different ways—set out to free us
from stable, reified, conventional categories and concepts have ended up
as brand names in their own right. So it is with the creative destruction
of narrative paradigms: your "knight's move," your deviation or defamil-
iarization, ends up becoming just another "new paradigm" (unless, as in
postmodernity, it chooses the path of what used to be called irony,
namely the use of pastiche, the play with a repetition of dead forms at a
slight remove).

Such are, in my opinion, the consequences of Lukács's insights in the *Theory of the Novel*—insights which did not have the benefit, as we do, of generations of accumulated modernist experiments in this direction. Returning to *One Hundred Years of Solitude* with a view to demonstrating and validating what I have proposed, let's begin with its principal narrative paradigm, the family novel. It has been debated a good deal lately, the upshot being that it is no longer possible, if it ever was (and perhaps, indeed, in the West it never was). The *Bildungsroman* is not a family novel but a flight from the family; the picaresque novel turns on a hero who never had a family; and as for the novel of adultery, its relation to the family speaks for itself.

Someone, I think it was Jeffrey Eugenides, has claimed that the family novel today is only possible in the non-West, and I think there is a profound insight here. We may think of Mahfouz, for example, but I would argue that it is one of the greatest of all novels, the Chinese classic *Dream of the Red Chamber*, one should have in mind. After all, it is from China that we have the slogan that epitomizes the ideal of the family as the fundamental structure of life itself: five generations under one roof! The great manor or compound thereby includes everyone from the eighty-year-old patriarch to the newborn baby, including the intermediate generations of parents, grandparents and even great-grandparents, at the appropriate twenty-year generational intervals: patriarchy in its ideal or even Platonic form, you might say (overlooking the often malign role of the various matriarchs and uncles in the process). Folk wisdom through the ages has—along with many philosophers, beginning with Aristotle—assimilated the state itself to this patriarchal or dynastic family, and it is this deep ideological archetype that *One Hundred Years of Solitude* brings to the surface and makes visible. The extended family founded by José Arcadio Buendía is the "mythic" state, which will only later, in its days of prosperity, be infiltrated by personnel of the professional or official state, in the person of a "magistrate" and his police, who are at once assigned a minor and inconspicuous position, along with the other hangers-on of any city-state, such as merchants and booksellers. And, just as an extended family has its own service personnel—gardeners, electricians, pool maintenance specialists, carpenters and shamans— so also these appear and disappear punctually in the entourage of the Buendía family, of which they may be considered honorary members.

The family considered as its own city-state has, as the anthropologists teach us, one fundamental problem: it is endogamy, the centripetal tendency to absorb everything external into itself, risking the danger of inbreeding (the intermarriage of cousins and even incest), and all the consequences of triumphant identity, including repetition, boredom, and that fateful genetic mutation, the family pigtail. What is not the family, to be sure, is the other and the enemy. Still, the law of endogamy does have its own way of thinking inoffensive otherness; it has its own thought categories for acknowledging difference and relegating it to a subordinate and intermittent, indeed cyclical and harmlessly festive category. It calls such incursions from the outside *gypsies*. These bring, as the opening pages of *One Hundred Years of Solitude* so memorably show us, radical difference, in the form of trinkets and inventions: magnets, telescopes, compasses, and, finally, the only true miracle achieved by these swindlers and con-artists, the wonder that testifies to their authentically magical power: "Many years later," the immortal first sentence of the novel reads, "as he faced the firing squad, Colonel Aureliano Buendía was to remember that distant afternoon when his father took him to discover ice." Ice! An element with inconceivable properties, a new addition to the atomic chart. The existence of ice in the tropics is "memorable" because it is remembered, as Benjamin might have put it. It marks, in that opening sentence, the dialectical nature of reality itself: ice burns and freezes simultaneously.

So, it is the raw material of the "family novel" which will, in this opening section, be worked over for all its resources and all its possibilities of musical variation, structural permutation, metamorphosis, anecdotal invention, the production of endless episodes which are all, in fact, the same, structural equivalents in the myth of "magic realism," whose production and reproduction is itself what is then tautologically described as "mythic." Yet the identity of this seemingly irrepressible and irreversible proliferation of familial anecdotes is betrayed by the repetition of names down through the generations—so many Aurelianos (seventeen of them at one point), so many José Arcadios, even with some Remedios and Amarantas thrown in on the distaff side. Harold Bloom is right to complain of "a kind of aesthetic battle fatigue, since every page is crammed full of life beyond the capacity of any single reader to absorb."

I would add to this an embarrassment the literary commentator is loath to confess, namely the difficulty of keeping the characters' names separate from one another. This problem is rather different from students' complaints about impossible Russian patronymics and matronymics (and now Chinese or non-Western ones), and worthier of attention in its own right as a symptom of something historically more important: namely, the renewed significance of generations and the generational, in an overpopulated world henceforth doomed to synchrony rather than diachrony. I can remember when, in the development of that now respectable literary genre the detective story, a writer of some originality (Ross Macdonald) began to experiment with multi-generational crimes: you could never remember whether the murderer was the son, the father or the grandfather. So it is with García Márquez, but deliberately, in a spatial world beyond time itself ("No one has died here yet"; "the first person born in Macondo" and so on). Everything changes in Macondo, the state arrives, and then religion, and finally capitalism itself; the civil war pursues its course like a serpent biting its own tail; the town grows old and desolate, the rain of history begins and ends, the original protagonists begin to die off; and yet the narrative itself, in its rhizomatic strings, never grows extinct, its force remaining equal to itself until the fateful turn of its final pages. The dynasty is a family of names, and those names belong to the inexhaustible narrative impulse, and not to time or history.

So, as Vargas Llosa has observed, there lies behind the repetitive synchronicity of García Márquez's family structure a whole diachronous progression of the history of society itself, against whose shadowy, inexorable temporality we follow the structural permutations of an ever changing yet static family structure, whose generations ring the changes on its permanency, and whose variations reflect History only as symptoms, not as allegorical markers. It is this dual structure which permits a unique and unrepeatable solution to the form-problem of the historical novel and the family novel alike.

But the family narrative has one last trick up its sleeve, a final desperate move at its moment of saturation and exhaustion: the absolute structural inversion or negation of itself. For what defined the autonomy of Macondo and allowed its luxurious exfoliation of endogamies was its monadic isolation. Yet as in the ancient cosmologies of atomism, the very concept of the atom produces a multiplicity of other atoms, identical to itself; the notion of the One generates many Ones; the force of attraction that pulls everything external into the internal, that absorbs all difference into identity, now subverts and negates itself, and the repulsion into which attraction suddenly turns acquires a new name: war.

With war, *One Hundred Years of Solitude* acquires its second narrative paradigm, only apparently a mirror-image of the first, whose secondary, eccentric filial protagonist now suddenly becomes the hero. The war novel, to be sure, is itself a peculiar and problematic kind of narrative: if you like, it is one manifestation of a deeper structural necessity of all narrative, namely what the screenwriters' handbooks recommend as conflict, and what narrative theorists such as Lukács (and Hegel) see as the essence of the pre-eminence of tragedy as a form.

The Latin American version of the war novel, however, is a little more complicated than it looks. Colombia's institutionalized civil war, the Austrian-style alternation of its two parties, is at first memorialized in Aureliano's identification with the Liberals, but is then transformed by his repudiation of both parties in the adoption of guerrilla warfare and generalized social "banditry." Meanwhile, in the country of Bolívar, this atomization is modified by a truly Bolívarian pan-Americanism (of the type aspired to by both recent Latin American revolutions, the Cuban and the Venezuelan), which is itself but a figure of that "world revolution" onto which the original Soviet revolution had hoped to open. The ambiguity is not only that of South America as a distinct geographical and ethnic "autonomous zone" in a world history of which it nonetheless wishes to be a central part; but also of the imbrication of these various autonomies—from village to nation-state to region—between which the representation freely moves. We remember that the mythic founder, José Arcadio, set out from the Old World "in search of an outlet to the sea" (discouraged by his discovery of a primal swamp, he settled on the halfway position of Macondo). The space of independence (and solitude) is thus something like the attempt to become an island. The sea here figures that ultimate boundary and end of the world otherwise socially and economically embodied for Latin America by the US. (It is true that the other great regional autonomous zone in which García Márquez's Cartagena participates is the Caribbean, but it scarcely has the importance in *One Hundred Years of Solitude* that the regional centrality of the Cuban revolution had in García Márquez's own life.)

This would be the moment to speak about politics, and of *One Hundred Years of Solitude* as a political novel, for, despite Colombia's eternal civil war, the enemy is always the US, as Porfirio Díaz's inexhaustible sigh reminds us: "Alas, poor Mexico, so far from God and so close to the United States!" But these gringos, a strange and alien race, whose very approach tenses the muscles and always arouses suspicion, are here personally reduced to the self-effacing Mr. Brown then replaced by the faceless banana company, which brings with it capitalism, modernity, union-busting, bloody repression and an inevitable relocation (an uncanny anticipation of the US's own plague of factory expatriation decades later). It also brings the desolation of eight years of rain: a world of mud, the worst possible dialectical synthesis of flood and drought. But what is truly and artfully political about this sequence isn't just its mythic symbolism, or even the way in which the combined form-problems of the representation of villains, foreigners, and collective actors are skillfully circumnavigated, but, rather, the redeployment of García Márquez's supreme theme, which is not memory but forgetting. The plague of insomnia (and its resultant amnesia) has long since been surmounted; but a specific—one wants to say, a surgical—amnesia is here revived: no one but José Arcadio Segundo can remember the massacre of the workers. It has successfully, magically and yet naturally been eradicated from the collective memory in that archetypal repression which allows all of us to survive history's immemorial nightmares, to live on happily despite "the slaughterhouse of history" (Hegel). This is the realism—yes, even the political realism—of magic realism.

There is, however, something peculiarly sterile and skeletal in this context about the war paradigm as such: warfare cannot provide the anecdotal richness of the family paradigm, particularly when it is reduced, as in this novel, to the stark reciprocity of enemy sides. What emerges isn't so much a war novel as a play of executions, beginning with that famous first sentence ("as he faced the firing squad"), and a set of surprise reversals (Aureliano will not be executed—twice over—but his brother José Arcadio will be, along with various alter egos). Here, at this temporal rather than geographical "end of the world," what the execution promises is a momentary halt in that breathless continuity of filled time and perpetual narrativity which Bloom deplored, thereby making room for a new kind of event altogether: namely, memory ("Colonel Aureliano Buendía was to remember"). The representation of memory as an event transforms this temporality altogether: utterly unlike the familiar Proustian version, it comes as a thunderbolt in its own right. Nostalgia is anecdotal; memory here is no resurrection of the past, in this filled space of unremitting sentences, of something like a Churrigueresque narrativity. There can be no past in that traditional sense, nor any real present either (what there is, as readers of the novel already know, is a manuscript, to which we will come in a moment).

But the structural reversals that make up the eventfulness of the novel do draw their most intense off/on energies from the war material, and this very precisely in the characterology of Aureliano (who for this reason most often seems to be the novel's protagonist, even though it has no protagonist except for the family itself and the space of the named collectivity). García Márquez is behaviorist in the sense that the characters have no psychologies, depth or otherwise; without being allegorical, exactly, they are all obsessives, possessed and defined by their own specific, all-encompassing passions. Secondary characters are marked by mere functions (plot or professional); but when the protagonists withdraw from their obsessions, it is into the *néant* of closed rooms and shuttered houses, as with Rebeca, who persists forgotten into her old age in a kind of narrative sequestration, where the distraction of the novelist (or better still the impersonal chronicler) is rigorously the same as the forgetfulness of society (and of the family) as such; without their anecdotal captivations, they do not simply become normal, they disappear.

Or else their passions suddenly mutate into new missions, new demonic possessions: this is what is paradigmatic about Aureliano, who moves from the fascination of ice in childhood, through the alchemy of his year-long handicraft (in his father's laboratory) of little golden fish-trinkets, to the political vocation of war and rebellion, which seizes him as soon as Macondo threatens to be absorbed into the institutional reification of a state, and falls away again like a deconversion and a fit of dejection at the end of the age of revolutions, at which moment he reverts to his handicraft and his closed quarters: in Macondo only cease-less activity sustains life.

In Macondo only the specific and the singular exist: the great abstract schemas of dynasty and war can only preside over minute and empiri-cally identified activities. It is clearly in some unique, not to say impos-sible coordination of these narrative levels that the specificity of García Márquez's narrative solution lies: not in the unification of episodic poetic inventions within the continuity of a single bizarre character's life (as in the parallel generic line of the mega-novels of Grass and Rushdie), but, rather, in a unique structural constellation, perhaps the last thing to call which is "magical realism." Indeed, let's stop using this generic term for everything unconventional and consign it to the bin in which we keep such worn-out epithets as "surrealistic" and "Kafkaesque." Alejo Carpentier's original version is that the real itself is a marvel (the "real

maravilloso"), and that Latin America is in its paradigmatic uneven-
ness—in which computers coexist with the most archaic forms of peasant culture and on up, through all the stages of the historical modes of
production—itself a wonder to behold. But this can only be observed
and told absolutely deadpan, and with the unsurprising undeniability of
a simple empirical fact. García Márquez's "method," he tells us, must be
"to tell the story . . . in an imperturbable tone, with infallible serenity,
even if the whole world resists, without for one instant calling into doubt
what you are saying and avoiding the frivolous and the truculent
alike . . . [this is] what the old ones knew, that in literature there is nothing more convincing than your own conviction." So nothing remarkable, nothing miraculous, about the fact that Mauricio Babilonia, a man
who is all love, pure love, should constantly be surrounded by a swarm
of yellow butterflies ("accompanied by a stupendous odour of grease");
nothing tragic about the fact that he should be shot like a dog by someone whose plans he hampers; nothing magical about the fact that a
priest disturbed by the utter absence of God or religion in Macondo
should seek to call its citizens to decency and piety by levitating a foot
above the ground (after fortifying himself with a cup of hot chocolate);
or that Remedios the Beauty should rise into heaven like a windy tangle
of backyard sheets. No magic, no metaphor: just a bit of grit caught in
transcendence, a materialist sublime, drying the wash or changing the
oil caught in an angelic perspective, celestial grime, the Platonic Idea of
Socrates' dirty toenails. The storyteller must relate these things with all
the ontological coolness of Hegel confronting the Alps: "Es ist so" (and
even then, without the philosopher's ontological emphasis).

Not "magic," then, but something else must be evoked to account for
the undeniable singularity of García Márquez's narrative invention and
the form that allows it to come into being. I think it is his uncanny, rapt
concentration on his immediate narrative object, which isn't without
resemblance to Aureliano's awakening to the world "with his eyes open":

> As they were cutting the umbilical cord, he moved his head from side
> to side, taking in the things in the room and examining the faces of
> the people with a fearless curiosity. Then, indifferent to those who
> came close to look at him, he kept his attention concentrated on the
> palm roof, which looked as if it were about to collapse under the
> tremendous pressure of the rain.

Later on, "adolescence . . . had restored the intense expression that he had had in his eyes when he was born. He concentrated so much on his experiments in silverwork that he scarcely left the laboratory to eat." It is interesting, but not particularly relevant for our purposes, that, like his own sequestered characters, García Márquez himself never once left his house during the writing of *One Hundred Years of Solitude*; what is essential for grasping the peculiarities of the novel is this notion of concentration itself which, far more than vague ideas of the magical or the "maravilloso," give us the key to its episodic narrative.

We might draw back and sketch a long development between Aristotelian logic and Freudian free association, passing through the eighteenth-century psychology of associationism and culminating in Surrealism, on the one hand, and Jakobsonian structuralism (metaphor/metonymy), on the other. In all these frameworks, what matters is temporal succession and the movement from one topic to another, as when Aureliano's nascent vision moves from object to object, or as the emplacement of the objects of this or that "memory theatre" remind the speaker of the order of his remarks. I want to suggest that, far from the baroque disorder and excess of that "magic realism" with which he is so often taxed, the movement of García Márquez's paragraphs and the unfolding contents of his chapters are to be ascribed to a rigorous narrative logic, characterized precisely in terms of a peculiar "concentration," which begins with the positing of a specific topic or object.

From a relatively arbitrary starting point—the gypsies and their peculiar mechanical toys or playthings, the wife's family, the construction of a new house (to mention just the openings of the first three chapters)—an association of events, characters, objects, is followed with all the rigor of Freudian free association, which isn't free at all but, in practice, demands the utmost discipline. That discipline demands exclusion rather than the epic inclusion so often ascribed to García Márquez's narrative. What does not arise in the specific line of associated topics must rigorously be omitted; and the narrative line must lead us wherever it goes (from the curse of the pigtail to the slander of Prudencio Aguilar, his killing, the haunting by his ghost, and as a consequence the attempted abandonment of the haunted house, the exploration of the region, the founding of Macondo, its peopling by their children, the organ which is far from being a pigtail, etc.). Each of these follows rigorously on its predecessor, whatever shape the series takes under its own momentum, but it is not the form of the narrative sequence but, rather, the quality of its transitions as they emerge from García Márquez's rapt concentration on the logic of his material, as well as the sequence of topics that emerge from that undistracted stare, from which neither abstraction nor convention can move him. This is a narrative logic which is somehow beyond subject and object alike: it does not emerge from the unconscious of some "omniscient narrator"; nor does it follow the habitual logic of daily life. It would be tempting to say that it is embedded in the raw material of that Latin America Carpentier characterized as "maravilloso" (owing, I believe, to the coexistence of so many layers of history, so many discontinuous modes of production). Anyway, it isn't really appropriate to credit some exceptional storytelling genius to a fictive entity called García Márquez's "imagination." Rather, it is an equally indescribable or unformulatable intensity of concentration which produces the successive materials of each chapter, which then, in their accumulation, result in the appearance of unforeseeable loops and repetitions, "themes" (to name another literary-critical fiction), finally exhausting their momentum and beginning to reproduce themselves in static numerical patterns.

This concentration, however, is the quality we consume in our unique reading, and which has no real equivalent in *The Tin Drum*, say, or *Gravity's Rainbow*, or *Midnight's Children*, even though their momentum is analogous, as are the associations from which their episodes are constructed. We have no ready-made literary-technical terms with which to approach the strange mode of active contemplation that lies at the heart of this compositional process (and of reading too). It would be philosophical and pedantic to hearken back to the notorious Fichtean formula—"the identical subject-object"—which has had its day in fields beyond the aesthetic; but there is a sense in which it remains the most satisfactory characterization, and incites us to an essentially negative approach to these narrative strings. No, there is no point-of-view here, no implied narrator (or reader either). There is no stream of consciousness, or style indirect libre. There is no initial order, challenged and ultimately restored. No digressions either; the string pursues its own internal logic without distraction and without realism or fantasy. The great images—ghosts who grow old and die, the lover emanating yellow butterflies—are neither symbols nor metaphors, but simply designate the string itself, in its inexorable temporal progression and its stubborn repudiation of any distinction between the subjective and the objective, the inner feeling and the external world. The starting points alone are arbitrary, but they are given in the family itself, less a genre or a subject matter than a network of points, any of which can serve until the associations begin to peter out and are broken off. The dialectic of quantity into quality leaves its mark as the episodes pile up and begin to burden what used to be new references with layers of memory. And, indeed, this is what, for want of a better word or concept, García Márquez calls the narrative logic of his strings: "memory," but memory of a strange and unsubjective kind, a memory within the things themselves of their future possibilities, threatened only by that contagious epidemic of insomnia that threatens to wipe out not only the events but the very meaning of the words themselves.

It would be philistinism of the most unreceptive and boring kind to pronounce the word "imagination" here, as though García Márquez were a real person and not (as Kant thought of "genius" itself) simply the vehicle of a physiological anomaly, like his own characters, the bearer of that weird and inexplicable gift we have called concentration, the inability to be distracted by what is not implicit in the narrative sequence in question. Our happy accident as well as readers, if we are able in much the same way to lose ourselves in that precisely situated oblivion in which everything follows logically and nothing is strange or "magical," a hyperconscious yet unreflexive attention in which we are unable to distinguish ourselves from the writer, in which we share in that strange moment of absolute emergence which is neither creation nor imagination: participation rather than contemplation, at least for a time. It is a defining characteristic of the spell of the marvelous that we are unaware of our own bewitchment.

Still, certain features of the work of art in general offer privileged access to what the Frankfurt School used to call their truth-content; among these, temporality has always played a significant role in the more productive analyses of the novel as a form. Just as Le Corbusier described the dwelling as a "machine for living," so the novel has always been a machine for living a certain kind of temporality; and in the multiple differentiations of global or postmodern capitalism, we may expect a far greater variety of these temporal machines than there were in the transitional period we call literary modernism (whose experimental temporalities, paradoxically, seemed initially on the face of it far more varied and incomparable).

The novel is a kind of animal, and just as we speculate about the way in which a dog experiences time, or a tortoise, or a hawk (both in its limits and its possibilities, and granted that we assess these in terms of our own human temporal experiences), so also each distinctive novel lives and breathes a kind of phenomenological time behind which non-temporal structures can sometimes be glimpsed. This is why, for example, I have insisted on grasping what is here called the act of memory as a punctual experience, an event that interrupts the anecdotal yet irre-versible flow of narrative sentences and is at once reabsorbed into them as yet another narrative event. Thus, what seems as if it might be the pause and distance of a moment of self-consciousness turns out to be another instance of unreflexive consciousness, that unremitting atten-tion to the world which is itself shaped and tensed by a contradictory ontology in which everything has happened already at the same time that it is happening afresh in a present in which death scarcely exists, although time and aging do. Repetition has become a popular topic in contemporary theory, but it is important to insist on the varieties of repetition of which this temporal one—past and present all at once—is a unique type.

This particular temporal structure then intersects with another, in which fundamental historical breaks are registered: the founding of Macondo is one such "break," but it is reabsorbed owing to the tendency of mythic events to loop back into themselves. The arrival of the banana company, which registers the traumatic event of US economic coloniza-tion, is assimilated into the continuity of everyday life in Macondo as its agents and actors become part of the secondary personnel of Macondo; and then wiped away altogether by the misery of the years of rain which renders its presence invisible. Here too then, temporality as a form-problem reflects that more general dilemma I have characterized as endogamy, in which the autonomy of the collective and its internal events must somehow find a way of defusing external shocks and assim-ilating them into its fabric, whether by marriage, warfare or, in this case, by a naturalization that turns the socio-economic into acts of god or forces of nature. Historical temporality becomes natural history, albeit of a miraculous kind; while its recipients retain the option of withdraw-ing into the real interior space of crumbling buildings.

Such withdrawals, the long-awaited deaths of the principal protago-nists, indeed the very indices of capitalist modernity itself in the impe-rialist penetration by the banana company of Macondo's ever more threatened autonomy, and with all this the gradual exhaustion of the dual plots or narrative paradigms (the cyclical repetition of names; the gradual enlargement and effacement of military rivalries into ideological conflict and the dialectic of guerrilla resistance and "total war"): all of this betokens increasing impatience with the paradigms whose structural originalities have been exhausted and which, after their two-part development, give way to the interminable repetition of tale-spinning and the piling up of anecdote on fresh anecdote. (Where does the break take place? This is the historian's unnamed vice, the hidden jouissance of periodization: a deduction of the beginning of the end times, of "when it happened," or in other words when it all stopped—the opposite of the Freudian primal scene. I would personally select the moment in which "Colonel Gerineldo Márquez was the first to perceive the emptiness of the war," but I leave it to others to identify their own secret "break.")

This kind of memory-event is utterly different from what happens in the great predecessor, Faulkner's *Absalom, Absalom!*

> Once there was—Do you mark how the wisteria, sun-impacted on this wall here, distills and penetrates this room as though (light-unimpeded) by secret and attritive progress from mote to mote of obscurity's myriad components? That is the substance of remembering—sense, sight, smell: the muscles with which we see and hear and feel—not mind, not thought: there is no such thing as memory: the brain recalls just what the muscles grope for: no more, no less: and its resultant sum is usually incorrect and false and worthy only of the name of dream.

Faulknerian memory is profoundly sensory, in the tradition of Baudelaire—the odor that brings a whole moment of the past back with it. Despite its assignment to a poetic avant-garde, this is the mainstream Western ideological conception of time and the body, where that of García Márquez is on the contrary a reversion to chronicle time, the time of miracles and curiosity, of heightened attention, of the memorable, the exceptional event (Benjamin's storyteller)—what generally goes down in collective or folk memory, even though here it is the "folk memory" of an individual character. And the other way round: for is not all of Faulkner somehow transmitted via memory as such, so that events, soaked in it, are no longer to be distinguished as present or past, but only conveyed by the interminable murmur of the remembering voice?

No such voice in García Márquez: the chronicle records but does not evoke, does not fascinate and immobilize us, rapt, in the web of a personal style; and the absence of style is also in general the mark of the postmodern.

"The history of the family was a machine with unavoidable repetitions," Pilar Ternera says towards the end of the novel, "a turning wheel that would have gone on spilling into eternity were it not for the progressive and irremediable wearing of the axle." We can recognize the onset of this final section by the emergence of sheer quantity as its organizing principle, and above all the apotheosis of those dualisms dear to structuralism in general, in which content gives way to pattern and empty formal proliferation; but also, as I have already hinted, by the signs of modernity that begin to show up in the village like so many unwanted strangers who must somehow be accommodated.

The denunciation of imperialism would scarcely be a novelty for Latin American literature: the genre of the "great dictator novel" would be another version (García Márquez himself took it up in his next book, *The Autumn of the Patriarch*)—the portrait of the political monster who is alone powerful enough to resist the Americans. Here, however, the analysis is more subtle: only the rain can force the banana company out of the country, but the cure leaves its own insuperable desolation behind it—the very epitome of "dependency theory."

The ways in which this penetration of "Western modernity" is registered in temporality itself are more problematic, for it brings with it what we now call "daily life" but what the novel's title has already identified as "miserable solitude," the absence of the miraculous event, whose boredom must now be filled by mindless rote work: in the case of Amaranta, sewing, whose "very concentration gave her the calmness that she needed to accept the idea of frustration. It was then that she understood the vicious circle of Colonel Aureliano Buendía's little gold fishes." But this introduction of "understanding" into the sheer activity of the chronicle is already a contamination, and points towards other kinds of narrative discourse the novel means to avoid. So, also, the notion of "truth," which appears at the very moment when José Arcadio Segundo finds that the memory of the workers' massacre has been, in Orwellian manner, effaced from collective memory. Truth then becomes the negative in a quasi-Hegelian sense, not the interminable listing of events of the chronicle, but rather the re-establishment of old events in the place of their distortion or omission. But this is also another kind of discourse, another kind of narrative, from the one we have been reading.

This is the twin face of the exhaustion and onset of readerly boredom to which Harold Bloom gave voice: for here the chronicle mode has fallen into deterioration, and the novel itself has begun to lose its reason for being, threatened by psychology on the one hand and depth analysis on the other. The chronicle mode was itself a kind of archaic utopia, but of a more subtle and effective kind than in those outright indigenista novels of which Vargas Llosa so bitterly complained. The chronicle took us back to an older kind of time and place, an older mode of origin. Now suddenly for the first time we begin to grasp the novel as itself a duality, the existence, alongside García Márquez's impersonal yet contemporary narrative, of the old parchments in Sanskrit in which Melquíades composed the same history in another, more authentic form. And, at this point, *One Hundred Years of Solitude* paradoxically becomes a trendy text espousing all the ideological furor of 1960s "écriture"; for in an unexpected final flourish, a concluding originality arises to match that of the novel's beginning, and when "real life" finally coincides with the confabulation of the parchments everything ends up in a book, just as Mallarmé had predicted, and the novel swirls away in a gust of dead leaves, just as Macondo is wiped out by the wind.

13

The Religions of Dystopia

Who will recount the pleasures of dystopia? The pity and fear of trag-edy—pity for the other, fear for myself—does not seem very appropriate to a form which is collective, and in which spectator and tragic protago-nist are in some sense one and the same. For the most part, dystopia has been a vehicle for political statements of some kind: sermons against overpopulation, big corporations, totalitarianism, consumerism, patri-archy, not to speak of money itself. Not coincidentally, it has also been the one science-fictional sub-genre in which more purely "literary" writers have felt free to indulge: Huxley, Orwell, even the Margaret Atwood of *The Handmaid's Tale*. And, not unpredictably, the results of these efforts have been as amateurish as analogous experiments in the realm of the detective or crime story (from Dostoevsky to Nabokov, if you like), but including a message or thesis.[1] So-called mass cultural genres, in other words, have rules and standards as rigorous and profes-sional as the more noble forms.

But Atwood can now be considered to be a science-fiction writer, I'm happy to say, and this is not meant to disparage. In any case, it might be

"Then You Are Them: On *The Year of the Flood* by Margaret Atwood," *London Review of Books* 31(17), September 10, 2009.

1 The mark of the amateur here is topicality, among other things: in *Flood*, the reference to "the Wall they're building to keep the Tex refugees out", or the list of saints' names—"Saint E. F. Schumacher, Saint Jane Jacobs . . . Saint Stephen Jay Gould of the Jurassic Shales," etc. Perhaps Atwood's SF apprenticeship comes with *The Blind Assassin* (2000).

argued (but not here), that, at this moment of time, all fiction approaches science fiction, as the future, the various futures, begin to dissolve into ever more porous actuality: and the end of the world seems to approach more rapidly than the unified world market itself.

Oryx and Crake was a brilliant tour de force, in which two dystopias and a utopia were ingeniously intertwined. What may now surprise us is that Atwood has decided to go on living in that universe, which, however, did not have a to-be-continued sign attached to it. The wonderful cliff-hanger of the earlier novel is thereby somewhat spoiled (we need a technical term for this inverted *in medias res*, as though *Robinson Crusoe* broke off with the footprint). But perhaps we do not pick the world, which, on the contrary, picks us. Or perhaps, as the protagonists of *Oryx* were males, it seemed only fair to write a sequel for the female characters. *The Year of the Flood* is neither sequel nor prequel, but, rather, both at once, in what might better be called a parallel narrative, where the godlike figures of the first book (the figures who became gods, let us rather say) are reduced to secondary roles and walk-on parts. Religion is still very much in question in the new novel, but it is a different kind of religion, as we shall see.

All the characters and their stories are thereby diminished, but this is no weakness: it results from an enlargement of narrative perspectives to include the deep space of institutions and collectivities, and a rather different kind of historicity from that projected by the individual fable of the first version. Here, we are more clearly able to perceive the break-down of modern capitalist society into the various private contractors to whom social needs are outsourced, and behind them the enormous corporations that have replaced all the traditional forms of government. ("The Compounds were where the Corps people lived—all those scientists and business people Adam One said were destroying old Species and making new ones and ruining the world.") Here, also, we glimpse the forms of resistance aroused by the devolution in which what we still consider social and technological progress consists—they range from the survival of the most sadistic to the banding together of small groups and the formation of new religions or, more ominously, to what is called "bioform resistance." Food and sex are obviously the most immediate needs: they are supplied by SecretBurgers, into which all available protein matter is dumped, and AnooYoo spas, accompanied by hosts of dreary fly-by-night dollar stores, whose multiplicity scarcely arouses the free-market exhilaration of the cyberpunk visions of the world to come. A faceless power center is embodied in the CorpSeCorps, which, as in medieval society (and quite unlike Orwell's universal surveillance), keeps tabs only on what it needs to know and does not hesitate to organize para-political goon squads when necessary; anything more destructively criminal can then be dealt with in the Painball facilities, in which teams of convicts are organized to kill each other off. The well-being of the elite is assured by the HelthWyzer institutes, of which the reader has already heard something in *Oryx*, along with various scientific think-tanks that have, among other things, devised new species to supply human replacement organs, such as the memorable pigoons. *Oryx* gave us the view of this system from the inside and as it were from above, even though there really does seem to be no oligarchic ruling elite nor any totalitarian party or dictatorship on the old-fashioned modernist dystopian model; *The Year of the Flood* gives us the view from below—always, as we well know, the most reliable vantage point from which to gauge and map a society.

A second dystopia then sets in with the Flood—the Waterless Flood, as this lethal plague is characterized in the sequel. Readers of *Oryx* know that it is man-made, but like the original, it fulfils its purpose, namely to cleanse the world of the toxic garbage of human society, leaving the few survivors (mostly people trapped in inaccessible and thereby uncontaminated spaces) to start something new. It is an interesting theoretical question whether to distinguish this generic version—Apocalypse or the end-of-the-world story, Mary Shelley's *The Last Man* and the post-nuclear landscapes—from the densely inhabited dystopias of various kinds of which these books have also given us a sample. My current feeling is that the post-catastrophe situation, in reality, constitutes the preparation for the emergence of Utopia itself, which, to be sure, in Atwood's new instalment, we reach only by anticipation (of which I will speak in a moment). The originality of *Oryx* was to have offered the glimpse of its creation: literally, out of the test tube of the mad scientist who, from sheer loathing of human nature as it currently is, invents a tribe of noble savages perfect in every way (the "made-on-purpose people" as someone calls them), physically, biologically, in their social relationships as well as in their existential experience—save that, inasmuch as they have few enough problems to solve, their conceptual equipment has not had to develop commensurately. We do not have to be so skeptical and disabused of the Rousseau revival inaugurated by Lévi-Strauss and so many others in the 1950s and 1960s to find this tribal vision altogether ironic. Its future must remain as open a question as that of the survivors themselves, and it is another interesting formal and generic question whether

Utopia (or dystopia either, for that matter) could have any ending or closure, in the sense of the old Aristotelian narrative—any closure save that of absolute destruction and death, that is.

Perhaps it will also be retorted that our noble savages here do have another defect, a most significant one indeed: they believe in God; or, rather, they believe in a god, the eponymous Crake himself, their maker (as well as their lawgiver), who now enjoys the authority of Lycurgus, namely of the dead. We're not supposed, at least since Freud, to believe that this kind of confidence in a Big Other is a satisfactory foundation for either collective or individual existence. But Atwood has another kind of religion up her sleeve, and it is perhaps the most stimulating new feature of *The Year of the Flood.*

Religion is, of course, right now a hot theoretical topic, what with all kinds of violent postmodern fundamentalisms and even the left revival of St. Paul as a theorist of cultural revolution; but it is a tricky topic as well, since even to call it "religion" is to reify it and confirm its status as a non-secular phenomenon. The concept is thereby booby-trapped, and you have implicitly acknowledged "belief" in the throes of an effort to deny such a thing in the first place. But if you call it something else, ideology, say, or ritual, or existential illusion, you at once lose its curious specificity. Meanwhile, any emphasis on the invention of specific religions by individuals, the necessarily "made-on-purpose" features of these pretentiously redefined "belief systems," also at once reduces them to something like home-made furniture and demands a supplement in the form of deep time, ancient cultural custom, or revelation itself—so that the representation of a new religion like that, here, of Atwood's Gardeners, is itself a delicate matter.

And so it is a pleasure to report that this one, with its prophets, its sermons, its taboos, and even its Hymnbook, wears astonishingly well: ecological, communitarian, cunningly organized in decentralized units, each with its "Ararat" of supplies stashed away against the inevitable Waterless Flood of plagues to come and police repression as well, and despite its regressive primitivism utilizing computerized information and informers strategically planted among the elites. Functional hierarchy (the Adams and the Eves) is here made palatable by cooperative egalitarianism and a serene acceptance of the frailties of human nature. Even Adam One, whose sermons are a model of biopolitical saintliness, is also admirably Machiavellian in the tactics of group survival. Perhaps the Hymnbook deserves independent publication:

The Creatures need no lesson books,
For God instructs their Minds and Souls:
The sunlight hums to every Bee,
The moist clay whispers to the Mole.

Regressive it all is, however (and it is always helpful to wonder what politics today could possibly be otherwise). Here for example is this Utopia's dystopian vision of history:

According to Adam One, the Fall of Man was multidimensional. The ancestral primates fell out of the trees; then they fell from vegetarianism into meat-eating. Then they fell from instinct into reason, and thus into technology; from simple signals into complex grammar, and thus into humanity; from firelessness into fire, and thence into weaponry; and from seasonal mating into an incessant sexual twitching. Then they fell from a joyous life in the moment into the anxious contemplation of the vanished past and the distant future.
The Fall was ongoing, but its trajectory led ever downward.

Is this religion not itself ideology?
And is this book not the expression of an ideological doctrine? In a post-feminist age, whose great writers (Ursula Le Guin, Toni Morrison, Christa Wolf) are not women writers but just writers, Atwood does not easily fit some category labelled feminist: *The Robber Bride*, whose male figures are mostly not even violent but simply inept (the masculine "masquerade," said Lacan, borrowing the concept from Helene Deutsch and adapting it to "masculinity" and machismo, is mostly ridiculous), positions the very center of evil in woman. Is Atwood then some kind of ecologist? But Nature, in her work, goes all the way back to her 1972 novel *Surfacing*, with its terrifying Deleuzean *devenir-animal*. Yet there is a category into which she squarely fits and without which she cannot fully be understood, a category of which at least 300 million English-speakers generally need to be reminded: she is a Canadian, and no little of her imaginative power comes from her privileged position above the border of the lower 48. The Fall is not properly grasped unless it is understood to be a fall into Americanism, as the magnificent rant from *Surfacing* reminds us:

It doesn't matter what country they're from, my head said, they're still Americans, they're what's in store for us, what we are turning into.

They spread themselves like a virus, they get into the brain and take over the cells and the cells change from inside and the ones that have the disease can't tell the difference. Like the Late Show sci-fi movies, creatures from outer space, body snatchers injecting themselves into you, dispossessing your brain, their eyes blank eggshells behind the dark glasses. If you look like them and talk like them and think like them then you are them.

When the narrator was little, the idea of evil was Hitler; but in the world of grown-up violence and Nature, a more sickening metaphysics begins to develop: "The trouble some people have being German, I thought, I have being human ... then I realised it wasn't the men I hated, it was the Americans, the human beings, men and women both." It is a disease you can observe: "Second hand American was spreading over him in patches, like mange or lichen. He was infested, garbled, and I couldn't help him: it would take such time to heal, unearth him, scrape down to where he was true." But "American" is also technology, mechanization, mass production: "The machine is gradual, it takes a little of you at a time, it leaves the shell. It was all right as long as they stuck to dead things, the dead can defend themselves, to be half dead is worse. They did it to each other also, without knowing."

This then is the world of Atwood's dystopia, for which, in this global near future, the term American is no longer necessary. Its colors have a loathsome pastel quality, like drugstores; its bunny suits and fluffy fabrics reflect the bad taste of infantile mass production; the bloody physical violence is that of cartoons rather than Hitler. If there is aesthetic pleasure here, it is that of a syrupy nausea that repeats on you; so that the end of the world has some of the cleansing, bracing effect of sand and waste landscape, of the seashore. But it is still better to think of it in Adam One's reassuring words:

What a cause for rejoicing is this rearranged world in which we find ourselves! True, there is a certain—let us not say *disappointment*. The debris left by the Waterless Flood, like that left by any receding flood, is not attractive. It will take time for our longed-for Eden to appear, my Friends.

But how privileged we are to witness these first precious moments of Rebirth!

14

Fear and Loathing in Globalization

Has the author of *Neuromancer* really "changed his style"? Has he even "stopped" writing science fiction, as some old-fashioned critics have put it, thinking thereby to pay him a compliment? Maybe, on the contrary, he is moving closer to the "cyberpunk" with which he is often associated, but which seems more characteristically developed in the work of his sometime collaborator Bruce Sterling. In any case, the representational apparatus of science fiction, having gone through innumerable generations of technological development and well-nigh viral mutation since the onset of that movement, is sending back more reliable information about the contemporary world than an exhausted realism (or an exhausted modernism either).

William Gibson, now the author of *Pattern Recognition*, has certainly more often illustrated that other coinage, "cyberspace," and its inner network of global communication and information, than the object world of late commodification through which the latest novel carefully gropes its way.[1] To be sure, Sterling celebrated the hackers, the heroic pirates of cyberspace, but without Gibson's tragic intensity—portraying them as the oddballs and marginals of the new frontiers to come. The rush and exhilaration of his books, rather alien to the cooler Gibson, has

---

"Fear and Loathing in *Globalization: On Pattern Recognition* by William Gibson," *New Left Review* 23, September/October 2003.

1   William Gibson, *Pattern Recognition* (New York: Putnam, 2003).

always seemed to me to derive as much from global entrepreneurship, and the excitement of the money to be made, as from paranoia.

But that excitement also expresses the truth of emergent globalization, and Sterling deserves more than a mere paragraph or parenthesis here. The novels are often episodic, but stories like those collected in *A Good Old-Fashioned Future* are authentic artifacts of postmodernity and little masterpieces in their own right, offering a Cook's tour of the new global way-stations and the piquant dissonances between picturesque travelers and the future cities they suddenly find themselves in. Tokyo, to be sure (Tokyo now and forever!), in which a Japanese-American federal prosecutor from Providence, Rhode Island, finds herself entangled in a conspiracy waged through ceramic cats; but also the California of misfit inventors, in which a new process for manufacturing artificial (and aerial) jellyfish threatens to convert all the oil left in the ground in Texas into so much worthless *Urschleim*. Finland then offers an unsurprisingly happy hunting ground for meetings between '60s-style terrorists and the former KGB, along with ruthless young ecological nationalists, veteran industrial spies, and an aged Finnish writer of children's books immensely popular in Japan.[2]

Meanwhile, Bollywood actors in flight from the Indian tax system have the luck to happen on the biggest mass grave in history, in Bolton, in an England decimated by the plague and now good only for making cheap movies on location; while, in Germany, in Düsseldorf, the new institution of the *Wende* is explored, in which—observed by a "spex" salesman from Chattanooga—all the destructive collective movements of the time, from football hooligans to anti-modern moral majorities, periodically coincide in a ritual "turbulence." Indeed, it is Chattanooga, its burnt-out downtown future megastructure now a rat's nest of squatters, which serves as the stage for a more complex and characteristic encounter: between a de-sexed bicycle repairman (new gender movements have proliferated in this future, including that of Sexual Deliberation, which artificially eradicates the sex drive) and the private police of a long-serving and now senile congressional stalwart, whose artificial identity replacement (the so-called mook) risks being unmasked by an unwanted package in the mail. Finally, classic science fiction returns with the discovery in a Central Asian desert, by twenty-first-century bounty-hunters, of an enormous artificial underground cavern, in which the Zone (the latest future form of the old East Asian Co-Prosperity Sphere, now run by China) has housed three world-sized human

---

2   Bruce Sterling, *A Good Old-Fashioned Future* (New York: Bantam Books, 1999).

communities as an experiment in testing the viability of 400-year-long space flights. I have only incidentally mentioned some of the wacky SF technology taken for granted in these tales: more significant are the priorities of global cyberpunk, in which technological speculation and fantasy of the old Toffler sort takes second place to the more historically original literary vocation of a mapping of the new geopolitical Imaginary.

Paperback seismographs

This is why such Hunter-Thompsonian global tourism has real epistemological value: cyberpunk constitutes a kind of laboratory experiment in which the geographic-cultural light spectrum and bandwidths of the new system are registered. It is a literature of the stereotypes thrown up by a system in full expansion, which, like the explosion of a nova, sends out a variety of uncharted signals and signs of nascent communities and new and artificially differentiated ethnies. Stereotypes are pre-eminently the vehicle through which we relate to other collectivities; no one has ever confronted another grouping without their mediation. They are allegorical cartoons that no longer convey the racist contempt of the older imperialism and which can often (as Žižek has observed of the ethnic jokes popular in the old Yugoslavia) function as affectionate forms of inclusion and of solidarity.

Indeed, an inspection of this literature already provides a first crude inventory of the new world system: the immense role—and manifest in Gibson's evocations, all the way down to *Pattern Recognition* itself—of Japan as the monitory semiotic combination of First World science-and-technology with a properly Third World population explosion. Russia now also looms large, but above all in the form of its various Mafias (from all the former Republics), which remind us of the anarchy and violent crime, as well as of the conspiratorial networks and jobless futures, that lurk just beneath the surface of capitalism. It also offers the more contemporary drama of the breakneck deterioration of a country that had already reached parity with the First World. Europe's image ambiguity—a kind of elegant museum or tourist playground which is also an evolutionary and economic dead end—is instructive; and the absence of Islam is a welcome relief, in a moment in which it is reality, rather than culture or literature, that is acting on the basis of that particular stereotype.

This new geopolitical material marks a significant historical difference between these commercial adventure stories and the equally cynical gonzo journalism of an earlier period; indeed, the affinities and
distinctions between the cultural products of the '60s and '70s and those
of the '90s and '00s would be well worth exploring further. Equally
significant is that these protagonists—busy as they are in locating rare
products, securing secret new inventions, outsmarting rivals, and trad-
ing with the natives—do not particularly need the stimulus of drugs
(still a preponderant, one may even say a metaphysical, presence in so
recent a world-historical expression as David Foster Wallace's 1996
Infinite Jest).

eBay imaginary

But it is by way of its style that we can best measure the new literature on
some kind of time-continuum; and here we may finally return to the
distinctiveness of *Pattern Recognition*, where this style has reached a
kind of classical perfection. I will define it as a kind of hyped-up name-
dropping, and the description of the clothes selected by the protagonist
(Cayce Pollard) for her first day in London is a reliable indicator:

> a fresh Fruit T-Shirt, her black Buzz Rickson's ma-1, anonymous black
> skirt from a Tulsa thrift, the black leggings she'd worn for Pilates,
> black Harajuku schoolgirl shoes. Her purse-analog is an envelope of
> black East German laminate, purchased on eBay—if not actual Stasi-
> issue then well in the ballpark.

I have no idea whether all these items actually exist, but eBay is certainly
the right word for our current collective unconscious, and it is clear that
the references "work," whether or not you know that the product is real
or has been made up by Gibson. What is also clear is that the names
being dropped are brand names, whose very dynamic conveys both
instant obsolescence and the global provenance and neo-exoticism of
the world market today in time and space.

A further point is that, little by little, in the current universe, everything
is slowly being named; nor does this have anything to do with the older
Aristotelian universals in which the idea of a chair subsumes all its individual manifestations. Here, the "high-backed workstation chair" is

almost of a different species to the seat in the BA 747 "that makes her think of a little boat, a coracle of Mexcel and teak-finish laminate." But there are also exercise chairs, called or named "reformers": "a very long, very low, vaguely ominous and Weimar-looking piece of spring-loaded furniture," which can also be translated into another language, where it becomes "a faux-classical Japanese interpretation in black-lacquered wood, upholstered with something that looks like shark-skin." Each of these items is on its way to the ultimate destination of a name of its own, but not the kind we are familiar with when we speak of a "Mies chair" or a "Barcelona chair." Not the origin, but rather the named image is at stake, so that an "Andy Warhol electric chair" might be a better reference.

In this postmodern nominalism, however, the name must also express the new, and fashion: what is worn-out, old-fashioned, is only useful as a cultural marker: "empty chrome stools of the soda-fountain spin-around kind, but very low, fronting on an equally low bar," where it is the "low," the "very low" that connotes Japan. And, in Moscow, the table "flanked by two enormous, empty wingback armchairs" only stands for back-wardness. This is probably why Gibson's Russian episode is less interest-ing: he brings a residual Cold War mentality to this built space, "as though everything was designed by someone who'd been looking at a picture of a Western hotel room from the eighties, but without ever having seen even one example of the original." Current Soviet and Central European nostalgia art (*Ostalgie* in German) is far more vibrant and exciting than this, reflecting on an alternate universe in which a complete set of mass-produced industrial products, from toilet seats to windowpanes, from shower heads to automobiles, had been invented from scratch, altogether different from the actually existing Western inventory. It is as though the Aztecs had beaten Cortéz and survived to invent their own Aztec radio and television, power-vehicles, film genres, and popular culture.

At any rate, the premise here is that Russia has nothing new to offer us in this field (the Sterling aesthetic offers much better chances of appreciating what is genuinely new, world-historically innovative, in Eastern nostalgia art); and the conclusion to be drawn is that name-dropping is also a matter of knowledge, and an encyclopedic familiarity with the fashions of world space as those flow back into the boutiques or flea markets of the West. What I have called name-dropping is therefore also to be grasped as in-group style: the brand names function as a wink of familiarity to the reader in the know. Even the cynicism (taking the word in Sloterdijk's, rather than in its post-Watergate sense) is a joyous badge of group adherence, the snicker as a form of hearty laughter, class status as a matter of knowing the score rather than of having money and power. In-group style was, I believe, the invention—or better still, the discovery—of Thomas Pynchon, as early as *V* (1963), even though Ian Fleming deserves a reference ("Thank you, Commander Bond," murmurs Cayce, as she pastes a hair across the outside apartment door). But, just as we no longer need drugs, so we no longer need Pynchon's staples of paranoia and conspiracy to wrap it all up for us, since global capitalism is there to do it more efficiently; or so we are told.

Birth of an aesthetic?

Nonetheless, *The Crying of Lot 49* remains a fundamental paradigm and, as with Hunter Thompson, the differences are historically very instructive indeed. For the post-horns and the other tell-tale graffiti have here been replaced by something like a "work of art": the clues point, not to some unimaginable reality in the social world, but to an (as yet) unimaginable aesthetic. It is a question of an unidentified film of some kind which has come to be known, among insiders, as "the footage," and which shows up in stills and clips in the most unlikely places (billboards, television ads, magazines, the internet), in "one hundred and thirty-four previously discovered fragments . . . endlessly collated, broken down, reassembled, by whole armies of the most fanatical investigators." Indeed, as one might expect, a whole new in-group has formed around the mysteries of the footage; we are experiencing, one of the characters observes, the "birth of a new subculture." A worldwide confraternity comes into being, committed to this new object and passionately exchanging and arguing contradictory theories about it. The footage thus makes *Pattern Recognition* over into something like Bloch's conception of the novel of the artist, which carries the unknown unrealized work of art inside itself like a black hole, a future indeterminacy suddenly shimmering in the present, the absent Utopian sublime suddenly opening up like a wormhole within the empty everyday:

> Light and shadow. Lovers' cheekbones in the prelude to embrace.
> Cayce shivers.
> So long now, and they have not been seen to touch.
> Around them the absolute blackness is alleviated by texture.
> Concrete?

They are dressed as they have always been dressed, in clothing Cayce has posted on extensively, fascinated by its timelessness, something she knows and understands. The difficulty of that. Hairstyles too.

He might be a sailor, stepping onto a submarine in 1914, or a jazz musician entering a club in 1957. There is a lack of evidence, an absence of stylistic cues, that Cayce understands to be utterly masterful. His black coat is usually read as leather, though it might be dull vinyl, or rubber. He has a way of wearing its collar up.

The girl wears a longer coat, equally dark but seemingly of fabric, its shoulder-padding the subject of hundreds of posts. The architecture of padding in a woman's coat should yield possible periods, particular decades, but there has been no agreement, only controversy.

She is hatless, which has been taken either as the clearest of signs that this is not a period piece, or simply as an indication that she is a free spirit, untrammeled even by the most basic conventions of her day. Her hair has been the subject of similar scrutiny, but nothing has ever been definitively agreed upon.

The problem, for the group forming around this artifact, as indeed for all group formation, is that of the contradiction between universality—in this case, the universality of taste as such—and the particularity of this unique value that sets us off from all the others and defines us in our collective specificity. A political sect (as we now seem to call these things) wishes simultaneously to affirm the universal relevance of its strategy and its ultimate aims, and at one and the same time to keep them for itself, to exclude the outsiders and the late-comers and those who can be suspected of insufficient commitment, passion, and belief. The deeper anxiety of the practitioners of the footage website and chat-room is, in other words, simply that it will go public: that CNN will get wind of this interesting development; that the footage, or the completed film, the identified and reconstructed work of art, will become, as they say, the patrimony of mankind, or in other words just another commodity. As it turns out, this fear is only too justified, but I omit the details, as I hate people who tell you the ending; except to express my mixed feeling that Pynchon's solution was perhaps the better one, namely to break off *Lot 49* on the threshold of the revelation to come, as Oedipa is on the point of entering the auction room.

After all this, it may come as something of a surprise to learn that the footage is not the central issue of this novel, even though it supplies the narrative framework. Yet it ought already to have been clear that there is a striking and dramatic contradiction between the style, as we have described it, and the footage itself, whose "absence of stylistic cues" suggests a veritable Barthesian "white writing." Indeed, it is rather this very contradiction which is the deeper subject of *Pattern Recognition*, which projects the Utopian anticipation of a new art premised on "semiotic neutrality," and on the systematic effacement of names, dates, fashions, and history itself, within a context irremediably corrupted by all those things. The name-dropping, in-group language of the novel thus revels in everything the footage seeks to neutralize: the work becomes a kind of quicksand, miring us ever more deeply in what we struggle to escape. Yet this is not merely an abstract interpretation, nor even an aesthetic; it is also the existential reality of the protagonist herself, and the source of the "gift" that informs her profession.

Commodity bulimia

Cayce Pollard's talent, lying as it does halfway between telepathy and old-fashioned aesthetic sensibility, is in fact what suspends Gibson's novel between science fiction and realism and lends it its extraordinary resonance. To put it simply (as she does), Cayce's business is to "hunt 'cool'"; or in other words, to wander through the masses of now and future consumers, through the youth crowds, the "Children's Crusade" that jams Camden High Street on weekends, the teeming multitudes of Roppongi and Shinjuku, the big-city agglomerations of every description all over the world, in order mentally to detect the first stirrings of anything likely to become a trend or a new fashion. She has, in fact, racked up some impressive achievements, of which my favorite, mildly redolent of DeLillo, is the identification of the first person in the world to wear a baseball cap backwards (he is a Mexican). But these "futures" are very much a business proposition, and Cayce is something like an industrial spy of times to come. "I consult on design . . . Manufacturers use me to keep track of street fashion"; these modest formulas are a little too dry, and underplay the sheer physicality of this gift, which allows her to identify a "pattern" and then to "point a commodifier at it."

There is here, no doubt, something of the specialized training of the authenticator of paintings and the collector of antique furniture; but its uncanny temporal direction condemns Cayce irredeemably, and despite her systematically black and styleless outfit, to the larger category of fortune-tellers and soothsayers—and occasionally puts her in real physical danger. This new métier thus draws our world insensibly into some science-fictional future one, at least on the borders, where details fail to coincide. The job of one character is to start rumors; to drop the names of products and cultural items enthusiastically in bars and nightclubs, in order to set in motion what would in Pynchon have been a conspiracy, but here is just another fad or craze.

But Cayce's gift is drawn back into our real (or realistic) world by the body itself; she must pay for it by the nauseas and anxiety attacks, the commodity bulimia which is the inevitable price of her premonitory sensibility—no doubt nourished by obscure traumas, of which the latest is her father's mysterious disappearance in Manhattan on the morning of 9/11. It is as if the other face of the "coming attraction," its reification and the dead-end product of what was once an active process of consumption and desire itself, were none other than the logo. The mediation between these two extremes of *energeia* and *ergon*, of process and product, lies no doubt in the name itself. I have argued that in the commercial nominalism of the postmodern, everything unique and interesting tends towards the proper name. Indeed, within the brand name the whole contradictory dialectic of universality and particularity is played out as a tug of war between visual recognition and what we may call the work of consumption (as Freud spoke of the work of mourning). And yet, to paraphrase Empson, the name remains, the name remains and kills; and the logo into which the brand name gradually hardens soaks up its toxicity and retains the poison.

Cayce's whole body is a resonator for these omnipresent logos, which are nonetheless louder and more oppressive in certain spaces (and places) than in others. To search for an unusual item in Harvey Nichols, for instance, is a peculiarly perilous activity:

> Down here, next to a display of Tommy Hilfiger, it's all started to go sideways on her, the trademark thing. Less warning aura than usual. Some people ingest a single peanut and their head swells like a basketball. When it happens to Cayce, it's her psyche. Tommy Hilfiger does it every time, though she'd thought she was safe now. They said he'd peaked, in New York. Like Benetton, the name would be around, but the real poison, for her, would have been drawn. This stuff is simulacra of simulacra of simulacra. A diluted tincture of Ralph Lauren, who had himself

diluted the glory days of Brooks Brothers, who themselves had stepped on the product of Jermyn Street and Savile Row, flavouring their ready-to-wear with liberal lashings of polo knit and regimental stripes. But Tommy surely is the null point, the black hole. There must be some Tommy Hilfiger event horizon, beyond which it is impossible to be more derivative, more removed from the source, more devoid of soul.

These nauseas are part of Cayce's navigational apparatus, and they stretch back to some of the oldest logos still extant, such as her worst nightmare, Bibendum, the Michelin Man, which is like that crack through which the Lacanian Real makes its catastrophic appearance. "National icons," on the other hand, "are always neutral for her, with the exception of Nazi Germany's . . . a scary excess of design talent."

Now it is a little easier to see the deeper meaning of the footage for Cayce: its utter lack of style is an ontological relief, like black-and-white film after the conventional orgies of bad technicolor, like the silence of solitude for the telepath whose mind is jammed with noisy voices all day long. The footage is an epoch of rest, an escape from the noisy commodities themselves, which turn out, as Marx always thought they would, to be living entities preying on the humans who have to coexist with them. Unlike the footage, however, Gibson's novel gives us homeopathy rather than antidote.

It does not seem anticlimactic to return to the future and to everything also auto-referential about this novel, whose main character's name is homonymous with that of the central figure in *Neuromancer*. Indeed, the gender change suggests all kinds of other stereotypical shifts of register, from active to passive for example (from male hacker to female future-shopper). Is it possible, however, that Cayce's premonitions of future novelty can also stand as the allegory of some emergent "new Gibson novel"? *Pattern Recognition* does seem to constitute a kind of pattern recognition for Gibson, as indeed for science fiction generally.

15

The Novel and the Supermarket

A well-known writer came over. We said hello, I was embarrassed, I knew he didn't like what I wrote. He had mentioned this once and been ironic, which made this even harder. But he didn't want to say just hello and congratulate me, he wanted to talk, and he spent at least five minutes refining his attitude to me and my books, he couldn't say straight out that he didn't like them, that they were bad in other words, but nor could he not say that, so what came out of his mouth was impossible to grasp because I didn't understand the basis.

Q. Can I read this before reading the other five books in the series?

A. Yes, because this one begins with the publication of the series and people's reactions to it, and so it takes place on a higher, more self-conscious level, so to speak. It also recapitulates some of the material in the earlier books, particularly the father's death in Book 1. Actually, if you want to begin here with Six, maybe you ought to read Book 1 first.

Q. Is this fiction or autobiography?

A. I don't know. He uses both words, and sometimes calls it a novel. Indeed, sometimes he seems to think of each individual volume as a

"Itemized: On *My Struggle: Part 6. The End* by Karl Ove Knausgaard," *London Review of Books* 40(21), November 8, 2018.

separate novel, which may give us a clue. As for autobiography, he does use real names, which is part of the uproar over this volume. He is accused not only of involving real people in his own personal story but of revealing potentially embarrassing personal facts about them as well, such as his wife's depression. "Have you considered the consequences of writing about your children? . . . How will it be for them when they grow up?" his mother-in-law asks. Meanwhile his uncle is planning to sue him (this is the story part of the first few hundred pages of the novel, which has about 1,100 of them, incidentally).

Q. Is it anything like Proust?

A. Not at all, except that, as in Proust, all the characters from the earlier parts of the novel reappear at the end. Here, though, they reappear as readers of what he wrote about them, they complain, write to the publishers, publish damaging newspaper exposés, hate him, or else assure him they don't mind at all (which is yet another, more unusual way of marking their changed relationship to him).

Q. Does anything happen in it?

A. Mostly he takes his three kids to school, goes home to write, sits on the balcony and smokes, picks them up in the afternoon, shops and buys them ice cream. But each volume has some overriding theme, such as the death of the father, or, here, the fallout from the publication. These segments do generate a certain narrative suspense in their own right, such as waiting to see what the uncle will actually do, besides writing vicious emails. So, in fact, if you really want to know what happens in this book, what happens is that Karl Ove writes, or is distracted by his family from writing, or has to get away for a few weeks to write, etc. We know what he wrote, of course, because it is in the other volumes; but, here, we do not yet know what he is writing, if you see what I mean. Spoiler: much has been made of the last sentence of the six volumes of *My Struggle* (*Min Kamp* in Norwegian), "Afterwards we will catch the train to Malmö, where we will get in the car and drive back to our house, and the whole way I will revel in, truly revel in, the thought that I am no longer a writer." This is, in fact, the conclusion of a book about how writing takes you away from your family and maybe from life itself, and how it is there to fill up time and to distract you from your boredom and potential misery (and maybe also from the burning wish to "become a writer"). In any case, the person whose name appears on the cover has published several books since this one so the question of whether, like Rimbaud, he plans to stop writing altogether is a misunderstanding of this final sentence.

Q. Will I like it better if I start with this volume and go back and read the others afterwards or should I start with them and work my way up to it, in which case by that time I may have started to get bored with it?

A. These questions seem to be getting less and less productive.

~

I will add, however, that whatever bother he has caused his family and his friends, he has also made trouble for his reviewers, who cannot deal with this the way they deal with an ordinary book (whether it is a famous masterpiece or a worthless paperback). Actually, the truly most frequently asked question is: do I have to read this, is it any good? A question to which there may or may not be a satisfactory answer, but which can, at least, be smothered by the information that people do seem to be reading it and that it has been translated into more than thirty languages around the world and has sold hundreds of thousands of copies and become a literary sensation, on the order of Roberto Bolaño or Elena Ferrante (both also somewhat autobiographical, it should be added). So, the more satisfactory response would be to take a poll (preferably worldwide) and find out what its readers think. I believe the result would be that they cannot tell you whether they think it is good or not either, but also that they all agree it exercises a certain fascination that keeps you reading. This fascination is what a proper reviewer would have to analyze. Otherwise, you are reduced to the status of the art teacher, moving from pupil to pupil and saying, this part is really good, there is something wrong with the anatomy of this figure, there's something missing in the lower left part of the picture, that part has an interesting color combination, etc. I'm afraid I will have to do that too, since I agreed to review this book.

At any rate, the parts with the children are quite delightful, it is good there are three of them for variety, and we look forward to a daily life with them which is not an event but a lively routine (at least until, at the end, their mother, Linda, starts to have the problems I have mentioned). The writing

is, however, undistinguished, at least in translation: only Norwegians will
know how it really feels, and indeed where it belongs in their culture, literary or otherwise. You do not read it for the style, except for the conversations, which are often unobtrusively witty and entertaining. Here is some
banter between Karl Ove and his best friend, Geir Angell Øygarden:

> "You've done nothing wrong," said Geir.
> "But I have, obviously," I said. "I'm trying to live with it."
> "Your dad's dead. Your grandma's dead."
> "And your empathy's dead."
> "Look who's talking."
> "Imagine there's a life after this," I said. "If we take that thought
> seriously. Only the body dies. The soul lives on in the world to come,
> in whatever form. What if it's true? I mean, really true. It struck me
> the other day. What if there is life after death? It'd mean my dad's out
> there somewhere waiting for me. And he's going to be angry as hell."
> Geir laughed.
> "You can relax. He's dead as a dodo."
> "Gunnar isn't, though."
> "But what can he do? OK, he can sue you. But for what? Defaming
> your father's name? He wasn't exactly Jesus, was he?"
> "Gunnar says I'm a Judas. In which case he must be Jesus, since he's
> the one I'm betraying."
> "If he was Jesus, that makes your grandmother the Virgin Mary.
> And your grandfather was Joseph, the carpenter. Besides, Jesus didn't
> have a son to betray him."
> "I wonder if it was actually Brutus he meant. He was a kind of son.
> Brutus Juliussen. Et tu, Brute? No, I only ate one."
> "You don't have to say everything that comes into your mind, you
> know. Kids do that. Adults can put their utterances through quality
> control first."
> "I remember crying when I read about Julius Caesar. His death. I
> always did whenever I read biographies. Because of course they all
> die. Thomas Alva Edison. Henry Ford. Benjamin Franklin. Marie
> Curie. Florence Nightingale. Winston Churchill. Louis Armstrong.
> Theodore Roosevelt."
> "You read Theodore Roosevelt's biography when you were a kid?"
> "I did, yes. There was a series. About twenty of them, I suppose.
> One on each. Most were about Americans. A lot of presidents. Walt

Disney, I remember him. Robert Oppenheimer. No, I'm joking. But Abraham Lincoln, at any rate. And when they died, no matter how, I always cried. But in a good way."

"Because it wasn't you!"

"No, no—it wasn't that. It was more that they'd overcome all this injustice in their lives and eventually succeeded in what they wanted to do. It would have been a lot sadder if they died before achieving what they were meant to. Like Scott. [Scott of the ill-fated Antarctic expedition.] Scott was bad, I was out of it for days."

"He probably wasn't happy about it either."

"Whereas Amundsen's death was a bit more ambiguous. He did what he set out to. And then there was something decent about him vanishing while trying to save someone else."

This is distinctive dialogue, interesting, the characters talk with style but are not mannered. It makes one wonder whether dialogue isn't a place where some originality can still be achieved. If you think of DeLillo's transitional novels, for example, the weirdness comes, he tells us, from the transcription of the private languages people invent when they are alone together. Maybe this is where invention goes when the plots of modernism become familiar, conventional, and boring. Plays are not prose, Gore Vidal observed; and to be sure, dialogue in the novel is not yet drama. But Beckett's plays (and maybe even his novels) come out of a private kind of dialogue (or monologue); and his period, the breakdown of the modern, was certainly also a glorious moment in the theatre, across the world. And then one thinks of the electrifying impact Hemingway's stories must have had on readers in the 1920s and 1930s: people's voices talking to each other like that. So, Knausgaard is probably right to cling to his characters' exchanges, as one place, at least, in which you can tell the truth (one of his obsessive ambitions) and keep on being a real writer.

What about the rest of it? Can you tell the truth by listing what you buy in the store? (Would it be lying if you left something out?)

I . . . turned to the shelves of fresh-baked bread. They had seven rolls for ten kronor, so I took one of the paper bags meant for loaves and put the rolls inside, scrunched the top end together and dropped it in the basket, then moved on to the milk and dairy, grabbing a packet of coffee and a one-and-a-half litre of Pepsi Max on the way.

Now, it would be dishonest to leave this passage without saying that it includes history, that it is preceded by the memory that there were once at least five or six kinds of bread with their own names, and followed with a memory of the supermarket of his childhood and what that was like, before it returns to the present day as he picks up a carton of milk, etc.

But I want to situate this passage, a scoop out of a seemingly endless and relatively homogeneous stream of detail, somewhere in the history of writing. "Surface writing" (designed for "surface readers")? That's already too visual, and besides, we really are not seeing these items. The second-by-second account of muscular and gestural movement, frame by frame, as we find it in Wyndham Lewis, early Peter Weiss, the Beckett of *Watt* (the turn of the century Germans even had a word for it: *Sekundenstil*)? But it is not analytic; it does not break conventional gestures, conventional acts and names ("I took a carton of milk") into the "neural unconscious" of the instinctive flexing of joints and muscles. Stream of consciousness? Mr. Bloom would have been embarrassed to have navigated a store like this in so literal and impoverished a state of mind; and as for Proust and childhood memory, *n'en parlons pas*. Naturalism and Zola were the high point of that "description" against which Lukács railed; their "thick" accounts wanted to show the way things worked as well as where they came from (and everything else they may have stood for symbolically); their American descendants (Nabokov among them) would have looked into their brand names, as the latter began to populate just such supermarket shelves in the 1950s.

None of that here. What about more recent cultural diagnoses? A greater hunger and thirst for reality? An increasing disgust or impatience with the fictional? An appetite, not for realism (which remains fictional even when it is its opposite), but for the Real itself wherever we can still find it? Not autobiography: that is far too retrospective and tarted up by wish-fulfilment, false memory, or even regret and remorse. But something else: a different combination of ingredients maybe (the French decided to call it "autofiction" at one point)—one which at a pinch you might call on to explain the fascination of Ferrante as well, of Bolaño, or Sebald—where "experiment" is no longer a matter of novelistic form but of its raw material, of "experience" itself? But what I am trying to put in doubt, with all due respect, is whether this is really experience either; or, rather, what kind of experience it is if daily life (a new existential category, only current since World War II) is not the right term for it.

I will call Knausgaard's kind of writing "itemization." We have, in postmodernity, given up on the attempt to "estrange" our daily life and see it in new, poetic or nightmarish, ways; we have given up the analysis of it in terms of the commodity form, in a situation in which everything by now is a commodity; we have abandoned the quest for new languages to describe the stream of the self-same or new psychologies to diagnose its distressingly unoriginal reactions and psychic events. All that is left is to itemize them, to list the items that come by.

So, it is not only the objects Karl Ove buys and uses that are itemized here: it is the people, the emotions and feelings, the thoughts, that are itemized as well. This is why the innumerable sentences in these thousands of pages—varied as they may be—fail to pass the supreme test of any postmodern aesthetics, which is the achievement of heterogeneity (virtually the magic key word in our current situation). Variety being the spice of life, we have to conclude, regretfully, that these pages do not quite enliven the palate. Here is the distilled quintessence, as Witold Gombrowicz, one of Knausgaard's great masters and forebears, put it in his own diary:

Monday
Me.
Tuesday
Me.
Wednesday
Me.
Thursday
Me.

Karl Ove too is locked up inside his own identity; but it does not take this form. Nor does it take the form of the boredom with self either—that great peerless theme of David Foster Wallace's in his last book, *The Pale King* (2011).

Q. Does anything happen in these books?

A. Yes, but not where you think. Let's first follow a certain consequence of itemization to its conclusion. There are feelings and emotions in these

volumes, and they are the usual ones—love, grief, apprehension, inferiority, anger, etc. But they are not expressed; they too are itemized. There
are personal relations and tense interpersonal situations; but these too
are not exactly dramatized, they are simply listed, and noted down.

As for thoughts, well, there we must open a parenthesis (without, for
all that, going into a lengthy theoretical digression on the novel of ideas,
if there is such a thing). I find myself growing impatient when, instead
of going on about his children, his friend Geir, his wife, other family
members or meetings in the street, Karl Ove stops to give us some
thoughts. They offer his ideas about life and death, about human relations and political relations, about art, about books and writers too,
contemporary as well as classical. Indeed, those are often the most interesting moments: the long and admiring pages on Handke's *A Sorrow
beyond Dreams* raise the question of truth and fiction far more
profoundly than I have done here and can stand as a memorable testimony to this ostracized writer. The thoughts on the visual arts are for me
even more striking: the secret of painters, if not of viewers as well.

> What does it mean to see? With the Impressionists, the question is:
> what does it mean to experience seeing? . . . One doesn't have to think
> too hard to understand . . . the reason that painters and sculptors
> spent all their time during their crucial formative years of youth copy-
> ing others or mechanically reproducing models of objects. They
> weren't doing it so they could learn to copy reality . . . They were
> doing it so as to learn how not to think. This is the most important
> thing of all in art and literature, and hardly anyone can do it or even
> realises it is the case.

And there is much of interest on Celan as well as on Kafka. But, just as
he wavers between calling his own book(s) novels or autobiography, so,
here too, he occasionally uses the word "essay"; and it is here that we
must draw the line, at the four-hundred-page "Hitler essay" which interrupts the story of Karl Ove's own publications and takes us, with much
intelligence and erudition (there is a bibliography at the end), through
the life of the young Hitler before the fateful departure for Munich. This
is, ostensibly, a reply to the first volume of Ian Kershaw's now canonical
biography, and, quite rightly, takes issue with a literary and formal problem raised by biography in general, and Kershaw's in particular—viz.
the inevitable projection backwards onto the youth of what we know

about the man. (Recall the story by Alphonse Allais of his discovery, in a dusty provincial museum, under glass, of the skull of Voltaire as a child.) For Kershaw, who knows the outcome, everything the young Hitler does is tainted in advance: not an act, not a feeling or an interest, a watercolor or a musical enthusiasm that is not sinister (Wagner!), or at the very least mediocre (failed artist, etc.). Here, too, Karl Ove is raising a form-problem (among other things) and implicitly rethinking his own written life, *Min Kamp*, in a discussion of its eponymous predecessor, which is also juxtaposed with one of the foundational works of his own national literature—to wit Knut Hamsun's *Hunger*, about a similarly desperate youth. At least he does not go as far as his unhappy Danish contemporary, Lars von Trier, who effectively ostracized himself by observing that he could sometimes understand Hitler (as though anyone could understand!).

But all of this—the essay or essays scattered throughout this enormous final volume, where it might be argued that he ought at least to be allowed to draw a few conclusions—is not to be judged on the basis of its interest (some of it is interesting, some jejune or embarrassing, some simply conventional) but rather on generic (I won't say aesthetic) grounds; and this, however much you are willing to sacrifice on the altar of heterogeneity, is a value I also personally prize. But these essays are not narrative, they are opinion—that *doxa* the Greeks so sharply distinguished from *episteme* or "knowledge." I am willing to argue that this opposition has its literary and formal version, and that there is, in fact, something we may call narrative truth. Knausgaard's accounts of his own opinions are not the narrative of someone thinking, arguing, discovering plausible or pernicious ideas; they are simply a collection of his own personal thoughts, which he might better have projected in a truly rhetorical and literary form, i.e. the essay. There have been remarkable essays in which an author effectively tells the story of his own opinions. Here, however, we already know what Knausgaard is doing, and where the flaw lies: he is itemizing them. He has already discovered and thought them through; now he is listing them for us, no matter how elaborate the entries.

So, let's reverse the argument, though it wasn't necessarily wrong, for there is something rather different running through all this, which is a kind of thinking, even if one cannot quite call it a thought: it is the

constant preoccupation with the pronouns, the "I," "we," "it," a kind of
"you" . . . The "he" and "she" get absorbed in the narrative; on the
abstract level Heidegger's "das man" fights it out with Levinas's Other;
the "I" gets lost in ruminations about identity; the "we" becomes the
collectivity of Nazism: "an extreme reinforcement of the we, and the
attendant weakening of the I," a kind of banal philosophical psycholo-
gizing which leads the author to rather sterile personal dead ends
("Personally I have never felt myself to belong to any we") and disquisi-
tions on the permanence of death and war that become interesting only
when one thinks of them as a matter of daily life and how one narrates
that (the death of the father or the sordid, littered, and messy rooms left
after his death).

The form—the format—dictates the overriding impression of someone locked into his own subjectivity and desperately peering out of the
window; but this is Karl Ove's mistake (and Gombrowicz's), if not our
own. Karl Ove is perfectly normal, a good deal more "normal," one
would say, than most writers and certainly than most first-person writers. The mistake lies in not understanding that there is no "normal" and
that everyone is a neurotic: neurosis is the very structure of human
subjectivity, of Dasein. Only other people are "normal," at least some of
them. Knausgaard has here hit on the great reality, the great mystery, of
the world, which has little enough to do with nature, death, or whatever
other grand metaphysical themes I'm forgetting here. It has to do with
the hapless attempt of a biologically incomplete being to claim some
mental or spiritual completeness; as well as with the inevitable failure of
a group of these beings, a group of any size, to constitute some kind of
whole. The "I" and the "we" stand for those two failures, those two structural impossibilities: the Centered Self and the General Will, or the
Dictator and the Family, if you prefer. I would not say that his book
agonizes over this dilemma; rather, it finds itself, by some lucky historical accident, in the very crosshairs of it, wriggling between its two horns.

Oddly enough, however, none of this leads us to the center of this
dispersed and seemingly random meditation which is the absent "you"
itself. The real "you" here is not the "you" of the characters, not the "you"
of the relationships with the lovers, the best friend, the children, the
family. If I wanted to be melodramatic about it, I would say that we get
closer by deducing that the real "you" in this book is, as with *Hamlet*, the
uncle: for it is the uncle who, reading Book 1 (just published at the
beginning of this one), flies into a rage, denounces Karl Ove's lies and

distortions (his brother was not a drunkard, there weren't empty bottles all over the apartment he shared with their mother—indeed, shared for many more years than the nephew claims), the uncle who writes letters to the publishers, denounces the writer and his own hostile mother, threatens a lawsuit; constitutes, in fact, that "ideal reader" of whom the great critics have talked so much.

This is, then, the concrete emotion that courses through these pages and stands in sharp contrast to the feelings and emotions so conscientiously itemized along the way: the writer as victim, the writer as "someone in danger of losing his independence, a person held captive and paralyzed by the power of another, who fawningly acts like him, pale, bloodless and ghostlike." That other is the Karl Ove of the novel, about whom the narrator writes and who is supposed to be the narrator. Then there is the more philosophical "I," the "I" of Gombrowicz and "immaturity," the Sartrean "I":

> Perhaps because I have always had such a weak ego, always felt myself inferior to all others, in every situation . . . I am inferior to the female assistant in the shoe shop when I go in to buy shoes, she has me in her hands, so to speak, full of an authority to which I yield. But the worst for me are waiters, since their role is so obviously to serve and be there to please.

Yet the waiters who secretly judge you are at least "there." The uncle (who was "there" and whom the novel-reminiscence of Book 1 portrayed quite differently) is no longer present, even though he still very much exists. What about those who judge you without being there at all, without even existing (in that sense); what about all those others to whom you are incomprehensibly opening yourself, submitting, recounting your every thought and daily action, without those things being in the least bit guilty, so that your telling of them, as in Rousseau, becomes a "confession"? Or, maybe, as Paul de Man thought, it is the act of telling them that makes them guilty and that turns the telling itself into a confession *avant la lettre*? But is it really guilt at all? Is this really a confession? Toril Moi has suggested that what troubles Knausgaard (without, perhaps, his having any great awareness of the distinction) is not guilt but shame. Guilt demands expression and, above all, confession; but the openness which Moi sees as the therapy for shame is not a redemptive act of that kind but, rather, a stance towards life itself, one which is fulfilled in the attention to details of everyday life unassociated with the ostensibly shameful matter as such. This is, no doubt, as demanding a life-discipline as confession, but here it is fulfilled, not so much in conduct, ethical or not, but in the aesthetic, in the voluminous pages which itemize the day's content and that of the life itself.

But to shift levels for a moment, and to abandon the aesthetic for the ethical, Knausgaard's is perhaps less a therapy than a solution to the problem of what to do with himself and his life—namely, to write it down item by item. This, no doubt, involves memory (although the truth he seeks doesn't lie in memory but in what Moi, perhaps drawing on Hölderlin and Cavell, calls openness, in telling everything rather than in telling the truth in some classical juridical context). And, since, despite everything, Proust is always the reference here, let's point out that it is precisely here that we can glimpse the ultimate contradiction in the Proustian enterprise too, a contradiction of which he is almost aware, and which he certainly evades as swiftly as possible. I'm thinking less of my readers than of my book, he tells us. "For they would not really be my readers, according to me, but rather the readers of themselves, my book being little more than one of those magnifying glasses offered by the optician of Combray; my book thanks to which they would be offered the means of reading themselves." But what do Proust's experiences (and Knausgaard's) offer us, who have had different ones? The universal? We have to understand the premise of both writers: it is not introspection they offer, or reading either, but writing. And Proust's rather hapless apologia suggests that the lesson both writers offer us is simply, go and do thou likewise, write out the book of your own life the same way we do. I must confess that I do not find the prospect of a utopia in which everyone is diligently scribbling down his or her experiences—daily or life-long—terribly appealing. When would we have time to have any experiences in the first place? As if there were not enough books in the world already, with many more to come from all around an awakened and literate, self-conscious, publishable world.

At any rate, the "you" here, the judge, the absent other, is the reader yourself (or in this instance myself): this "being-for-the-reading-other" makes for a new kind of otherness, a new kind of interpersonal relationship quite unique from a literary perspective and which is also quite different from the psychological discoveries of a Dostoevsky or a Henry James, the discovery of new kinds of feeling and emotion or reaction. As readers, we are closer to Karl Ove than in any ordinary novel or autobiography, where, in any case, the "I" of the first-person narrative pushes the reader further away than the conventional third person (with whom we have "empathy"). The new intimacy is stranger and stronger than those because the author is aware of our presence in his mind and of our inevitable judgment on him, just as the reader is aware at every moment that he is expecting our judgment, anticipating a condemnation even more fateful and inevitable than that of Josef K., even if the judgment claims to be positive. This is, of course, the real story of this particular novel: how will the people talked about in it react, since they cannot but react in one way or another (and the uncle's reaction is actually a kind of relief). More crucial for Karl Ove himself is the reaction of his wife and eventually, when they grow up, of his children. But the reaction that is most important for me, the reviewer, is what he will think of my reaction, of what I will do with our newfound intimacy. It is a situation which has either never before been staged by literature, or else has existed (as my being-for-others) at every moment of everyone's life.

I believe that this is a unique and as yet untheorized human relationship: not new certainly, but unnamed, and not subsumed under any of our pronominal categories—not "I-you," or "them-us" or "we," but a peculiar absent presence of an otherness which is neither the big Other nor the crowd of eyes; and its shame is permanent, its openness an ever possible vulnerability to some unknown consciousness which is not an entity and can never really be reached by us in any active way. Knausgaard's achievement is to have foregrounded this immeasurably strange relationship which is there all the time but to which we so rarely attend directly.

Q. Does anything happen in this novel?

A. Well, this is what happens in it—writing—and as for its events, they are not really to be found in the observations (or, as we have seen, in the "thoughts"), but, rather, in what Karl Ove does after he takes the children to school and before he picks them up, in between the cigarettes and coffee on the balcony during what is literally a coffee break—that's to say, the writing of the sentences themselves. A lot of literary "thinking" was devoted, especially in the 1960s, to writing about writing, to the production of textuality, to sentences whose content was the sentence itself; and a lot of self-designating or auto-referential literature thereby generated which we can now thankfully consign to secondhand book-shops, if we can still find any. What Knausgaard is doing is not the "production of text" in that sense; or maybe it actually is: the real thing itself, which the 1960s were dreaming of but could not really imagine.

And this is, then, finally, the fascination that Knausgaard, maybe unwit-tingly, ends up exercising on his readers. We do wonder why we take such satisfaction in the notation of all these daily things: the people who pass by in the street below the balcony, the things we have to buy in the store, the chance exchanges at the kids' school, or what we see on the occasional trips, at lectures or at conferences . . . It is what a different postwar theoretical philosophy called redemption; all these insignifi-cant moments of an insignificant daily life are here redeemed, by the ordinary, undistinctive sentences which write them down. They have not been transformed or lent some higher meaning; they remain what they were before, transient and of no particular interest. Nor are they lifted into the timeless eternity of classical literature, posterity, and the canon: you can dip into them wherever you like, and they will not be any more quotable or Virgilian; they will, in fact, remain quite as nonde-script as before. But Knausgaard has written them, and written about writing them, and this is the story, not of his own experiences, but of the writing of these non-reflexive sentences, about which we do not even feel his writer's cramp or his aching shoulder, his blurred vision. We just feel them being written as we continue to read, and do not even have to be told (as he has told us) that he never rewrites or corrects anything. Nor is he more than very occasionally conscious of this continuity:

> Always and yet never the same. When I see the image in my mind's eye I am transported there, and with all my being I am aware not only of my own existence but of my own self, for a brief moment it floods my consciousness, and in those few moments I am quite oblivious to my own problems, the things I have done or need to do, the people I know, have known or will know in the future, and everything that connects me to the social world is gone.

So, even if I cannot advise you to read it, I can certainly advise rereading it, as one might leaf through a journal or a diary and follow a few paragraphs before putting it down again. And for what ought to be the most frequently asked question, I would have the answer "Yes, it has a happy ending, which might run something like this":

In the bus going home Vanja slept with her head in Linda's lap while Heidi sat limply on mine dozing. Her little body registered all the bus's jerks and jolts as at first we drove from traffic lights to traffic lights through the town, then onto the motorway along the coast where the blazing sun hung above the dark blue sea.

Happiness wasn't in my nature, but happy was how I felt.

Everything was light and airy, my emotions were lofty and uncomplicated, the mere sight of a bulging wire fence or a stack of worn tires outside a garage opened my soul, and a rare warmth spread through my insides.

16

Temporalities of the Sea

Recently a happy accident put me in possession of a rarely seen film by Andrzej Wajda, *Smuga cienia*, from 1976. It is an adaptation of Joseph Conrad's short, openly autobiographical novel *The Shadow-Line* (1916). Wajda conceived the film as a modest docudrama based on Conrad's last mission at sea. The British government, in the thick of World War I, had enlisted the aging celebrity for a brief, hopefully not too dangerous foray in the North Sea to hunt for German U-boats. The trip was undertaken without incident and—as its captain, James Sutherland, recorded—without any great satisfaction either. Conrad wrote very little during the war, with the exception of *The Shadow-Line*, which draws on memories of his first command in the British merchant navy some thirty years earlier. So, it seems Wajda ended up combining these two episodes, the North Sea expedition and the first command, in a scenario from which Captain Sutherland and the U-boats disappeared altogether.

F. R. Leavis would not have approved of *The Shadow-Line*, whose broken-backed structure is perhaps no less objectionable than the double plot Leavis deplored in Daniel Deronda. Nearly a third of the novel is given over to bureaucratic machinations on shore, which Wajda wisely shortened but was unable to omit entirely. This opening part of the book turns on the inexplicable decision of the unnamed protagonist, the Conrad figure, to abandon his position as mate on "an Eastern ship" and return to England, effectively giving up his career. He doesn't say

---

"Time and the Sea: On Joseph Conrad," *London Review of Books* 42(8), April 4, 2020.

why (*acte gratuit*? existential choice?): there is a lot of speculation, people try to dissuade him, rumors abound. The hum of activity is calculated to heighten the shock of what happens next, an unexpected reversal. The captain of a barque has died at sea, and his place is offered to the protagonist, who accepts it just as impulsively as he had earlier decided to drop out of the game.

First command in Conrad is as romantic as first love and is never disillusioned. An alternative version of the unique experience is offered by Marlow in "Youth" (1898), where the longing "to see the East" encounters as many obstacles as in *The Shadow-Line* but reaches a different and more wondrous conclusion (Francis Ford Coppola borrowed it for *Apocalypse Now*, his film version of *Heart of Darkness*). Touching shore at long last in the dark, Marlow wakes from the sleep of exhaustion to a silent dawn:

> I opened my eyes . . . and then I saw the men of the East—they were looking at me. The whole length of the jetty was full of people. I saw brown, bronze, yellow faces, the black eyes, the glitter, the colour of an Eastern crowd. And all these beings stared without a murmur, without a sigh, without a movement. They stared down at the boats, at the sleeping men who at night had come to them from the sea. Nothing moved.

For the human animal, the experience of being looked at is profoundly ontological, and often traumatic. Conrad wanted to leave London, an acquaintance testified, because "the crowd in the streets so terrified him. 'Terrified? By that dull stream of obliterated faces?' He leaned forward with both hands raised and clenched. 'Yes, terrified: I see their personalities all leaping out at me like tigers!'" This "first contact," the enigmatic silence of otherness, is the moment of imperialism: Achebe called it racism in his denunciation of *Heart of Darkness*. It is carefully excised from *The Shadow-Line*, where there are only European sailors, the stay in Bangkok is non-exotic, and the destination is Australia.

This is perhaps the moment to say something about Conrad's relationship to empire. I would suggest that what is asphyxiating about *Heart of Darkness* is not, in the first place, what so exasperated Achebe, but a personal crisis in Conrad's life that is rarely discussed: the historical transition to steam, the replacement of the sailing ship by machine power in the 1870s and 1880s, a development repugnant to the seamen of Conrad's generation. It surely played a part in his change of profession, his abandonment of maritime commerce for the perilous new métier of writing for a living. Indeed, I conjecture that Conrad unconsciously projected this existential choice onto the unmotivated decision that opens *The Shadow-Line*. Conrad's choice may be interpreted as a response to what might be called the dialectic of success.

The shift from sail to steam power made "freshwater shipping" possible, to the great contempt of traditional seamen. This is the kind of work into which, in *Heart of Darkness*, Marlow is forced by his assignment in the Congo. ("What more did I want? What I really wanted was rivets, by heaven! Rivets. To get on with the work—to stop the hole. Rivets I wanted.") The steamboat facilitated the prodigious expansion of the British Empire into such backwaters, the aquatic capillaries of world conquest. The age of empire is a success that brings discomforts and sacrifices along with it ("Winner loses," as Sartre liked to put it): from the literary standpoint, a loss of the romance of the sea and adventures of exploration, to be replaced by a more worldly realism, if not the mysteries of syntax. Marlow's story also illustrates the modern dilemmas of employment and unemployment that have only been exacerbated by automation and computerization in the present.

It is historically unsurprising that, in the context of an emerging mass culture, nostalgia for older forms should express itself in their revival and imitation as high-art products. The adventure story was promoted into literature. A taste for this "canon," from Stevenson to Kipling, from gaucho stories to Westerns, was formative for Borges, whose admiration for Conrad was well known. It is a mistake to consider Borges a modernist; rather, when he was awarded the Prix Formentor in 1961, marking his belated arrival on the world literary stage (along with Beckett, who shared the prize that year), it was a harbinger of the postmodern return to plot, to intricacy and intrigue, and away from the densities of poetic language. Conrad's "postmodern" reversion to plot was, however, combined with a different kind of modernist supplement, namely the work of style. Conrad dealt with his traditional raw material according to a stylistic strategy very different from Borges's superposition of alternating plots and narrative paradoxes; yet the affinity betrays a deeper contradiction in the literary production process common to their respective historical moments.

Conrad as modernist? Not exactly. Ian Watt's idea of Conrad's style as "delayed decoding"—the bewildering perceptual fragmentation of an act or object only then belatedly identified—is more appropriate to, say, his friend and collaborator Ford Madox Ford, whose sentences (*Parade's End!*) provoke just such reading operations and can, therefore, unlike Conrad's mature writing, certainly be looked at through the optic of modernism. Watt's reading of Conrad is more suggestive when applied to plot: in Conrad's bravura moments, it is the plot that displays the technical prowess of delayed decoding, and obliges us to remain in suspense with regard to one part of the plot, while the other, known and comprehended part waits for completion.

Still, what Conrad does with plot betrays the fundamental contradiction in modernism between plot and sentence. *The Shadow-Line* articulates this contradiction in terms of work and class. The "first command" (the initial title of *The Shadow-Line*) designates a personal and sentimental experience, yes, but, to be blunt about it, it also literally signals a shift from labor to management. In *The Shadow-Line*, it would be wrong to interpret the first mate's resistance to the new captain as mere jealousy, or frustration at his inferior status. The captain is endowed not only with a different kind of authority, but engages in a different kind of activity, involved with knowledge rather than production, at least at sea. In port, the captain is obliged to supervise the delivery and loading of cargo, as well as managing relations with the imperial authorities and the shipping company. Here, the implementation of Taylor's "scientific management"—in which there is a separation between the manager's knowledge of the totality of the production process and the laborer's carefully delimited individual tasks—is not yet complete: an ambiguity attested by the undecidable status of the eponymous protagonist of *Nostromo*, whose power and prestige derive from the uncertainty as to whether he is taking orders or giving them.

A surprise awaits us in *The Shadow-Line*, however. As well as the ill will, paranoid fantasies, and physical debilitation of the first mate, Mr. Burns, and amid the many misfortunes that meet the ship itself, another disaster occurs: a contagion that lays the crew low and leaves no one to perform even the most menial duties. The honest steward, Ransome, is the one man on board still able to function (though he has a heart condition, and so the captain's first command will be Ransome's last voyage). His loyalty, trustiness, and reliability are Conrad's ethical sweetening of the pill of imperialism's "material interests." None of this, however, alters the fact that under these circumstances the captain has to become a worker again, racing back and forth between mast and wheel, securing loose cargo, patrolling the deck, holding the watch on all sides, doing the work of three or four men at once.

And what is productive labor when it comes to the sea? Productivity is normally defined in terms of work on raw materials, the transformation of nature by human effort and toil into useful objects. But the crew's struggle against the sea does not produce anything in that sense: it effects distribution rather than production, circulation rather than industry. The question has literary implications as well. Godard once remarked (in *Passion*) that, bodily and material as they were, neither sex nor labor could really be represented.

A little prestidigitation is required. The struggles of the *Odyssey* were set down to the ill will of a god. In *The Shadow-Line*, Burns in his delirium rambles about the malevolent power of the dead captain (the novel's title designates the boundary that must be crossed to escape his baleful influence). In an "author's note" written in 1920, Conrad went to great lengths to deny that the novel was a ghost story, but I think he protests too much and that his concern had more to do with marketing strategy and a desire to distinguish his work from the competition. In any case, Conrad's storms are intelligent enough: "A furious gale attacks a man like a personal enemy, tries to grasp his limbs, fastens upon his mind, seeks to rout his very spirit out of him."

Today, our own "struggle against nature" has as much to do with the global marketplace, with extraction, with containers and the delivery of goods and cheap labor, as it does with producing the commodities themselves. Marxian debates about value and immaterial labor are scarcely exotic or superfluous when they concern a system in which universal consumerism tends to conceal production in favor of distribution, a category that includes not only circulation and exchange as such, but also the full-blown ideology of communication and information that has become our dominant mode of understanding in a media society. The captain is now the locus of information that Taylor wished the manager to be; but the laborers have gone below deck.

Or else their place has been taken by the labor of language, which, it turns out, identifies what is unique about Conrad in literary history as well as what is most ambiguous—in some good, ever tantalizing way—about his solution to his literary dilemma. This dilemma can be characterized philosophically as the tension, if not the contradiction, between the universal and the particular; but that is no doubt a most pretentious way of saying it. In fact, the increasing gap that characterizes "the modern" is what I have called a "contradiction" between the overall plot and the individual sentence, or the "fabula" and the "syuzhet," as the Russian Formalists put it, the raw material of the story and its realization in sentences or in dramatic acts. Conrad's solution to this quintessentially modern form-problem is disarming: labor becomes the central theme at both levels, which thereby echo each other. I have already discussed the way the plot deals with the question of labor through the genre of the sea or adventure tale; in language, labor is a matter of what Conrad and Ford liked to call "impressionism," the shouldering of the burden of "le mot juste" bequeathed to them by Flaubert (who never used the expression but suffered the thing itself his whole life, thereby becoming the inescapable ideal and martyr of the writerly art). Conrad and Ford here violate a staunch British tradition and demonstrate fealty to a foreign language. In Conrad's defense, it must be said that he thought in French, and that writing in English was for him a kind of translation process. The pair reveled in professional discussions on the rendering of qualia, and on the lack of "clean edges" in English words as opposed to French ones: they would ask themselves "how we would render . . . a ten-acre patch of blue-purple cabbage. We would try the words in French . . . we would try back into English."

This commitment to precision finds a striking contradiction—if it is not, in fact, a confirmation—in Henri Bergson's sense that it is language which first imposes a spatializing deformation on experience. Noun, verb, adjective: the noun reifies the object by classification, the verb turns an act into a thing, the adjective ornaments this frozen reality like a Christmas tree. Leavis, indeed, saw the adjective as Conrad's weak point and his gravest temptation: *Heart of Darkness* is notoriously a sink of adjectives, of which the famous "horror" is the distillation, a symptom that reveals Conrad's fundamental uncertainties and hesitations about the implications of that text. In fact, the doctrine of "le mot juste" is, for him, essentially adjectival propaganda and, far from yielding precision, only really works when a slight gap between word and thing displays the writer's virtuosic choice of an elegant and eye-catching substitute, his expertise in sidestepping cliché, the perfect word conveying not the thing itself but rather the bravura gesture of the writer. In Conrad, however, "le mot juste" becomes a formula for translation from French to English, and the equivalent in literary production of the hesitation in the fabula between the status of captain or manager and that of subordinate or common seaman.

Why English? Conrad's choice wasn't made only for commercial reasons (he was always desperate for income), or even because English was the world's *lingua franca*. Here it is worth taking a fresh look at Conrad's Toryism, which has so often been a cause of reproach, or met with an indifferent acknowledgment of his singularity. Everyone knows by now that the apolitical is itself a political choice, even when it isn't replaced by an ideological alternative such as aestheticism (which certainly characterizes Conrad as well, but in an idiosyncratic way, not quite comparable to that of other fin-de-siècle European or Victorian figures). The political is a unique kind of passion in its own right, but mid-nineteenth-century Poland (a land under foreign occupation, like Ireland) was in any case a boiling cauldron of social forces and political passions. Conrad's father, Apollo Korzeniowski, was a distinguished poet and translator who took part in numerous patriotic actions (fortunately for him, he was in exile during the most dramatic of these, the Warsaw uprising of 1863). In this, he was opposed by other members of his family, notably his uncle, Conrad's lifelong patron and a resolute abstentionist, who ran his estate and didn't trouble himself with militancy or subversive anti-Russian activity. In all this turmoil, which affected not only his own family but social life in general in the period following the great revolutionary awakening of 1848, one can imagine the young Korzeniowski seeking some serenity in the form of an attempt to escape politics altogether.

That is exactly what he did. Figuratively (though it is a figure that would be literally dramatized again and again in his writings), he jumped ship. At the age of sixteen he signed aboard a French vessel. Leaving Poland meant leaving politics behind forever. The problem was, however, that no nation-state at the time could match the extraterritorial isolation provided by the ship itself. Every nation in Europe was wracked by political antagonisms, from the Commune and its republican sequel in France, to the various ethnic nationalisms and official state patriotism of Central and Eastern Europe (and of the post-Civil War US, to the idea of which so many oppressed Europeans took flight). The one place Conrad found tranquility was in a supranational system from which such domestic tensions appeared, to a foreign observer at least, to have been banished: namely, the British Empire. This is not to say he didn't have any political opinions (he loathed Leopold II, for example, though he evaded the Irish question and the fate of his friend Roger Casement); but, here, he was at least free from the strife in Poland, and the empire's seemingly neutral non-national framework was what eventually decided his choice of language, too (that is, his decision to write in English rather than French; for obvious reasons, Polish doesn't come into it). In English, his literary constructions would be sheltered from national concerns, just as his various vessels and cargo ships were from the flags under which they navigated, whose provenance only came into play in port (and even in port the worldwide network of British naval and maritime outposts served as something of a universal shield against local jurisdictions). To call all this "Toryism" is a gross oversimplification of a complicated existential situation, which obscures the political as well as the historical meaning of Conrad's texts.

In *The Shadow-Line*, imperialism safely bracketed, the decks seem to be clear for a straightforward account of the author-protagonist's first encounter with space and the sea. Yet what happens is in a sense the opposite. Not the subtle and probing, exhaustively varied, sometimes overpowering trials of *Typhoon* ("It was as if Nature itself were an intelligent being trying deliberately to destroy them"), but rather indifference, and as it were the absentmindedness of God. Far from being storm-battered, the unnamed ship is beset by something worse: no sooner does it leave harbor than the wind falls and the vessel is fatally becalmed. The violence of the tempest, in which time is virtually abolished by the urgency of tasks to be performed, is raw material with which words, from the *Odyssey* to Conrad himself, can deal just as well as film images. Language cannot, however, begin to compete with cinema when it comes to the windless emptiness of time at a stop: "calme plat, grand miroir/De mon désespoir." Baudelaire's great lines, which serve as the epigraph of *The Shadow-Line* (and are then borrowed back by Conrad's French translator André Gide for the cruise sequence of *Counterfeiters*), capture the desperation of the ship in its doldrums and the slackness of the sails whose imperceptible stirring Wajda starkly underscores, along with the idle impotence conveyed by the captain's aimless rushing back and forth across the deck. ("All the ills of man come from this, the inability to sit still in a room.") And suddenly we understand: it isn't so much the genius of Wajda and the glorious images of this magnificent ship in full span that convey the metaphysical significance of this moment. It is the inexorability of the projector and the unreeling film, and the condemnation of the audience to immobility throughout the ordeal, which are the condition of what we now perceive: the emergence of pure empty Time, devoid of content, Proustian or otherwise.

This is the real or "simple" time beyond human temporality that Bergson sought to express in an eloquent language nonetheless doomed to remain human. The Greeks were seemingly unable to dissociate time from movement: even the tortuous Aristotelian formula ("Time is the number of motion with respect to the before and after") was unable to do without it, while it is the very movement of the sentence that led Derrida to his judgment of futility: "In a sense, it is always too late to talk about time." Even the contemporary versions of Bergson's insistence fall back, tainted by movement, when they evoke the "arrow of time." Still, Wajda's camera is able to share Conrad's glimpse, through the gap between his adventure stories and his Flaubertian art-sentences, of that Bergsonian time beyond temporality, which, neither eternity nor living present, neither ephemerality nor fulfilment, beyond all ennui and anxious waiting, neither an ending nor a beginning, consists in the essence of pure and empty Time in itself and as such, the Time of changeless yet irreversible succession.

17

A Businessman in Love

When I ask myself why this extraordinary novel—*Lalka* (*The Doll*, 1890) by Boleslaw Prus, nom de plume of Aleksander Glowacki—is so little known, so little read in the West, the first answer that inevitably arises has to do with the so-called small-power languages.[1] Never mind the fact that Polish is the oldest Slavic literary language, with a rich Renaissance literature dating from a period in which Poland was the largest country in Europe—a language that also boasts the greatest romantic poet in any language (he will figure significantly in *The Doll*). Never mind the heroic stereotype of the Poles as the Irish of the East, in their gallant doomed revolts against the powerful imperial neighbor and overlord (it will also be a question here of the greatest of those failed revolutions, the Warsaw uprising of 1863, in which the author also fought). Never mind the central significance of Poland for European Jewry—they also play a profoundly historical role here—nor its peculiar class system—a numerous petty and impoverished nobility and small bourgeoisie, only slowly emerging in the towns—so alien from the Western experience of snobbery that the readers of Proust or of English

---

"A Businessman in Love: On *The Doll* by Bolesław Prus," in *The Novel*, Vol. 2, ed. Franco Moretti (Princeton: Princeton University Press, 2007).

1 The English translation by David Welsh (New York: Twayne, 1972) is not altogether complete, but its pages are referenced here in the text. UNESCO has published a complete translation into French in three volumes (*La poupée*). For more on Prus, see Czeslaw Milosz, *History of Polish Literature* (New York: Macmillan, 1969).

literature in general would find its social content incomprehensible. *Mais quoy, ils ne portent point de haut de chausses.*

But perhaps they are remote from us, and too exotic, after all: a businessman in love! Such is the subject of this long masterpiece of postnaturalism, and to put it this way is, for the Western reader, to evoke comedy and caricature. Here, we do not have the hungry young arriviste of Zola's diptych (*Potbouilli/Au bonheur des dames*) or of Maupassant's *Bel ami*: indeed the radical difference of Paris as the very capital of Western modernity will furnish a stunning bravura excursion at the center of *The Doll*:

> Wokulski walked on and looked attentively at the buildings. What splendid shops! Even the most paltry looked better than his, although it was the finest in Warsaw. Stone houses: almost each floor had great balconies and balustrades along the entire façade. "This Paris looks as though all the inhabitants must feel the need of constant communication, either in the cafes or on their balconies," Wokulski thought. The roofs were impressive too, high, loaded with chimney-stacks, prickly with chimney-pots and spires. A tree or lamp or kiosk or column mounted with a globe rose every few paces along the streets. Life was effervescent here, so powerfully that it was unable to use up its energies in the never-ending traffic, in the swift rush of people, in the erection of five-story houses, so it had also burst out of walls in the forms of statues or bas-reliefs, and out of the streets in the shape of innumerable kiosks.
>
> Wokulski felt he had been extricated from stagnant water and suddenly plunged into boiling water which "storms and roars and foams." He, a grown man, energetic in his own climate, felt like a sensitive child here, impressed by everything and everyone. Meanwhile, all around him, the city "seethed and boiled and roared and foamed." Unable to see any end to the crowds, carriages, trees or dazzling store windows, or even of the street itself, Wokulski was gradually overcome with stupefaction. He stopped hearing the passers-by chattering, then grew deaf to the cries of the street traders, finally to the rattle of the wheels. (373)

> "It's a marvelous city; isn't it?" she exclaimed, suddenly looking into his eyes.
>
> "Let people say what they choose, but Paris—even conquered—is still the center of the world. Did it give you that impression?"

"It was very impressive. After a few weeks there I seemed to gain strength and energy. Not until I went to Paris did I really learn to be proud of the fact that I work for a living."

"Pray explain . . ."

"It's very simple. Here, human labor produces poor results: we're a poor and neglected country. But there, work illuminates like the sun. The buildings, covered from roof to side-walk in ornaments like valuable caskets . . . And those forests of pictures and statues, whole regions of machinery, and that chaos of factory and craftsmen's products! In Paris I realized that man only seems to be a frail, weak being. In reality, man is a creature of genius and an immortal giant, who can erect cliffs with as much ease as he creates from them something more delicate than lace." (449–50)

The Doll is no bedroom farce, nor is it to be ranged under the category of that novel of adultery that is virtually the central genre of Western European, nineteenth-century literature and the most profound expression of its critical negativity.[2] But this Polish novel is also not to be assimilated to the Russian tradition: Catholicism, urban life, logical positivism, and coloniality, along with the literary traditions I have mentioned, beside which a late-developing Russian literary language is little more than an upstart, combine to produce a very different novelistic discourse, in which the city/country opposition is insignificant, compared with the Russian great estates; the nationalism is oppositional and political; and the mystical and transcendental overtones of Dostoevsky (or in a different way, of Tolstoy) are wholly absent.

Perhaps I should have said that their place is taken by a rather different kind of mysticism: the secular one of romantic love, whose high priest was Mickiewicz, and which is here diagnosed as that fatal sickness recognized in a tradition that runs from the Greeks to Proust. But rarely has this disease been visited on so interesting a character as the protagonist of *The Doll*. I choose my terms carefully and prefer this specification to the conventional laudatory terms of "complicated" or "complex" precisely because we never really get to know Stanislas Wokulski or to find out how "complex" he is, despite chapters of third-person point-of-view narrative in which his feelings are generously exposed and his own thoughts about them faithfully recounted.

---

2   See Herbert Marcuse, *Eros and Civilization*, or T. W. Adorno, *Minima Moralia*.

Here, indeed, we touch on one of the formal peculiarities of *The Doll*, an external or structural design, which, although no innovation, has far deeper consequences for the content of this only seemingly conventional work. This is the alternation of two modes of narrative: Wokulski's third-person chapters, which sometimes wander, in highly un-Jamesian carelessness, over onto other figures; and a recurrent set of first-person narrative chapters told in the voice of Wokulski's faithful clerk—to be sure an interesting person in his own right, particularly in his own intersection with History, but probably for most readers a "flat" rather than a "round" character, and one, in any case, wholly given over (in that, not unlike the Serenus Zeitblom narrator of *Doctor Faustus*) to devotion to his master. These are not yet the "pseudocouples" of Beckett,[3] but it is time to admit that we have here yet another version of *Don Quixote*, the one that might have emerged had Sancho written his memoirs and shared his anxious concerns about the knight's obsessions with his readers.

But it is precisely those obsessions that make Wokulski enigmatic, and even—I do not hesitate to use this theoretical term anachronistically, for nineteenth-century realism—undecidable. More is at stake than some mere alternation between inside and outside, between Wokulski's consciousness and the judgments other people draw from his behavior. There is an undecidability posited by his consciousness itself, which has a family likeness with Proust's "intermittences du coeur" but includes more brutal discontinuities across a void no Proustian narrative voice is there to conceal.

This void is social and historical, as well as existential: such is the first of the many originalities of this wonderful novel. It is an open wound left by Poland's subalternity; by the underdevelopment of a commercial bourgeoisie; by the utter absence as well of Wokulski's childhood (he seems to appear full-grown, and out of nowhere); and, finally, by the signal event I have already alluded to, the abortive revolution of 1863, in which the youthful protagonist fights, spending an equally unmemorialized decade in Siberia for his pains. We will return to this encounter with History later on, which I will not enlist in any characterization of *The Doll* as a national allegory (although I believe it to be one), contenting myself with observing that the literature of small or non-First-World

---

3   See the discussion of this figure in my *Fables of Aggression: Wyndham Lewis, the Modernist as Fascist* (Berkeley: University of California Press, 1979), pp. 58–61.

powers is more likely to be political than that of the hegemonic countries because politics is for their citizens unavoidable and History necessarily intersects existential experience in them, whereas the mark of First World affiliation is our individual capability of avoiding history altogether and of retreating into private lives in which, in general and for most of the time, we are protected from it.[4]

As for Wokulski's youth—we first meet him retroactively in this novel as a mysterious, darkened, looming "bearded figure in a sealskin overcoat" on his return from Siberia—it is itself already a juxtaposition of unrelated dimensions. He has a passion for science and invention, which is to say, for Western modernity, but, utterly impoverished, he has to earn his living as a waiter. Nevertheless, he becomes a rich businessman—in fact he marries for money, not the most endearing trait for a romantic hero-to-be, and he has as uncle a romantic nobleman, now deceased, but still fondly remembered. Yet he himself surely counts as one of the foremost representatives of the rising bourgeoisie and is indeed made to wear the stigma of a mere businessman, even though he is also an adventurous entrepreneur, capable of taking dramatic risks and throwing himself into dangerous wartime expeditions. He uses his wealth and power brutally:

> Thus thought Wokulski as he coolly eyed Maruszewicz. But the decayed young man, who was moreover very nervous, wilted under the gaze like a dove eyed by a spotted snake. First he turned a little pale, then sought to rest his weary eyes on some indifferent object, which he looked for in vain on the walls and ceiling of the room, until finally, drenched in a cold sweat, he knew his wandering gaze could not escape Wokulski's influence. It seemed to him that the sombre merchant had caught hold of his soul with grappling-irons, and there was no resisting him. So he shifted his head a few times more, then finally sank with complete surrender into Wokulski's gaze. (212)

Yet he frequently indulges in Dostoevskian acts of charity, without the salvational aura, in sordid scenes and surroundings that enable a properly naturalist glimpse of the new urban and industrial miseries, in a novel mainly confined to the privileged classes.

---

4   See my "Third World Literature in the Era of Multinational Capitalism," *Social Text* 15 (Fall 1986): 65–88.

"A horse?" Wokulski whispered, and somehow his heart ached. Once, last March, as he had been crossing the Jerusalem Way, he had seen a crowd of people, a black coal-wagon standing across the street by a gate, and an unharnessed horse a few feet away. "What's happened?" "Horse broke its leg," one of the passers-by replied cheerfully; he had a violet scarf on, and kept his hands in his pockets.

Wokulski looked at the culprit as he passed. It was a lean nag with its ribs showing, and kept lifting its back leg. Tied to a small tree, it stood quietly, looked with its rolling eye at Wokulski and gnawed in its pain at a branch covered with hoar-frost.

"Why should I be reminded of that horse just now?" Wokulski thought. "Why do I feel this pity?"

He walked thoughtfully up Obozna and felt that, in the course of the few hours spent by the river, a change had come upon him. Formerly—ten years ago, a year ago, even yesterday—while walking about in the streets he never met anything unusual. People passed by, droshkies drove along, shops opened their doors hospitably for customers. But now a new kind of idea had come to him. Each ragged man looked as if he were shouting for help, the more loudly because he said nothing but only cast a fearful glance, just as that horse with the broken leg had done. Each poor woman looked like a washerwoman, supporting her family on the brink of poverty and decline with her worn hands. Each pitiful child seemed condemned to premature death or to spending days and nights on the garbage heap in Dobra Street.

It was not only people who concerned him. He shared the weariness of horses pulling heavy carts along, and the sores where their horse-collars had drawn blood. He shared the fright of a lost dog barking in the street for his master and the despair of a starving bitch as she ran from one gutter to the next, seeking food for herself and her puppies. And on top of these sufferings he was even pained by the trees with their bark cut, the pavements like broken teeth, dampness on broken pieces of furniture and ragged garments. It seemed to him that every object like this was sick or wounded, complaining: "See how I suffer . . .," and that he alone heard and understood their laments. And this peculiar capacity for feeling the pain of others had been born in him only today, an hour ago. (82–3)

I want to celebrate, as a narrative and novelistic achievement, the consequence of this heterogeneity, namely, that these multiple traits and features are not unified into an organic totality, a psychologically coherent if protean figure; but, rather, all remain at a distance from each other, in an additive or external way, which leaves its central subject as an absence. Wokulski—vehicle as we shall see of a grand passion if there ever was one—is a cipher. I do not know any other nineteenth-century novelistic protagonist of whom this can be said, but I also wish to underscore the undramatic, un-Dostoevskian quality of this enigma, so different from the interminable monologues and confessions through which the Russian characters seek to express, if not already to construct, their mysteries. It should also be added that Prus's dialogue has nothing in common with these great Russian confrontations but, rather, crackles with the dry wit we find everywhere at the end of the century from Gissing to Galdós and Fontane (and even going back as far as George Eliot, but leaving the French naturalists out of it).

What is this void at the center of Wokulski's being? The thing called passion, certainly, about which we need to report that his first glimpse of Isabella Lenska in a theater is the pretext for an all-absorbing lifelong obsession, which leads him to make a fortune in business (risking his own life in the Balkan wars) and then secretly to support her father, an impoverished nobleman incapable of believing in his own bad luck and pennilessness or of living according to his means. Indeed, almost everything Wokulski does is in one way or another dependent on winning the esteem of this extraordinarily beautiful but still unmarried young woman, about whom one cannot tell whether she is empty-headed and frivolous or cold and unapproachable, whether she is afraid of Stanislas's plebeian energy or simply contemptuous of his social standing (a tradesman!).[5] Isabella is thus also enigmatic, after her fashion, and it is important that we not blame her for Wokulski's fate. This is not the *belle dame sans merci*: we are given to witness her astonishment at this force of nature that her limited social circle has not hitherto allowed her to observe.

> On meeting Wokulski, she had for the first time made the acquaintance, not only of a new personality, but also of an unexpected phenomenon. It was impossible to define him in a single word, or

---

5   Yes, of course Isabella is in *some sense* the eponymous doll, in all her beauty and uselessness. But the title actually springs from a later interpolated episode in which a little girl is falsely accused of having stolen a doll she admires in the apartment of a miserly and quite peculiar neighbor (in fact, it is Wokulski who has given her the doll from his own emporium).

even in several hundred words. He was unlike everyone else, and if it was at all possible to compare him to anything, then perhaps it was to a place through which one travels all day, and where valleys and mountains, woods and lakes, water and desert, villages and towns are to be found. And where too, beyond the mists of the horizon, some vague landscapes appear, unlike anything known before. She was amazed and wondered whether this was the play of an excited imagination—or was he really a supernatural being, or at least a super-drawing-room one. (219)[6]

Nor are the casual flirtations that drive Wokulski to the edge of madness anything more than her social being—indeed, we are able to observe her gradual but not unwilling reconciliation to the idea of marrying this remarkable, but also very wealthy, commoner.[7] It is Wokulski who makes a final decision in the matter, and we may conjecture that perhaps in that like all great passions this one is not only doomed to failure but, in some more obscure fashion, wedded to it. The grand passion cannot be "successful" without abolishing itself; the very word *success* is vulgar in relationship to it; as in the very first modern novel (after the obvious predecessor), *La Princesse de Clèves*, the only way to preserve a grand passion and to keep faith with it is to avoid its consummation. Not that Wokulski takes that path either, exactly.

But, now, we have to look more closely at the thing itself, about which it would be wrong to think that it is something psychological, or even an emotion or feeling of some sort: it is rather a metaphysical experience, an experience of the Absolute, that "mystic point where all his memories, longings and hopes coincided, a hearth without which

---

6   This entire chapter (14) documents Wokulski's enigmatic personality by way of an enumeration of Isabella's changing impressions and opinions of him.

7   Wokulski's great mood swings, as T. S. Eliot noted about Hamlet, are insufficiently motivated by his frequent suspicions and attacks of jealousy. The world changes abruptly, from one moment to the other: "He became pessimistic. The women looked ugly, their colorful dresses barbarous, their flirtations hateful. The men were stupid, the crowd vulgar, the band out of tune. Entering the stand, he sneered at its squeaking steps and old walls, stained with rain leaks" (199). This metonymic *Stimmung* is, however, also capable of shifting to the metaphoric: "Unutterable rage was fuming within his heart. His hands were becoming like iron bars, his body taking on such strange rigidity that surely any bullet would rebound from it. The word 'Death' crossed his mind and for a moment he smiled. He knew Death does not attack the bold; it merely confronts them like a mad dog, and glares with green eyes, waiting for a muscle to twitch" (206).

his life would have neither sense nor meaning" (75). I believe that bourgeois or individualistic psychology is poorly placed to grasp such a phenomenon, which only the absent center of a properly unspeakable event (unspeakable because prohibited by Russian censorship), namely the failed revolution of 1863, can explain. Only a philosophy of the "event" (such as Alain Badiou is currently developing)[8] can convey the unity of form and content (or theory and practice) inherent in this supreme moment, in which History touches its Absolute, and whose loss can be redeemed only by the analogous absolute of Wokulski's love-passion. But I do not even want to claim, as Lukács will in various places,[9] that the lovepassion is the substitute for a political passion that was not fulfilled: that love is the second-best after the historical defeat, that it is something like the culture of the world-historical experience of defeat. *Defeat* is, no doubt, a nobler word than *success*, but I am inclined to see these two Absolutes—revolution and Wokulski's passion—as somehow profoundly interrelated, by way of subterranean "vases communicants." What we take to be the inhuman center of Wokulski's subjectivity and the impersonal nature of his obsession, the primal void around which the more seemingly human and psychological traits of this personality seek inconsistently to reunite themselves, is, rather, that deeper interrelationship of the absolutes, that unconscious or even metaphysical unity of individual and collective that makes Wokulski over into a vehicle for these unidentifiable and, indeed, untheorizable drives. *The Doll* is thus, all appearances to the contrary, a great political novel, a narrative whose absent center is a primordial political impulse that is never mentioned and that is everywhere present in its absence.

It is a reading confirmed by the more *gemütlich* subplot, the story of the faithful clerk Rzecki, whose one great adventure turns out to have been the Revolution of 1848 and his enlistment in the Hungarian revolutionary army, his subsequent picaresque wanderings across a henceforth counter-revolutionary Europe, his nostalgia for Napoleon, and his lifelong memory of the fallen comrade Katz (significantly, foreshadowing Wokulski's own fate, the latter seems to have committed suicide). All the warm sympathies of the novel, the affective pleasures of friendship

---

8   See, for example, *L'être et l'événement* (Paris: Seuil, 1988), section 4.

9   See, for example, his discussion (in *Essays on Realism*) of Hulot's passions in *La cousine Bette*.

and mourning, take refuge in this subplot, as though in flight from the icy inhumanities of the principal one.

Still, let's not exaggerate: we have already seen Wokulski's charities, which are often moving indeed. We should also talk about his passion for science and invention, which is truly childlike and full of an infectious enthusiasm. For Paris and its modernities are, in fact, personified for Wokulski by an anomalous figure, Geist (even the name is no doubt significant), something of an eremitical if not alchemical scientist, in pursuit of unique chemical combinations and substances, which, in ancient times, would have been identified as the philosopher's stone, or, at the very least, that gold into which the magicians transformed lead, but which today would merely make lots of money. Geist's laboratory is a perpetual temptation for Wokulski and the old man, "a Moses leading an unborn generation into the Promised Land" (404); and it constitutes Isabella's opposite number in the struggle for the hero's soul.

How are we to understand this vision of science, whose experimental puttering reminds us less of the Curies than of the monumental and absurd, tragic father figure of Céline's *Mort à credit*, less of the laboratory than of the home workshop, from *La recherche de l'absolu* onward? The word to be pronounced is *positivism*, and we need to set ourselves back into a late nineteenth-century intellectual climate in which the ideals of Auguste Comte have triumphantly made the tour of the world, leaving their slogans embedded in the Brazilian flag and their spirit faithfully venerated everywhere that "development" is sought after. Poland has its own folk periodization for this matter, which it is instructive to distinguish from the Russian-style (revolutionary/anarchist) chronologies of the "man of the fifties, man of the sixties, man of the seventies," and so forth. Here, in Poland, Wokulski's destiny is itself a figure for this particular historical periodization: one of the wiser characters, a Jewish doctor close to him, puts it this way: "two men are merged in him; a romantic of the pre-1863 kind, and a positivist of the '70s" (153) (here, Faust's "two souls in one breast" receiving social and historical specification).

With this, everything is said, at least on the ideological level. The great Mickiewicz, epic and lyric poet alike, and poet of revolution as well (his play *Dziady* [*Forefathers*] sparked another kind of failed revolution in Warsaw a century later, in 1968), is also a central player in this drama, which, just as much as *Don Quixote* or *Madame Bovary*, is also about the corruptions of literature. "I know, now," murmurs Stanislas, "by whom I am bewitched . . . All you poets have wasted my life . . . You have poisoned two generations . . . These are the results of sentimental views of love" (406). Thus, the novel as a form turns back on itself in autoreferentiality and designates that literary genre and language that is to be uprooted, canceled, negated, and utterly refused, if it is itself to come into being.

But it is not only positivism (and Monsieur Homais) that trivializes romanticism and transforms it into mere bovarism: the former is also trivialized unless we see it as a working ideology of industrial modernization itself. Early in the novel (and to be sure, in France, the very heartland of Western modernity for these Slavic tourists), Isabella, glimpsing an iron foundry, has a remarkable vision of the emergence of a whole new world, and the end of the old aristocratic one in which alone her privileged life has meaning:

> While traveling down from the mountains into a region of woods and fields under a sapphire sky, she saw an abyss of black smoke and white steam, and heard the dull rattling, creak and hiss of machinery. Then she saw the foundries, like the towers of medieval castles breathing flame, powerful wheels that revolved like lightening, great scaffolds that moved on rails, streams of molten iron glowing white, and half-naked laborers like bronze statues with sombre expressions. Over it all was a blood-red glow, the sound of rumbling wheels, bellows panting, the thundering of hammers and impatient breathing of furnaces, and underfoot the terrified earth trembled.
>
> Then it seemed to Isabella that she had descended from the heights of Olympus into the hopeless chasms of Vulcan, where the Cyclops were forging thunderbolts that might shatter Olympus itself. She recalled legends of rebellious giants, of the end of this splendid world of hers, and for the first time she the goddess, before whom senators and marshals bowed their heads, was afraid. (40–1)

It is of these terrifying energies that Wokulski himself is for her allegorical; indeed, it is this future that he emblematizes for her whole class. "I congratulate you on a complete triumph," remarks a knowledgeable lawyer on the occasion of the proposition of a business consortium Wokulski makes to a selected group of aristocrats; "the Prince is quite taken with you, both the Counts and the Baron too . . . They are all somewhat scatter-brained, as you will have noticed, but they're men of good will ... They want to do something, they're intelligent and educated—but they lack energy. A sickness of the will, my dear sir: their whole class is affected by it" (169). This is then the ultimate diagnosis of the specifically Polish misery, recorded with comical precision in the satiric pages of this tale of passion: but it is not in the light of some supreme value of passion (as, for example, in Stendhal) that the hilarious and cruel social panorama is staged. Rather, it is the failure of a whole class to undertake its historic mission that is indicted here, and it is in the space of that failure that the Jews of this novel find their opportunity.

> "I have noticed over the last year or two," observes Rzecki, "that dislike of the Hebrews is increasing; even people who, a few years ago, called them Poles of the Mosaic persuasion, now call them Jews. And those who recently admired their hard work, their persistence and their talents, today only see their exploitation and deceit.
>
> When I hear such things, I sometimes think a spiritual twilight is falling on mankind, like night." (145)

In the absence of a bourgeoisie, and in the debility of this aristocracy, the Jews have become the entrepreneurs by the end of the time span of the novel; and Wokulski's contempt for antisemitism (and the author's own) cannot save them from the malice and envy of their impotent competitors, nor indeed from a gamut of characterological traits that range from revolutionary enthusiasm to outright greed and avarice. It is an interesting document on the historic role of Jews in Poland's economy (and in a country so central to Jewish history and experience in general) and makes a fascinating juxtaposition to the picture of a glittering and cultured Jewish high society in Copenhagen in Pontoppidan's *Lykke-Per* (*Hans im Glück*, 1904).

The latter was also, the reader will recall, one of the works enumerated in Lukács's *Theory of the Novel* as an example of his first typological category, the so-called novel of abstract idealism, which centered on *Don Quixote*, and which was opposed to the ironies of "romantic disillusionment" (epitomized by *L'éducation sentimentale*). *The Doll* is also a novel of lost illusions but finally continues to keep faith with those illusions no less absolutely than *Don Quixote*. "All the same, Don Quixote was happier than I," thinks Wokulski toward the end. "He didn't begin to awaken from his illusions until the brink of the grave. But I?" (623).

Perhaps Prus's novel is that rare form that combines both of Lukács's types into one. At any rate, by the time Wokulski thinks this, he is also on the brink of the grave, a grave of his own choosing. Off stage, like the hero of *Pierrot le Jou*, he binds dynamite around himself, in a mountainous place associated with the less unhappy passion of his uncle, memorialized on stone by equally immortal verses of Mickiewicz. Fittingly, however, our last thoughts are for Rzecki: indeed, what can Sancho possibly find to do with himself after the disappearance of his master?

18

The Failure of Success

Once upon a time, when provinces still existed, an ambitious young provincial would now and again attempt to take the capital by storm: Midwesterners arriving in New York; Balzacian youths plotting their onslaught on the metropolis ("à nous deux, maintenant!"); eloquent Irishmen getting a reputation in London; and Scandinavians—Ibsen, Georg Brandes, Strindberg, Munch—descending on Berlin to find a culture missing in the bigoted countryside. So also Henrik Pontoppidan's hero, an unhappy clergyman's son who flees the windswept coasts of Jutland for a capital city which is itself narrow-minded and provincial in comparison with the bustling centers of Europe. Denmark has just lost a war, and an important territory, to Prussia: one in "a long row of national humiliations" in "a doomed country that, in the course of one man's life, had fallen into ruin, wasted away to a pale and flabby limb on Europe's body swelling with power." Denmark itself is to Europe as Jutland is to Copenhagen; and we must never underestimate the degree to which that "national misery," which is secretly a part of every national history and identity, is also part and parcel of the personal or psychic identity of its inhabitants.

In the Northern or Protestant countries, cultural dissatisfaction is indistinguishable from religious misery as well, and from a dogmatic Christianity whose doctrinal debates set the agenda for most of the

"Cosmic Neutrality: On *Lucky Per* by Henrik Pontoppidan," *London Review of Books* 33(20), October 20, 2011.

cultural and intellectual life of the Danish nineteenth century, from Kierkegaard's complex and subtle polemics all the way to Brandes's call for a secular national modernity in its closing years. Pontoppidan's 1898 novel (untranslated into English until now, despite his 1917 Nobel Prize) will not exactly tell the story of a moral and sexual revolt against the oppressive institutional power of the Church, but it breathes a properly Nietzschean hatred of Christianity that testifies to the tenacity of the grip of religion on this society, in revolt fully as much as in submission.

Our present-day postmodern religious fundamentalisms are far enough away from these nineteenth-century clerical struggles for the novel to have little more than historical interest for us, if this were all it registered. The title, however, sends us in another direction, that of the peculiar word "luck," and of the fairy tale to which it alludes (the German translation indeed borrows the Grimms' title, "Hans im Glück," for the novel itself). Luck, to be sure, plays a fundamental role in the *Bildungsroman* in general, and it may be worth recalling the paradigmatic ending of the first and most influential of them, Goethe's *Wilhelm Meister's Apprenticeship*, of whose hero it is said: "You make me think of Saul, son of Kish, who went forth to seek his father's lost asses and found, instead, a kingdom."

Yet this particular fairy tale is perhaps not so affirmative when it comes to the value of chance meetings. It tells of a country boy who seeks, not to make his fortune, but only to return home with it (he has just served an apprenticeship of the traditional seven years and received his accumulated savings in the form of a lump of gold). In the first of many chance meetings, admiring the alacrity of a passing horseman, Hans is offered the horse itself in exchange for the troublesome lump of gold, an offer he is happy to accept. Then, after being thrown by the horse, he is not unwilling to exchange it for a cow, led by a farmer who explains the advantages of its sustenance, in the form of milk, butter, and cheese. But it milks poorly, and a passing butcher persuades him of the benefits of a young pig, for which he gladly exchanges it; a bargain then soon enough replaced by the swap of a fat goose; and so on and so forth until he loses the final avatar—a grindstone—in a well and, no longer burdened by that weight either, joyously reaches home with nothing left in his pockets at all. "There is no man under the sun so fortunate as I," he cries happily as he greets his mother. We should take into consideration the possibility that this really is a happy ending.

So it is that the naive Hans becomes the very prototype of foolishness and good fortune all at once; and it is a modern and sophisticated version of this paradox that Pontoppidan offers us in this unusual novel. We must remember that, like the German *Glück*, and quite unlike what obtains in most other languages including our own, the Danish *lykke* has the double meaning of "luck" and "happiness"—a combination not necessarily obvious, but on which the German fairy tale also turns. Presumably, in the rural landscape of the Grimms, the combination implies that you would not be able to get out of the eternity of rural drudgery without some truly remarkable accidental encounter; or perhaps, on the other hand, that you would be very lucky indeed to know happiness in such a setting. At any rate, in modern (industrial) times the two meanings seem to separate from each other and to become relatively autonomous: you can be happy without luck, you can be lucky without necessarily knowing happiness.

And Per is himself lucky both physically and mentally: a robust and attractive physique endowed with an inventive, perhaps even genial mind, capable of imagining his vast Jutland engineering project at an early age and of drawing up its plans even before any formal or professional training. But he also knows that "you had to hunt down luck as if it were a wild creature, a crooked-fanged beast, the fairytale's golden-brush boar, capture and bind it—booty for the fastest, strongest, bravest."

This means contacts and even, if possible, a wealthy marriage. Indeed, the bias against this provincial Christianity secures a unique privilege for Pontoppidan (and his hero)—access to the world of Judaism. *Lykke-Per* is one of the few great European novels to make a central place for Jewish life and experience; but, unlike *Daniel Deronda* and its abstract discussions of Zionism, it offers a rare portrait of the glittering Jewish high society of Copenhagen, along with a glimpse of the misery of eastern Jewry, driven into exile by the pogroms. Jakobe, a gifted and intelligent young Jewish heiress (but one far less attractive than her younger sister) is Per's first fiancée, and the object of a passionate attraction which never reaches the fulfilment of marriage. Jakobe's life finally makes her into a co-protagonist of the novel, whose unexpected destiny (she founds a school for refugee children in Central Europe) poses the same question as Per's own, a question that at first looks like that of happiness or luck, but which proves to posit yet a third alternative, namely that of success. The originality of the novel lies in its tripartite permutation of these themes, as momentous for the form of the novel as such as it is for the existential fate of individuals themselves in this modernizing late nineteenth century.

The end of feudal society was famously dramatized by "la carrière ouverte aux talents"—the freedom of youths to follow their ambitions, and to become generals in their twenties or to leave their villages and seek their fortunes in Paris. It is true that literature was most often fairly selective about the content of such careers, and that abandoning the various handicraft skills of the village usually left the novelist with few options: politics, art, marriage into high society, and above all money, about whose source once again a high degree of generality was imperative. Henry James never specified the source of the Newsome fortune in *The Ambassadors*, and the apocryphal story—the production of chamber pots—is perhaps just another fable about form and content. For, even if money in general could easily be translated into something more exciting, such as power, the specificities of production—the content of the career—were universally discredited by spreading commodification (itself a kind of generalization or abstraction). One of the most decisive things that happened to narrative in the nineteenth century had to do with the problematization of its formal conclusions, which closed their narrative circuit in earlier and simpler societies either by way of a happy ending (in fairy tales, for example, or romances) or a catastrophic defeat. Those older endings had content, as we might put it in philosophical language; in the new world of money and business, the whole social variety of existential outcomes was slowly reduced to a new set of abstract categories: the opposition between success and failure. Winning the girl is success, losing the war is failure: these abstractions do not on the face of it involve earning or losing money, but it is, in reality, the abstraction of money as such that governs the new system and which begins to impose the new simplified classification in terms of the stark alternatives of winning or losing, success or failure.

The formal result, for the novel, is strange and paradoxical, yet momentous: all successes grow to be alike, they lose their specificity and indeed their interest. Success sinks to the level of emergent mass culture—which is to say, fantasy and wish-fulfilment. Only the failures remain interesting, only the failures offer genuine literary raw material, both in their variety and in the quality of their experience.

It is the spread of commodification into the far corners of society which will come to define the novelist's basic form-problem in the course of the nineteenth century, making it more and more difficult to write an interesting narrative about success. You would have to arouse the reader's interest in specific production techniques: something even

Zola was unable to do without a heavy dose of symbolism, without making them mean something else and something more. And you would have to earn the reader's sympathy for the successful men themselves, with their arrogance and their aggressiveness, their contempt for the rest of us, their supreme self-satisfaction and self-confidence. The last of this species—Zola's Octave (inventor of the first department store) and Maupassant's "bel ami"—still marry into money, but finally trace a route for their successors that leads out of literature into mass culture and the bestseller, whose fundamental drive is neither pity nor fear, nor comic joy and euphoria either, but rather wish-fulfilment, the fantasy of the lives of the rich and famous.

So little by little serious literature must abandon the story of success; nor is Per Sidonius successful in that sense. But the male novel had one last trick up its sleeve: the theme of renunciation, a world-weary gesture that runs all the way through the century from the aged Goethe to Henry James, and which offers the further advantage of a distant kinship with sainthood. Whether *Lykke-Per* has any relationship to this particular motif will bear heavily on our judgment of the originality of the novel.

As for failure, in a situation in which everyone agrees that tragedy as such has become problematical, it is scarcely sustainable either for male protagonists in the long run, tending to degenerate into self-pity or impotence, as in its classic embodiment in Flaubert's *Sentimental Education*. At best it could recover a more eccentric or pathological interest with the identification of the will to failure and the satisfactions of inferiority as passions in their own right.

After that the novel belongs to women, along with the opera and the ballet: marriage will then almost by definition constitute their failure, with the novel of adultery virtually the only form that can lay some claim to being a modern tragedy. This is why, after the end of the marriage comedy, which became so remarkable a vehicle in Jane Austen's hands, the stories and destinies of women come to offer the richest raw material for literature: they are stories of failure, epitomized in the novel of adultery.

It is women's compensation for their exclusion from the *Bildungsroman* as such, and it is questionable whether the latter has itself been able to survive the catastrophe of nineteenth-century "success," save perhaps for that one variant which does not depend on business society: the novel of the artist.

The problem is that the artist novel faces form-problems and contradictions of its own, which Ernst Bloch identified in a famous series of essays. For it is not enough to tell the reader that your protagonist is a genius, you must prove it somehow. But how? By inserting a work within the work, and giving a sample of his achievements (which may well be better than the novelist's own, but which ought, in any case, to be different)? The result is most often what Bloch calls a utopian hole or absence at the center of the work, a transcendence which can only be imagined, a space that only the future can colonize. Otherwise, it might be better to make these putative works failures as well, as in *Le Chef d'oeuvre inconnu* or Zola's Cézanne novel, *L'Oeuvre*; at which point the protagonist rejoins the long and dismal line of capitalism's outcasts and rejects.

Lykke-Per deftly sidesteps this second dilemma by making its genius an engineer and by submitting, as its work within the work, a project that can be imagined and judged on its own merits, indeed a project whose fundamental ambition conjoins the novel's theme of modernization and of the national destiny with that other even more fundamental one of luck, happiness, and success, which is to say of desire itself. National allegory is alone achieved at that price, the coincidence of the collective destiny with that of the individual.

Per's scientific gift (although it does not yet quite strike the note of the two cultures debate) is itself an implicit judgment on the major Danish intellectual and cultural figure of the period, Georg Brandes (a scarcely disguised character in the novel, and also, not coincidentally, a Jew). Brandes was a giant figure for all of Northern Europe, a tireless champion of the avant-garde, very much including Nietzsche, and a major player in that late nineteenth-century European cultural revolution which led both to modern art and modern industrial development.

Brandes/Nathan is thus an obligatory stop on the line of development of Per's *Bildungsroman*; but his repudiation is no less characteristic of the form, marking the abandonment of a vision of a purely aesthetic and cultural modernity for a more comprehensive development that includes the national and the economic as well.

Yet engineering does not really take us that far away from art, inasmuch as Per, like any "great artist" in embryo, has nourished the project of his *Hauptwerk* from adolescence on: it is (like the ending of *Faust*) the draining of the marshes and the opening of a series of waterways in Jutland that will shift the very position and strategic importance of Denmark in Europe itself:

Per's proposal is to move the south Jutland landing back to the old place, or rather a bit north of that, namely Tarp, at the mouth of the Varde River. From there, traffic could go further inland. This waterway, deepened and straightened, with the help of a couple of locks, would be connected with the Vejle river and together they would form the most southern of the two channels that, according to his plan, would unite in conjunction with the Belts, the North Sea and the Baltic.

He writes that only the completion of at least one of these lines of connection could bring a competition with the north German ports, especially Hamburg, whose growing business power, he contends, is the real danger that threatens Denmark's independence. Denmark's defeat in the battle for business markets that, secretly or openly, is the concern of international politics, will be more and more fateful; on the other hand, a victory would be a golden triumph and, gradually, Denmark would become the centre point of Europe, moving Russia's rising developing might and culture farther and farther east.

The plan is utopian and realistic/historical all at once, and I can only think of Saccard's dream of colonizing the Middle East (in Zola's *L'Argent*) as a comparable moment in the nineteenth-century novel. Yet it remains unfulfilled; and the novel stands or falls with this unresolved dissonance, in which the project is suspended at the very moment in which (unlike the manias of Balzacian characters, for example) it finds practical and financial support and could actually be realized.

But this is what happens with all Per's plans and desires: they are abandoned at the moment of success. His love affair with Jakobe dissolves at the very moment of marriage: one can't say that it is broken off by a quarrel, or that the love affair that seems to come between them is anything more than a pretext, even though he also "loves" the new infatuation (indeed, this one he goes so far as to marry, in a liaison that dissolves as readily as the old one). This is not, I think, the existential fear of commitment, on the order of Kierkegaard's seducer or Sartre's *Age of Reason*. Nor do we have to do here with Fourier's "butterfly temperament," or the more serious professional conquests of a Don Juan. What is authentic is Per's capacity for new enthusiasms, intellectual as well as sentimental: but this renewal of interests does not exactly result in their conflict, in some painful hesitation between two desires, or the proverbial clash between love and duty. Per knows a double success—he has been adopted (figuratively) by a wealthy older woman and taken to Rome to experience the treasures of the city and its high society (shades of James, whose characters were there at much the same time), and in his absence the great engineering project for the seacoast has been taken up by some influential people and seems on the point of realization—but then he receives a message urgently calling him back to Copenhagen to promote the scheme, which is the project of his life. His refusal to do so is not to be understood as the hesitation between two desires, two temptations, even though it does seem to be expressed in terms of indolence, new and luxurious pleasures, the inability of the will to throw off these weak and effeminate indulgences and to embrace his duty (or his destiny). In fact, Per is not a particularly pleasure-oriented figure, and Rome has nothing special for him, save as an excuse not to hurry back to Copenhagen.

No, I think the situation stands otherwise, and could perhaps be put like this: now that he knows the great project can be completed, he loses interest, he no longer needs to complete it. I think that what startled its contemporaries about this strange novel was not the representation of the usual motivations, but rather the sense of something new, one of those as yet unnamed and perhaps unnameable psychic discoveries for which the novelists of the period—from Dostoevsky to James—desperately searched, in the exhaustion of traditional narratives.

Perhaps the most plausible competitor in this struggle of interpretations is the now current topic of melancholia, which would seem very apt to describe the strange feeling-tone of a lack of feeling that characterizes Per. Lack of feeling does not here mean the absence of passion— Per has many and diverse passions—but, rather, the failure of any of his passions or interests to cut deeply, to make their mark on a fundamental indifference which is not experienced in anxiety (as in the various existentialisms) but rather as a kind of permanent ground-bass of existence. This cosmic neutrality can itself take on a range of tonalities: from the ecstatic encounters with a nature that generally takes the form of an inorganic sublime (from rocks and mountains to the mines in which Per works for a time), to a more properly melancholy calm, as when Per accompanies the coffin of his mother back to the tiny port village in which he and his brothers and sisters grew up:

> Per had already, for some time, been shipboard on the open sea. Like a giant floating sarcophagus, the ship's large, dark body glided over the peaceful surface in the twilight while smoke billowed over it like

mourning crêpe. The sky was covered with clouds and hung heavy and black over the horizon. Here and there was a rift in the clouds through which a few pale stars peeked down like angel eyes watching over the solemn journey of the corpse.

Pontoppidan's discovery, if we judge it to be that and do not reduce it to older narrative stereotypes, is something closer to the Freudian or Lacanian death wish: the idea that, beneath all our conscious desires, which may or may not be satisfied, beneath all the successes that ought to bring fulfilment and at least a passing moment of satisfaction, there persists some immortal drive that can never be silenced (except by organic death) and which, "in us more than us" and insatiable, renders both success and failure meaningless. But we must avoid the temptation of a religious or ascetic interpretation, and the accents either of asceticism or of existential pathos and Pascalian "misery." We must resist the temptation to see Per's final return to Jutland as a withdrawal from the world:

> The place had a special attraction for him personally and, as he now realised, just *because* of its sterile and sad deserted nature, its full solitude. It seemed to him that he never had looked so deeply into himself as at that moment. It was as if he saw the ground of his own Being uncovered and was staring at it. When, in spite of all the good fortune that had come his way, he wasn't happy, it was because he had not *wanted* to be happy in the general sense of the word.

"In the general sense of the word": yes, this turns out to have been the novel's project—to change the sense of the word, to modify our sense of what luck or happiness means. "Il faut imaginer Sisyphe heureux," Camus concluded superbly, at the end of his book on the uselessness of passion. In just that way we must imagine that the fairy tale of stupid Hans has a happy ending; and that Lucky Per himself has managed to get beyond success or failure.

19

Days of the Messiah

Hebrew is written from right to left: could you get a feel for it by numbering the pages of a book backwards, as in Olga Tokarczuk's *The Books of Jacob*? At least, you might think, you would know how many pages you had left to read without having to subtract; but there you would be wrong, as doing this has the effect of eliminating the very idea of a last page, which has turned out to be the first! Perhaps, then, it simulates the Messianic countdown itself: the time of waiting for the end time, or for Apocalypse, "a king on a white horse, riding into Jerusalem wearing gold armour, perhaps with an army, too, with warriors who would seize power alongside him and bring about the final order of the world." Unless "the coming Messiah is a suffering, aching Messiah, trodden down by the evil of the world and the misery of people. He might even resemble Jesus [the very thought is an abomination to believers], whose mangled body hangs in Korolówka from crosses placed at almost every crossroads." Wrong! Wrong! The third Messiah is nothing like that—did I mention he was the third? Yet another misunderstanding!

But, as for Hebrew, our interest in it is preceded by that of Father Chmielowski, a passionate bibliophile and the author (he is a real historical personage) of the first great Polish chrestomathy, *New Athens* (from which Jacob Frank will learn his Polish), a chapbook of the most interesting thoughts and sayings of the past, to which he has decided to add

"The Fog of History: On *The Books of Jacob* by Olga Tokarczuk," *London Review of Books* 44(6), March 24, 2022.

the wisdom of the Jews, so far closed to him. The learned rabbi, Elisha Shorr, to whom Father Chmielowski proposes an exchange of precious volumes turns out, however, to have given him not the Zohar, but merely a children's book (later on, Father Chmielowski, incapable of bearing a grudge, or indeed much else, will shelter the old rabbi's considerable library from harm during the persecutions). Yet he will have had the instructive privilege of entering Rabbi Shorr's labyrinthine warren of a town house, peopled by the most obscure members of a far-flung clan reassembling from distant parts to celebrate a momentous wedding. Does Father Chmielowski's path ever cross Jacob's? I cannot remember; but at least during that same visit he performs a kindness for a stricken Polish noblewoman (another real historical person) who will be of much service to the Messianic clan in future years.

It is at this wedding that Shorr and his intimates first get news of the appearance of a new Messiah in Smyrna, in those same Ottoman lands where the first Messiah, Sabbatai Sevi, began his mission. We are finally also indebted to this wedding party for the unfortunate mistake to which we owe *The Books of Jacob*. The Nobel committee was clever indeed to slip their prize to the person whose name appears on its cover, before anyone had had the chance fully to appreciate who Olga Tokarczuk is. For *The Books of Jacob* takes its place alongside the great postmodern meganovels by Pynchon or Perec, Bolaño or García Márquez; and it may be said to rival even *New Athens* itself, of which the equally historical poet Elżbieta Drużbacka says: "This volume is so strangely magical that an endless reading is permitted in which one picks and pecks here and there, always finding interesting matters which furnish multiple pretexts for reflexion on the immensity and complexity of the world, in the awareness that there is no way of knowing it in its entirety, but only by bits and pieces, little details and modest elements of comprehension."

At any rate, it is during the wedding party that an aged grandmother from a distant branch of the family has inconveniently taken it on herself to enter her death throes. This is more than an inconvenience, as the whole wedding will have to be postponed, at great expense. The elders consult as to which is preferable, a wedding or a funeral. Rabbi Shorr unwisely decides to postpone the decease by means of a magic amulet, which the dying woman, who has her own brand of wisdom and cunning, promptly swallows. She, Yente, our all-seeing eye, then enters the condition of the undead, her living corpse secretly transferred from one hiding place to another (one of them, a grotto and a place of pilgrimage, will later be visited by her own grandson Jacob Frank), while her spirit, separating itself from that undead body, rises to circle the earth like the Sputnik of later centuries and sees all that we are to witness, from Frankfurt to Smyrna, from Warsaw to Mount Athos, and, in particular, those chateaux and peasant villages of Podolia and the multitudinous roads on which weary Jewish merchants travel to ply their trade.

The center of it all, however, the happiest and most fulfilled time of the Messianic adventure, is the village of Ivanie, a small group of huts deserted after the plague and situated on the Dniester:

> Yente sees how Ivanie has a particular status in the hierarchy of being.
> The village isn't firmly planted on the ground . . . homes stooping over
> like living things . . . The words pronounced in Ivanie—great and
> powerful words—transgress the world's boundaries. Behind them lies
> a completely other reality . . . like holding silk embroidered in 56
> colours up to grey fustian—incomparable . . . like some strange living
> body revealed by a wound, like the juicy pulp that escapes from under
> broken skin.
> That's how the Shekhinah [the female principle of the Kabbala]
> comes into the world.

But this space—momentarily transformed into the longed-for dwelling of Jacob's followers—is not to be confused with Utopia, which we also visit, courtesy of Moliwda and the bogomils. Ivanie means land: "We're not allowed to buy land, settle down permanently. They chase us off in all directions"; "A man who does not have a piece of land is not a man." And this is the drive behind the sham conversions: to get the Polish aristocracy, to get the Church, to give the community their own land on the aristocrats' great estates; this is the deeper promise of Jacob, the drive behind the longing for the Messiah, however personal the fascination he exerts, his charisma, may seem.

We need to pause for a moment over this word, "charisma," which, in a sociological *petitio principii*, Weber borrowed from the religious tradition in order to explain another religious phenomenon which, however, it only served to name. Even less helpful will be the word "populism," which, once the name of a revolutionary movement, has today, with the help of Le Bon and Freud, become synonymous with the pseudo-concept of totalitarianism applied indiscriminately to phenomena of left and right alike. Yente does not make judgments of this kind: she has no lessons for us; her all-seeing eye simply registers history.

As for Jacob's charisma, we have our own testimonies. Is that of Nahman of Busk reliable? He is to be sure Jacob's "prophet," in the sense in which the various Messianic figures of history (often themselves not aware of their vocation) have needed a prophet of their own: John the Baptist for Jesus, Aaron for Moses, Nathan of Gaza for Sabbatai Sevi, the innumerable éminences grises throughout history, if not, indeed, the powers behind the thrones. Nahman is not exactly an éminence grise, but he does bear witness to Jacob's Messianic awakening:

> When I look at him, I see that there are people who are born with something that I cannot find the words for, something that means that others respect them and hold them in the highest esteem . . . He has only to enter any space, be it the most decrepit shed or the holiest chamber, and all eyes turn to him at once, pleasure and appreciation on everyone's faces, although he has not yet done or said a thing." Even children feel it: "These words make an enormous impression upon Hershel. From that moment forward, he wants to be like Jacob. And being close to Jacob evokes in him some incomprehensible excitement, produces a warmth that flows all through his small body, so that the boy feels safe and powerful.

Can this be physical, sensual even? This was murmured of Sabbatai Sevi: "They also said in great secret—which nonetheless travelled faster than it would have had it been a slightly lesser secret—that the Messiah was a woman [the Shekhinah is what's meant here]. Those who had been close to him had glimpsed his feminine breasts. His skin, soft and rosy, smelled like a woman's skin." Jacob's physical attractions are not of this kind. But let's hear from an enemy:

> The man who emerges from the carriage is tall and well built, and to his height is added a slim Turkish hat, which feels like an organic element of his stature. Dark, wavy hair pops out from under his hat, softening somewhat the emphatic features of a rather harmonious face. His gaze is insolent—so it seems to Pinkas—and he is looking slightly upward, so that you can see a bit of the whites at the bottom of his eyes, as though he were about to faint. He casts his eyes around the people standing about by his carriage and over the heads of the

rest of the crowd. Pinkas sees the movement of his prominent, nicely shaped lips. He is saying something to the people, laughing—and now his even white teeth gleam. His face gives the impression of youth, and his dark beard seems to conceal even more of that youth, maybe even dimples. He looks both authoritative and childlike. Pinkas senses how this person might appeal to women, and not only to women, but also to men—to everyone—for he is extremely charming. This makes Pinkas hate him even more.

From this I propose that we divert our attention to the testimony of the fascinating figure Moliwda, a gentile and Polish nobleman who has seen the world and ends up as a kind of ambassador from the true believers (whom we may also begin to refer to as the "anti-Talmudists") to the higher authorities of Crown and Church:

> Moliwda used to wonder whether Jacob could feel fear. Eventually he decided that Jacob would not recognise the feeling, as though he'd simply been born without it. This gives Jacob strength: people can sense that absence of fear, and that absence of fear in turn becomes contagious. And because the Jews are always afraid—whether it's of a Polish lord, or of a Cossack, of injustice or hunger or cold—they live in a state of extreme uncertainty, from which Jacob is a kind of salvation. The absence of fear is like a halo that radiates a heat that can warm up a chilled and frightened little soul. Blessed are those who feel no fear.

Still, that Jacob is not yet an event, his story not yet historical; the historians, interested only in facts and causes, have no place here. We are in what, by analogy to the fog of war, may be called the fog of history: only gradually do world-historical events and the institutions they leave behind them begin slowly to emerge, in shadowy outline. To be sure, History bursts into Podolia as an effective presence with the great Cossack pogroms of 1648 and gradually seeps away again when the apostasy of Sabbatai Sevi—the first Messiah's forced conversion to Islam in 1666—drains the villages of their Messianic hope. For world history is itself imaginary: it is the distant horizon of legendary events unfolding beyond the immemorial daily life and rounds of peasants whose time is incompatible with it. It is a distant frieze of events with a time of its own, some distant privileged time that flows uninterrupted on and on, as in that magnificent passage from Hebel which Walter Benjamin so admired:

> In the meantime the city of Lisbon was destroyed by an earthquake, and the Seven Years' War came and went, and Emperor Francis I died, and the Jesuit Order was abolished, and Poland was partitioned, and Empress Maria-Theresa died, and Struensee was executed. America became independent, and the united French and Spanish forces were unable to capture Gibraltar. The Turks locked up General Stein in the Veteraner Cave in Hungary, and Emperor Joseph died also. King Gustavus of Sweden conquered Russian Finland, and the French Revolution and the long war began and Emperor Leopold II went to his grave too. Napoleon captured Prussia, and the English bombarded Copenhagen, and the peasants sowed and harvested. The millers ground, the smiths hammered, and the miners dug for veins of ore in their underground workshops.

In Podolia itself, however, time is not yet historical, as Yente knows: "She had thought time flowed! Now she finds it funny. It's obvious that time spins around like skirts whirling in a dance." Nor are the inhabitants of this non-historical world to be judged like literary characters—round and flat, high and low, the great and the anonymous. As in few other novels, they all think all the time; stubbornly they all have their opinions on everything and anything, and are prepared to argue them vociferously at a moment's notice.

But we must be clear: this is a world of merchants (the peasants are Polish), a world of caravans and markets: "chaotic trails, unpleasant to the eye. Zigzags, twisting spirals, lopsided ellipses—the record of travel for commerce, pilgrimage, on merchants' expeditions, visits to families, homesickness, and flights. There are many bad people around, some of them really very cruel." A world, too, of chaotic enumeration: "The crowd gleams with its different colours, chatting in different languages, arraying astonishing goods for sale: fragrant spices, vivid carpets, brightly coloured rugs, Turkish delicacies so sweet you'll grow dizzy with pleasure, dried dates and raisins of every sort, beautifully dyed leather slippers stitched with silver thread." We must not forget either that Jacob is himself a merchant, though a lazy and self-indulgent specimen:

> Jacob never sits in the office, but rather at a little table having tea, dressed lavishly, like a Turk, in a blue-green Turkish caftan and a

dark-red Turkish cap. Before they get down to business, they always have to have two or three little glasses of tea . . . Jacob gives audiences of sorts . . . After just a few days of working in Abraham's warehouse, it has become the most popular place in all of Craiova.

But this is daytime! This is business! It is the matter of leisure we must look into, the matter of entertainment and relaxation, amusement, distraction, which we, in our day and age, sometimes call mass culture. For Jacob's contemporaries, the merchants, what we have to understand is that mass culture is theology. The endless, innumerable disputations over pipe and wine, the interminable hair-splitting of arguments that can become passionate in an instant: all this is diversion, down to the very shape of the letters whose kabbalistic meanings can be contemplated for hours. Here, socializing is called study and gossip prophecy, news of the most recent marriage no less riveting than that of the coming Messiah or the authority of some new rabbi whom one must visit as soon as possible. Wisdom is as widely distributed as beards, and one must search for it everywhere along the rivers and roads of south-east Europe, from Poland to Turkey, which carry letters full of matrimonial and theological gossip as far away as Spain, all the while unevenly tolerated in the German lands and the Ottoman Empire in languages ranging from Hebrew and Turkish to Polish, German, Ruthenian, Yiddish, and in kingdoms from the loosely ruled Poland of the feudal aristocracies to the Ottoman Empire, which peacefully shelters all conceivable religions and heresies in its bosom, for a price (Jacob grows up there). Sabbatai Sevi emerged there as well, in the midst of an extraordinary reawakening of Jewish and in particular kabbalistic speculation. The sultan presides over all this with amused tolerance until he is informed of Sabbatai's more impertinent claims, at which point he confronts Sabbatai with the ultimate existential choice, to die or to don the turban; after which this former Messiah once again enjoys a surprising measure of personal freedom.

   Alongside this historical experience of defeat suffered by world Jewry, there persisted a current of Sabbatianism willing to see conversion as an act of spiritual aggrandizement (Sabbatai's successor Baruchia also converted but, like Jacob, to Christianity). Yet it is not exactly to some Trinitarian doctrine in the three reunited Mosaic religions that they are attracted, so much as to Jacob's person. Their stories reflect not some abstract theology but, rather, the desire for land and the ferocious civil war within Judaism stimulated by the quest for patronage.

Are we not to presume some general worldview which, apart from the sacred books themselves, might qualify as what we call religion? Why not? It might be, at the very least, that "to create the world God had to withdraw from Himself, leave within His body a blank space in which the world could take up residence." And it might also be that the gleamings of the Shekhinah must be sought for in mud and excrement. As for God, "every now and then [he] wearies of his own luminous silence, and infinity starts to make him a little bit sick. Then, like an enormous, omnisensitive oyster, his body—so naked and delicate—feels the slightest tremble in the particles of light, scrunches up inside itself, leaving just enough space for the emergence—at once and out of nowhere—of a world." (Schelling also had such visions.) Or, contrariwise, "the spirit circles around us like a wolf around those trapped in a cave . . . It seeks the smallest hole to get through to those weak figures living in the shadow world."

"Why does the spirit like olive oil so much?" Jacob asks, in response to these theological visions. "Why all that anointing? Is it to make it slippery, so it will be easier for it to go inside of matter?" This palpable obscenity proves we have understood nothing of the Messiah or of Jacob himself, whose mission is virtually innocent of such theological niceties. We have been approaching this figure in a spirit of reverence, with hushed voices, as in church, as though he had a religious task or mission. What we have failed to understand is that the Messiah is come, not to fulfil the Law but to destroy it! Not to perfect it but rather to abolish it altogether. We have been trying to imagine the wrong kind of world: this is not the utopian world of Thomas More (or even that of Moliwda); it is the world of Sabbatai Sevi's blasphemies and orgies, his vilification and repudiation of the Talmud, his public consumption of pork, his disregard—indeed, cancellation—of the most sacred Jewish holidays, his pronunciation out loud of the sacred name of God on all occasions.

This is the very quintessence of transgression, the promotion of a Bataille-type mysticism to the very center of social life, the injunction to destroy order itself, absolutely. The scandalous violence of this Messianism marks the end not only of the Law but of Judaism itself, and signals the return to the lost innocence of Eden and the time before the Law. Sabbatai's psychotic outbursts in some sense formalize and lend authority to Jacob's anti-Talmudist program. The regrouping around the person of Jacob of the "true believers" (that is, the remaining Sabbatians), the return to Poland, the imprisonment of Jacob, his arrival in Vienna: these are not biographical facts but rather truly historical and collective convulsions occasioned by a figure who remains, as Moliwda concludes, ultimately inscrutable.

A new History emerges within Judaism itself, a struggle between the establishment rabbis and the disciples of Sabbatai, whose remnants reassemble around the figure of Jacob and, crossing their own Rubicon into Poland, begin to stage public disputations with the Talmudists (which is to say, the "real" Jews) and convert en masse to Christianity under the wavering patronage of the great prelates and a monarchy enfeebled by the death of King Stanislaw and the incursion of the Russians. Now as Podolia itself comes to have a history we can begin to speak of historical "facts" and properly historical (that is, Western) inquiries: how to explain Jacob Frank's success at court; had his beloved Nahman betrayed him, like Judas, in order to fulfil the prophecy; did his mission change after Częstochowa, substituting the preaching of ecumenicism for the drive for land, etc.? Do these Jews in fact still want land? No doubt—"a man who does not have a piece of land is not a man"—but land on the estates and under the protection of the nobility and the Church, indeed of the king himself. (For this is no Zionist argument for the state of Israel so much as it is the celebration of Poland itself, "paradisus Judaeorum.")

But, just as Jacob is not the beginning of this book—following Aristotle's reminder that a life is not a complete event—so it has no ending. It simply deteriorates like life itself: the movement follows Jacob into the West, the Germanic and French languages first of the Viennese court and Jacob's own "court" at Bruenn, and then of Offenbach near Frankfurt, with its emergent stock market; Frankism sinks into history (the West being somehow History for these Eastern Europeans), and the movement dissolves, though incompletely, as with any intense and innovative movement. "Strange deeds" become ceremonies, Jacob a kind of prince whose death is ritually celebrated as if he were a Polish archbishop. As I have noted already, the book itself has no ending, but breaks off as it approaches page one. By then a Jacob who has at least belonged to us for a time will have turned into a name and a fact in the history books, with a movement to be chronicled behind it.

Some historians, meanwhile, will wish to assess whether Jacob's politico-religious program changed significantly after his imprisonment. Gnostic apologists for Judas will excuse his betrayal by Nahman of Busk in the light of the latter's conviction that the Messiah must sink to the bottom of society and share the sufferings of its dregs. Liberal moralists will wish to read Tokarczuk's foregrounding of Jacob's insistence on the identity of the three Mosaic religions as a not-so-disguised plea for tolerance in an authoritarian Poland. Linguistic mystics will answer, with Nahman, that curses follow names and that it is no small thing to behold the revolutionary transformation of Shlomo Shorr into Franciszek Woloski, of Nahman of Busk into Pietr Jakubowski, indeed of Jankiel ben Yehuda Buchbinder into Jacob Frank himself. Historians, as they consider Gershom Scholem's dialectical view of the significant role played by Frankism in the emergence of modern Judaism, may or may not share his judgment on Jacob Frank as "unscrupulous and depraved." Poststructuralists and adherents of Bataille will revel in Jacob's "strange deeds" and celebrate him as an early exemplar of transgression; some readers will be troubled by this "populism," while others will conclude, with Moliwda, that Jacob is inscrutable.

The glimpse of an old and prosperous Jacob in Offenbach, checking his investments on the newly established Frankfurt stock exchange, may well lead Messianists sadly to conclude that he was, after all, just another fraud and conman, merely the most recent of false Messiahs. Yet hypocrisy is the tribute vice pays virtue, and it is no small thing to found a movement that sweeps across whole landscapes, languages, and generations. Even the false Messiah glows with that Messianism on which we warm our hands. Never mind! What is important here is that Olga Tokarczuk has learned to do the impossible: to write the novel of the collective.

The Messiah is something more than a figure and a person—it is something that flows in your blood, resides in your breath, it is the dearest and most precious human thought: that salvation exists. And that's why you have to cultivate it like the most delicate plant, blow on it, water it with tears, put it in the sun during the day, move it into a warm room in the night-time.

Index